TRANSNATIONAL SOCIAL SPACES

DAMES
Dansk Center for Migration
og Etniske Studier

**EUROPEAN RESEARCH CENTRE
ON MIGRATION & ETHNIC RELATIONS**

Transnational Social Spaces
Agents, Networks and Institutions

Edited by

THOMAS FAIST
University of Applied Sciences, Bremen, Germany

EYÜP ÖZVEREN
Middle East Technical University, Ankara, Turkey

ASHGATE

© Thomas Faist and Eyüp Özveren 2004

All rights reserved. No part of this publication may be reproduced, stored in a retrieval system, or transmitted in any form or by any means, electronic, mechanical, photocopying, recording or otherwise without the prior permission of the publisher.

Thomas Faist and Eyüp Özveren have asserted their right under the Copyright, Designs and Patents Act, 1988, to be identified as the editors of this work.

Published by
Ashgate Publishing Limited
Wey Court East
Union Road
Farnham
Surrey, GU9 7PT
England

Ashgate Publishing Company
Suite 420
101 Cherry Street
Burlington
VT 05401-4405
USA

Ashgate website: http://www.ashgate.com

British Library Cataloguing in Publication Data
Transnational social spaces : agents, networks and
  institutions. - (Research in migration and ethnic relations
  series)
  1. Turks - Germany - Social conditions 2. Turks - Germany -
  Ethnic identity 3. Turks - Germany - Cultural assimilation
  4. Transnationalism 5. Culture conflict - Germany 6. Germany -
  Relations - Turkey 7. Turkey - Relations - Germany 8. Germany
  - Ethnic relations 9. Germany - Emigration and immigration
  I. Faist, Thomas, 1959- II. Özveren, Eyüp
  305.8'9435043

Library of Congress Cataloging-in-Publication Data
Transnational social spaces : agents, networks and institutions / [edited] by Thomas Faist and Eyüp Özveren.
       p. cm. -- (Research in migration and ethnic relations series)
    Includes bibliographical references and index.

   1. Turks--Germany--Social conditions. 2. Germany--Ethnic relations. 3. Germany--Emigration and immigration. 4. Turkey--Emigration and immigration. 5. Group identity--Germany. 6. Immigrants--Cultural assimilation--Germany. 7. Immigrants--Cultural assimilation--Turkey. 8. Social integration--Germany. I. Faist, Thomas, 1959- II. Özveren, Eyüp, 1959- III. Series.

DD78.T87T73 2004
305.89'435043--dc22   2004007280

ISBN 978-0-7546-3291-7

Transfered to Digital Printing in 2012

Printed and bound in Great Britain by the
MPG Books Group Ltd, UK

Contents

List of Contributors	*vii*
Preface	*ix*

1   The Border-Crossing Expansion of Social Space: Concepts, Questions and Topics   1
Thomas Faist

PART I: RIGHTS AND STRUGGLES

2   The Transnational Dimension of the Bergama Campaign Against Eurogold   37
Zeynep Kadirbeyoğlu

3   Transnational Space Between Women's NGOs in Germany and Turkey: Current Situation and Future Expectations   59
Hanife Aliefendioğlu

4   German Migrants in Turkey: The 'Other Side' of the Turkish-German Transnational Space   91
Bianca Kaiser

5   Turkish Ultra-nationalism in Germany: Its Transnational Dimensions   111
Emre Arslan

PART II: ENTREPRENEURSHIP AND MANAGEMENT

6   Transnational and Local Entrepreneurship   143
Cem Dişbudak

7   Intercultural Encounters: German and Turkish Managers in Joint Ventures   163
Marita Lintfert

PART III: CULTURE, MEDIA AND EVERYDAY SOCIAL LIFE

8   Good Guys and Bad Guys: Turkish Migrant Broadcasting
    in Berlin   189
    Kira Kosnick

9   Transnational Ties of the Second Generation: Marriages of
    Turks in Germany   211
    Gaby Straßburger

Index   *233*

List of Contributors

- **Hanife Aliefendioğlu** has a PhD in Anthropology from Hacettepe University, Ankara. She has been involved in the activities of various civil society organizations and civil service departments concerned with women's rights. Currently she is Assistant Professor at Eastern Mediterranean University, Magusa, Turkish Republic of North Cyprus.

- **Emre Arslan** is a doctoral Student in the Department of Sociology at Bielefeld University. He graduated from the Department of Political Science at the Middle East Technical University, Ankara, and wrote his Master Thesis on *The Role of the Nationalist Action Party in Turkey* in the Department of Political Science at Bilkent University, Ankara. The subject of his dissertation is the reproduction process of nationalist myths among Turkish fascists in Germany.

- **Cem Dişbudak** received his Master of Science degree in 1996 in Economics from Oklahoma State University, USA and his PhD in 2003 in Economics from Middle East Technical University, Turkey. His main areas of interest are the economics of international migration, history of economic thought, macroeconomic theory, economic development, and the Turkish economy. Currently, he is a researcher at Muğla University.

- **Thomas Faist** is Professor of Political Science and Political Management and Director of the Centre on Migration, Citizenship and Development (COMCAD) at the University of Applied Sciences Bremen. He received his PhD from The Graduate Faculty, New School for Social Research in New York. He currently directs research projects on the politics of dual citizenship, funded by the Volkswagen Foundation, and on migration control and democracy in Europe, sponsored by the German Research Foundation (Deutsche Forschungsgemeinschaft).

- **Zeynep Kadirbeyoğlu** is a doctoral candidate at the Department of Political Science at McGill University. Her research interests are state-society relations with reference to development projects and participation. Among her publications are 'State Structures: Coercion vs. Co-ordination. Some Lessons for Turkey', co-authored with Fikret Adaman (*New Perspectives on Turkey*, Spring 1999) and 'Medieval Business Partnerships: Islamic vs. Western' (*New Perspectives on Turkey*, Fall 2001).

- **Bianca Kaiser** is Assistant Professor of International Relations and Director of the International Office at İstanbul Kültür University. Her research interests include Germany's EU policies, Turkish-German relations, and migration from the EU to Turkey. Her latest publications include 'German Foreign Policy after Unification: Normality or Assertiveness?' (*İstanbul Kültür University Journal of Social Sciences*, 2002) and *Almanya'nın Avrupa Politikası: 1949-2003* (İstanbul: Bağlam Yayınları, forthcoming).

- **Kira Kosnick** is research fellow at the University of Southampton, UK, where she is working for the EU Fifth Framework project 'Changing City Spaces' that studies cultural policy and migrant cultural scenes in European capital cities. She received her Ph.D. in cultural anthropology from The Graduate Faculty, New School for Social Research in New York, with a doctoral thesis on local Turkish minority media in Berlin. Her current research interests include the transformation and reconfiguration of urban space through transnational cultural practices.

- **Marita Lintfert** received her Master of Arts degree in German as a Foreign Language, English and American Literature and Sociology at the Bielefeld University. From 1996-2000 she was a lecturer at the Marmara University in İstanbul, Turkey. She is currently teaching at the Goethe-Institute Inter Nationes and at the Foreign Language Centre of the state of Bremen.

- **Eyüp Özveren** is Professor at the Faculty of Economics and Administrative Sciences, Middle East Technical University, Ankara. He studied economics and sociology. Formerly affiliated with the Fernand Braudel Center for the Study of Economies, Historical Systems and Civilizations of the State University of New York at Binghamton (USA), he has been involved in the world-systems analysis of large-scale, long-term social change. He is the author of numerous publications with a theoretical specialization in institutionalism and a geographical focus on the Eastern Mediterranean.

- **Gaby Straßburger** received her doctoral degree in Social Sciences at the University of Osnabrück, Germany. Since 2002 she has been coordinator of Community Work at the Institut für Stadtteilbezogene Soziale Arbeit und Beratung (ISSAB), Essen. She wrote her dissertation on *Marriage Behaviour and Partner Choice in the Context of Immigration.* She was contributor to the Sixth Official Family Report about *Families of Foreign Origin in Germany.*

Preface

This volume is the result of the meetings of the German-Turkish Summer Institute for doctoral students from Turkish and German universities. Advanced graduate students from the disciplines of political science, economics, sociology, anthropology, law and linguistics participated in two intensive two-week workshops which took place over two consecutive years in Bremen and İstanbul respectively. The meetings provided a forum for discussing the drafts for the chapters presented in this book.

This collection of essays represents a further step towards an operationalisation of the concept of continuous and dense sets of transboundary social and symbolic ties, which have come to be known as transnational social spaces. An earlier volume on transnational spaces which emerged out of a project at the University of Bremen was published in German under the title *Transstaatliche Räume* (Bielefeld: transcript Verlag, 2000) and in Turkish *Devletaşırı Alan* (İstanbul: Bağlam, 2003). The current book further explores the concept of transnational social spaces and uses new evidence, extending the analysis beyond the German end of transboundary ties and bringing in studies from both the Turkish and the German side of transnational spaces. The authors deal with topics such as social movements in the realms of the environment and gender, inquire into transnational nationalist organizations, analyse transboundary marriage patterns, take a closer look at transnational entrepreneurship, and investigate management strategies in multinational companies as well as focusing on the transnational use of mass media.

The meetings of the German-Turkish Summer Institute were made possible thanks to the financial support of the German Academic Exchange Service (DAAD) in Bonn, the Körber Foundation in Hamburg, the Robert Bosch Foundation in Stuttgart and the University of Bremen. The Middle East Technical University (METU), Ankara, provided institutional support for the organisation of the meetings. Thomas Faist hosted the first meeting in Bremen in August 2000, and Eyüp Özveren organised the second meeting in İstanbul and Balikesir the following year. Special thanks go to Professor Fikret Adaman from the Department of Economics at Boğaziçi University in İstanbul, who acted as the local host at the İstanbul meeting in 2001. We would also like to thank İskender and Sema Azatoğlu for their warm hospitality during our stay at İdaköy Çiftlik Evi. Vicki May helped to correct grammatical mistakes, although obviously we take full responsibility for the final version. Michael Wittig took care of formatting the text assisted by Stefan Schaa and Nicole Wynands. Thomas Faist would also like to extend his thanks to the School of International Migration and Ethnic Relations (IMER) at Malmö University, which generously afforded him time to arrange for the English edition of the book during his tenure as Willy-Brandt-Guest Professor in the Spring of 2003. Eyüp Özveren is grateful to Professor Oktar Türel, former Dean of the Faculty of Economics and Administrative Sciences, METU, Ankara, for his support.

August 2003, Malmö and Ankara

The Editors,
Thomas Faist and Eyüp Özveren

Chapter 1

The Border-Crossing Expansion of Social Space: Concepts, Questions and Topics[1]

Thomas Faist

Introduction

Social formations and non-state co-operation across borders have received growing attention since the early 1990s in various fields of the social sciences. In the study of social movements, analysts have coined terms such as 'advocacy networks' to encompass the co-operation of non-governmental organisations (NGOs) around the globe in policy areas such as human rights (e.g. Keck and Sikkink, 1998) and the environment. In the mid-1990s the concept of transnational relations also resurfaced in the field of international politics (Risse-Kappen, 1995) Unlike the earlier literature on inter-state interdependencies based on ties arising out of trade and foreign investment, this new wave has sought to establish the outlines of a global civil society. In migration research, authors have begun to study international migration in the context of sometimes dense and continuous transborder linkages between migrants, groups, communities and non-state organisations, alternatively labelled transnational social formations (Smith and Guarnizo, 1998), transnational social fields (Basch et al., 1994) and transnational social spaces (Pries, 2001).

One of the most important questions facing students of transnational relations viz. spaces concerns the way in which transnational ties between individual and collective actors become regularized or institutionalised. Institutions imply that there is a permanent locus of regularized and established principles, or a code of conduct that governs a crucial area of social (political, economic, cultural) life. Institutions are sets of procedures and norms which regulate social activities. They may range from highly formalised structures and processes at one end of the scale to relatively informal ones at the other end. Even relatively informal processes may themselves become institutionalised through repetition or

---

[1] I would like to thank my co-editor, Eyüp Özveren, for valuable criticism, suggestions and additions.

2   *Transnational Social Spaces*

convention over time. Think of religious communities of Turkish immigrants in Germany in the 1970s, some of which later institutionalized their relations with organizations in Turkey during the 1980s and 1990s (Faist, 1998). This broad definition encompasses regularized activities and procedures in social structures like families, all types of communities such as villages, ethnic, religious, national and diasporic communities, business enterprises, political parties, to list but a few examples. Even issue networks may be classified as relatively informal types of institutions. These are relatively loosely-knit co-operative social structures concerned with certain topics such as human rights. We would expect that relatively high degrees of institutionalisation lead to more stable transnational ties and ensure that we are not dealing with purely transient, short-term and epiphenomenal border-crossing ties. This book therefore seeks to establish the existence of and the mechanisms operative in transnational ties, relations, formations – and, to use a catch-all term – transnational spaces.

Even the German-Turkish Summer Institute that provided the framework for this study emerged as a sort of institutionalised social space which continued through manifold contacts after its formal conclusion. It is perhaps no coincidence that this volume has emerged out of a truly transnational effort. The essays developed out of contributions to the German-Turkish Summer Institute we organised in Bremen in 2000 and İstanbul in 2001 with the support of our universities, the University of Bremen and the Middle East Technical University in Ankara.

Given the distinct disciplinary backgrounds of the participants in fields as diverse as sociology, area studies, economics, political science and anthropology – not to mention the wide range of methodologies, concepts, theories and methods these disciplines employ – it is absolutely imperative to seek to formulate, and perhaps even agree on some common ideas and questions.[2] This is why we must first define the key terms used to analyse the transboundary exchange of persons, symbols, ideas and information, services, goods, and capital. Transnational, or trans-state[3] social spaces are the main focus of our attention here, and we elaborate

---

[2] On the selection of Germany and Turkey as the main states around or above which transnational spaces have formed, see Faist, 2000b, pp. 50-2.

[3] In one of my earlier publications (Faist, 2000b) I have used the term 'trans-state' in order to avoid the conceptual quagmire of conflated notions of 'nation' and 'state'. Quite obviously, there exist not only nation-states constituted by a single nation but also multinational states such as India, Belgium, Canada and, perhaps, Switzerland. In the strict sense of the term, 'transnational' refers to relations both among nations within sovereign states and across state borders. Therefore, strictly speaking, the term is of little analytical value because it replaces the category which should be at the centre of attention here – state and non-state actors and institutions – with one of the important correlates in modernity – nation. This is why the term 'trans-state' makes more sense when describing ties that criss-cross the borders of sovereign states. However, this use of terminology is likely to create confusion because established terms then acquire a new and different meaning. For example, following the new terminology, transnational relations would now apply to ties between nations in one and the same nation-state (e.g. the ethnic categories of Flemings and

on various types of transnational spaces. Our focus then shifts to the main dimensions of transborder exchange: 1. the degree of 'time-space compression' (Anthony Giddens) in transborder transactions: the extensity and intensity of flows and exchanges and 2. the organisation of exchange: infrastructure, institutionalisation and state regulation of transnational transactions. Third, we differentiate four types of transnational spaces according to the degree to which they are institutionalised and examine the emergence of dense transnational networks. Fourth, we sketch some of the impacts of the transboundary expansion of social space; casting a wide net over German-Turkish spaces and, in some cases, placing them in a wider comparative perspective. Fifth, the Summer Institute was in itself a transboundary network of individuals and organisations. It is therefore useful to reflect upon the goals of the Summer Institute, and the modes and rules of communication within the workshop itself.

Conceptualisation: The Transboundary Expansion of Social Spaces and Transnational Spaces

The focus of our analysis is on transboundary exchanges and transactions in networks, organisations and communities. Our point of departure is not state-to-state interactions (as, for example, in international relations) but the interaction between non-state actors across borders. However, these transboundary exchanges are always examined in terms of their legal and politico-institutional regulation.

By transboundary expansion of social spaces we mean processes that signify a transformation in the spatial organisation of social and symbolic relations, namely, ties and transactions – assessed in terms of their extensity, intensity, infrastructure, degree of institutionalisation and impact. These processes are visible and result in transboundary exchanges and networks of interaction, linguistic and cultural diffusion, legal regulation and political authority. Unlike globalisation, the transboundary expansion of social spaces is restricted to certain regions – in our case that region is predominantly the core and periphery of 'Europe'. Therefore, the type of transboundary expansion of social space we are concerned with is regionally specific. Regional specificity here refers to the transboundary clustering of transactions, exchanges, networks and interactions of actors in functional and geographical groupings of states.

By transnational spaces we mean relatively stable, lasting and dense sets of ties reaching beyond and across the borders of sovereign states. They consist of combinations of ties and their contents, positions in networks and organisations, and networks of organisations that cut across the borders of at least two nation-

---

Walloons in Belgium) and across states (e.g. the national category of Hungarians in both Hungary and Romania). Therefore, while it is important to avoid confusing 'state' and 'nation' it may suffice to point out the dilemma and continue using the established terms (an approach followed by Mandaville, 2001).

states. Transnational spaces differ from clearly demarcated state territories. Nonetheless, actors in transnational spaces may include state agents who operate on behalf of a national state government or an intergovernmental organisation. The important point here is that when referring to transnational ties, non-state actors are involved to a significant degree. Space here denotes the cultural, economic and political practices of individual and collective actors within territories or places. Thus, the term space not only pertains to physical characteristics, as in a more traditional geographical understanding. Space comprises the links between actors in different places, whereas place refers to one specific location (cf. Faist, 2004). Overall, the concept of transnational social spaces explores the principles by which geographical propinquity, which implies the embeddedness of ties in one locality, is supplemented or transformed by transnational exchanges. This further raises the question as to the transaction mechanisms embedded in social ties and structures, such as exchange, reciprocity and solidarity.

The smallest analytical unit in a social space is a tie, be it social or symbolic. Social ties represent a continuing series of personal transactions – communication between at least three actors – to which the people involved ascribe common interests, obligations, expectations and norms. Social ties can also be indirect, reaching individuals beyond the immediate realm of direct relations. Symbolic ties are continuing transactions with which the people involved link common meanings, memories, expectations for the future, and collective representations. Languages can be seen as highly complex sets of symbolic ties. Both social and symbolic ties may reach beyond the face-to-face relations between individuals, involving people speaking the same language, members of the same faith, class, profession, ideology, ethnicity (or) nationality (Faist, 2000a, chapter 4).

Social and symbolic ties can assume a more institutionalised form. Citizenship is an example of an institutionalised tie between and among citizens and to their states. Law is an important element in regulating social and symbolic ties between and among people, the relation of people to states and interstate institutions, and the interaction between states. In the present era of 'globalisation', there has been a shift away from purely state-centred politics to a new, more complex form of multi-level, global governance (Marks, 1997), and – of prime importance here – regional governance, as in the case of the European Union (EU).

In order to grasp both conceptually and empirically the transboundary ties of persons, networks and organisations in transnational spaces, we need to develop a typology signifying the main dimensions of the transboundary expansion of social spaces. These dimensions can be conceptualised in two ways: in terms of the 'time-space compression' of ties and in terms of the organisation of ties.[4]

---

[4] The main categories of transboundary transactions are derived from the study by Held et al., 1999.

The Border-Crossing Expansion of Social Space

Time-space Compression of Ties: Extensity and Intensity

Extensity Extensity refers to the extensity of activities and practices across frontiers. Events, decisions and activities in one state can be significant for persons and communities in another. Three aspects of extensity must be taken into consideration:

- The location of activities. Activities, events, decisions may take place in Turkey and Germany to roughly equal degrees; or more in one country or the other. Extra-territorial activities are for instance when Turkish construction companies in Germany employ posted, i.e. subcontracted workers not subject to German social security regulations.
- The actors involved. These are individuals, groups, organisations, and communities who speak certain languages, engage in code-switching, embark upon transnational business activities, and who classify themselves or are defined by others as hybrids.
- The fields covered refer to the areas of social life affected by transnational ties. These range from everyday family life to public life in politics or even full formal membership in political communities, i.e. citizenship.

Intensity Over the past roughly three decades, we have observed an intensification and growing magnitude of interconnectedness, patterns of interaction and exchange that transcend the constituent societies and states in the EU-Turkey region. The number of ties has multiplied. However, this does not tell us much about the density and velocity of ties:

- The density of ties is the number of connections and relations and the frequentcy of transboundary transactions in a given space and over a given period.
- Speed of transactions refers to the acceleration of transnational interactions and processes through the development of transboundary transport and communications systems. We can measure the velocity of the transnational diffusion of ideas, goods, information, capital and people.

Linkage Patterns in Networks, Organisations and Communities

Infrastructure Needless to say, transboundary exchanges among and between persons, organisations, communities, groups and networks cannot exist without some kind of infrastructural support which facilitates transactions or provides resources for making connections and facilitates exchange. Infrastructures thus influence the overall level of interaction capacity in every sector (politics, economics, and culture), and the potential magnitude of regional interconnectedness.

6 *Transnational Social Spaces*

- Modes of transportation and communication include communication technologies, languages, and migration networks. These are mechanisms and mediators that facilitate or hinder transnational ties and flows.
- Informal norms and procedures can be found among communities spanning borders such as professional associations, religious communities, and village communities.

Regulation: Law and State Policies Non-state actors always operate in spaces regulated by individual states or through bilateral state agreements, international regimes, international law and supra-state authorities.

- Formal norms and procedures refer to the degree of restriction or liberty to which the movement of persons (e.g., immigration restrictions in family unification, asylum etc., access to citizenship), capital, goods, information and services across borders is subjected. Transborder movements and exchanges are also determined by domestic (intra-state) regulations that indirectly have an effect upon the transboundary expansion of social spaces. Take, for example, the freedom of religion, guaranteed by constitutions. If freedom of religious expression is restricted, believers may emigrate abroad. Relevant norms and procedures can be implemented by an individual state (e.g. Turkey or Germany), through bilateral agreements (e.g. the contract worker agreement between Germany and Turkey in 1961), international regimes, or by supra-state authorities such as the EU (e.g. through the Customs Union or accession of Turkey to the EU).
- Hierarchies and patterns of authority: Relations between states and between non-state organisations are rarely symmetrical in terms of power and authority. Even states differ in their political and economic influence and weight. Asymmetrical relations are the rule. In the late 19th century, Western expansion, imperialism and military power were the dominant modes and instruments of state interaction between the European powers and the Ottoman Empire. Germany, albeit in military co-operation with the Ottoman Empire (e.g. in the building of the Baghdad railway), also took part in the race for a share of the Middle East. In the late 20th century, by contrast, economic instruments, competition and co-operation appear to have taken precedence over military force as dominant modes of interaction between European states and Turkey; although still in an asymmetrical context (cf. Özveren, 2000b).

Institutionalisation There are various types of transnational spaces with varying degrees of institutionalisation ranging from low, as in networks and contact and diffusion fields (e.g. tourism) to highly formalised groups such as kinship systems and larger aggregates such as village communities, multinational companies, religious communities, and diasporas (see Table 1.1 on page 7).

Types of Transnational Spaces, their Evolution and Alternative Concepts

Types of Transnational Spaces

Transnational spaces can be differentiated according to their degree of formalisation or institutionalisation (see above) and longevity. The degree of institutionalisation refers both to the internal characteristics of group organisation and the extent of common or shared values and symbols. On the one hand there are networks with low levels of formalisation, and on the other there are highly formalised institutions. Organisations are characterised by a high degree of formalised relations, for example in terms of hierarchy and control. Communities also show a high degree of formalisation, though not in terms of their internal organisational structure but their common values and symbols. How about: In terms of their common values and symbols, communities can also be said to show a high degree of formalisation, expressed, for instance, in national, religious, communal and family customs. There are four ideal types of transnational spaces: areas of contact and diffusion; small groups, particularly kinship systems; issue networks; and communities and organisations (see Table 1.1).

Table 1.1 Types of Transnational Spaces

Degree of Formalisation	
Low: Networks	**High: Institutions**
diffusion: e.g. fields for the exchange of goods, capital, persons, information, ideas and practices (1)	*small kinship groups*: e.g. households, families (2)
issue networks: e.g. networks of business people, epistemic networks, advocacy networks (3)	*communities and organisations*: e.g. religious groups, enterprises (4)

8 *Transnational Social Spaces*

(1) Diffusion: Contact Fields for the Exchange of Goods, Capital, Persons, Information and Cultural Practices This category comprises phenomena such as the exchange of goods, capital and services between businesses. People engaged in these transactions do not necessarily have sustained or close contact with each other. In some cases, strangers meet at the marketplace or at tourist resorts. Transboundary ties between individuals and organisations may also lead to a diffusion of language, e.g. specialist terms are borrowed from one language and incorporated into another. We also find social and cultural practices diffusing across borders – as in the action repertoires of social movements. Among immigrants, for example, we observe processes that partly point to cultural diffusion from the country of origin to the country of settlement. For example, Kurds in Turkey brought their traditional New Year's celebration (*Newroz* or *Nevroz*) to Germany, where it became an important symbol of common Kurdish identity. In order to take the wind out of the Kurdish separatists' sails, the Turkish government promptly responded by declaring *Nevroz* an official bank holiday in 1996.

(2) Small Groups: Kinship Systems Highly formalised transboundary relations within small groups like households and families, or even wider kinship systems, are representative for many migrants. Families may live apart because one or more members work abroad as contract workers (like the former 'guestworkers' in Germany) or as posted employees within multinational companies. Small household and family groups have a strong sense of belonging to a common home. A classic example for such relations are transnational families, who conceive themselves as both an economic unit and a unit of solidarity and who keep, besides the main house, a kind of shadow household in another country. Transnational families make use of resources inherent in social ties like reciprocity, and also resources existing in symbolic ties, such as solidarity. Economic assets are mostly transferred from abroad to those who continue to run the household 'back home'. This type of transnational space tends to be relatively short-lived, although it is internally much more highly formalised or institutionalised than contact fields for the exchange of goods, information, practices and people. As a rule, remittances from migrants in small relational or household groups are made only as long as the group is not yet re-united in one country or while the migrants are still alive.

(3) Issue Networks Transnational issue networks[5] are sets of ties between persons and organisations in which information and services are exchanged for the purpose

---

[5] A network is defined as a set of individual or collective actors – ranging from individuals and families to businesses and nation-states – and the relations that connect them. In contrast to organisations. networks have no formal membership status and no authoritative spokespersons. Networks consist of more or less homogeneous sets of ties between three or more positions or 'nodes'. Social networks encompass ties linking nodes in a social system – ties that connect individuals, groups. organizations. or clusters of ties, as well as people. Network patterns of ties comprise economic. political networks of interaction, as well as collectives such as groups (kinship groups or communities) and private or public associations. A network is a concept or

The Border-Crossing Expansion of Social Space   9

of achieving a common goal. Linkage patterns may concatenate into advocacy networks (e.g. human rights; Keck and Sikkink, 1998), business networks, or science networks (cf. 'epistemic communities' by Haas, 1992). These issue-specific networks have a high value-content and engage in areas such as human rights and environmental protection, providing resources to actors in intra-state political, social and cultural conflicts. Often, there is a common discourse concerning a specific issue such as human rights or a profession. In contrast to organisations with formal membership, access to these networks is not strictly limited to interested actors. While issue networks look back upon a long tradition in the realm of human rights, and are making steady progress in ecology, they are also emerging among migrants who have moved from the so-called third countries to the European Union (EU). Among the immigrant and citizenship associations are, for example, the European Citizenship Action Service (ECAS), the Migration Policy Group (MPG) – the latter network including the British NGO Justice, the Immigration Lawyers Practitioners' Association and the Dutch Standing Group of Experts on Immigration and Asylum. Some of these networks – usually headed by non-migrant EU citizens – have succeeded in bringing issues such as discrimination onto the agendas of Intergovernmental Conferences (IGC), and, ultimately, into the Treaty of Maastricht (1997) (Favell, 1998, pp. 9-11). From the mid-1990s onwards, the EU Commission itself sponsored another transnational NGO, the European Union Migrants' Forum (EUMF). This structure, however, soon gambled away its reputation with infighting between Moroccan and Turkish groupings, the exclusion of certain migrant groups and countries, and disinterest on the part of French organisations.

(4) Transnational Communities and Organisations Communities and organisations constitute highly formalised types of transnational spaces with an inherent potential for a relatively long life-span. Although these two sub-types partly overlap, they should for analytical reasons be distinguished. Close symbolic ties are characteristic of transnational communities, whereas a more formal internal hierarchy and systematically structured controls over social ties exist within transnational organisations.

Transnational communities comprise dense and continuous sets of social and symbolic ties, characterised by a high degree of intimacy, emotional depth, moral obligation and sometimes even social cohesion. Geographical proximity is no longer a necessary criterion for the existence of a community. Transnational

---

strategy for studying how resources, goods, and ideas are exchanged among through particular configurations of social and symbolic ties. An analysis of networks enables us to make statements about the potential for interaction between certain people. Indicators are size, density or connectedness, degree, centrality and clustering of positions. An added benefit of network analysis is that positions can be included which are not part of formal and tightly bound groups. Descriptions and explanations based solely on bounded groups sometimes overlook members' crosscutting involvements in various circles.

communities may describe a wider relational space spanning the borders of two or more states. Transnational communities can evolve at different levels of aggregation. The simplest type consists of village communities in international migration systems, whose relations are marked by solidarity extended over long periods of time. Members of such communities who are abroad or have returned home often invest in private or public projects for the benefit of the community in question (cf. Engelbrektsson, 1978).

The quintessential form of transnational communities consists of larger transboundary religious groups and churches. World religions, such as Judaism, Christianity, Islam, Hinduism and Buddhism existed long before modern states came into existence. Diasporas also belong to the category of transnational communities. Diasporas are groups that experienced the territorial dispersion of their members some time in the past, either due to a traumatic experience, or specialisation in long-distance trade. Jews, Palestinians, Armenians and Greeks can be named as examples here. Generally, members of diasporas have a common memory of their lost homeland, or a vision of an imagined one to be created, while at the same time the immigration country often refuses the respective minority full acknowledgement of their cultural distinctiveness (cf. Safran, 1991). Emigration from Turkey has included diasporic elements (Jews, Armenians, Arab Christians). Collectives from Turkey with substantial numbers abroad have used terms such as 'diaspora' to give disputed claims to independence more weight and legitimacy. Some Kurdish organisations, for example, recently claimed the right to nationhood or lesser forms of cultural and political autonomy (e.g. federalism). The 'ethnic revival' in Turkey has reached other 'mixed' groups as well, such as Zazas, among whom we find Alevis (a religious category) and Kurds (an ethnic category).

Transnational organisations differ from small groups like transnational families by virtue of an even higher degree of formal control and co-ordination of social and symbolic ties. Both state and non-state political organisations are marked by a specific form of bureaucratic rule, such as efficient instruments of administration and inherent tendencies towards an expansion of the spheres of competence and control (cf. Weber, 1988, p. 498). An early type of transnational organisation – international non-governmental organisations (INGOS) – developed out of issue networks like the Red Cross, Amnesty International and Greenpeace. At the other extreme there are organisations which are based in one specific country but whose sphere of influence extends abroad, as with the ethno-nationalist PKK (*Partiya Karkarên Kurdistan*). The PKK is not a non-governmental organisation but a para-state association because it seeks – at least until the late 1990s it sought – political autonomy for a territory named 'Kurdistan'. Their goal is mass mobilisation, without which they cannot succeed. Transnational enterprises constitute a further type of transboundary organisation. These businesses are differenttiated transboundary organisations with an extremely detailed internal division of labour.

The Evolution of Transnational Spaces

Technological progress in transport and communication play a major role in the formation and dynamics of transnational spaces. First of all, economic development has brought with it unthought-of possibilities in technological development, encounters in contact fields and the formation of transnational enterprises. The technological breakthrough in telecommunications and travel began as early as the 19th century and perpetuated the growth of the world market. New, improved means of transport and communication such as transocean steamship lines or telegraphy offered the necessary, albeit far from perfect prerequisites for speeding up transboundary commerce, migration and travel. In short, continuing technological progress in the fields of communication and transport considerably diminished the costs of bridging long distances. This tendency even intensified after the end of World War Two. All available empirical indicators suggest that since then financial markets have integrated at break-neck speed and foreign capital investment has intensified (for manifold data, see Beisheim et al., 1999). Although relative geographical immobility reigns supreme in a world with international migrants constituting only around 2 percent of the world population, the migration rate grew by about 1.8 percent p.a. from 1960 to 1990, and between 1985 and 1990 reached an annual average of 2.6 percent, though with a slight upward tendency (Zlotnik, 1999, pp. 22-23). Thus, a diversity of potentially global structural and technological developments lifted the constraints on territorially confined networks, communities and organisations. However, this did not translate directly into the complete globalisation of these spaces, but rather the opening up of a multitude of new, transboundary social spaces on a regional scale.

Second, within world regions such as North America, Southeast Asia and above all Europe, governments have responded to and guided transnational transactions with novel forms of politico-economic integration, ranging in terms of regulation and common rules from free-trade zones to customs unions, internal markets and economic union. In Europe, 'internal borders' that formerly restricted the flow of goods, people, capital and services have been abolished and replaced by new, reinforced borders at the outer frontiers of the EU. The EU has developed through all these stages consecutively since the mid-1950s, evolving from a low-intensity international regime of states to a federated network of governments and common organisations (like the EU Commission, for instance) with 'pooled sovereignty'. The EU was created by intergovernmental fiat. And nowadays a few policy areas are even regulated by qualified majority voting in the Council of Ministers – thus limiting the sovereignty and autonomy of member states (e.g. macro-economic indicators, EU-internal migration, gender equality, occupational health and safety). The EU is now more than an international regime, and has taken on more of a supra-state character. The intensification of economic and political ties between the member countries has exerted an inexorable attraction to the countries at the rim of the EU, first in Southern Europe, and later in Eastern and South-eastern Europe and even North Africa.

12 *Transnational Social Spaces*

Third, state and non-state actors within the countries involved have responded in a number of different ways that sometimes fostered the transboundary expansion of social spaces. An obvious example in the economic realm is the abandonment of étatist (state-led) and import-substitution development plans and their replacement with export-oriented development strategies such as tariff dismantling with a view to trade and foreign exchange liberalization. But there are also policies which were intended to regulate political and cultural life but which instead have actually accelerated the establishment of transboundary ties, often unintentionally. For example, the diffusion of the 'nation-state' idea around those parts of world still undergoing decolonisation often generates minority conflicts and refugee crises.[6] Turkey has been plagued for decades with conflicts related to the 'Kurdish question', sometimes cast in religious terms and nowadays – not least because of the diffusion of the nation-state model – revolving around demands for national minority rights and more cultural and political autonomy for Kurds, and even the formation of a new state. Such conflicts have been taken abroad, not only to adjacent countries in the Middle East (Iraq, Iran, Syria) but also to immigration countries in Europe (cf. Hocker and Liebe-Harkort, 1996). What may at first sight seem surprising is that it is not so much repressive policies that contributed to the export and import of conflicts, but the relative openness of political systems. For example, in Germany 'multicultural' policies have contributed to the trans-boundary expansion of immigrant politics and culture. If immigration states are liberal democracies and do not seek to assimilate immigrants by force, the respective immigrant minorities have greater chances of maintaining their cultural difference and ties to their country of origin. Multicultural policies in immigration states – such as the institutionalised teaching of the native language as well as the incorporation of religious confessions – possibly support not only integration but also the maintenance of various transnational communities and organisations. Other things being equal, the more liberal or tolerant the respective political regime is towards the immigrant minority with regard to the preservation of distinctive practices and institutions, the more likely the formation of transnational collectives will be. Multicultural policies give immigrants the opportunity to mobilise resources. This applies to Kurdish immigrants in Sweden and The Netherlands to an even higher degree than in Germany. The former countries have come to embrace 'multiculturalism' as a state strategy to integrate immigrants. This means that not only repressive policies and discrimination encourage the maintenance of transnational ties among immigrants, but also liberal multicultural rights and

---

[6] A *nation* is a cross-class community whose shared sense of identity, solidarity and interest is rooted in an ethnic identity and common historical experience (thus mixing real, imagined and interpreted notions) and whose central political project is the possession of a distinctive state in a bounded territory. *Nationalism* can be seen as both a psychological and a cultural affiliation creating a connection with the community of the nation, and a political and cultural project which seeks to achieve self-determination and to create and shape states. *National cultures* are the complex bodies of real and imagined practices, beliefs, rituals and attitudes that have emerged out of these projects.

The Border-Crossing Expansion of Social Space 13

activities. In short, a mix of flight-inducing politics and policies – not always repression – in the emigration countries and a framework of liberal-democratic conditions in the immigration states seem to be particularly conducive to transnational mobilisation in the areas of politics and religion.

Selected Fields and Issues in the Analysis of Transnational Spaces

The organisation of ties and the impact of transnational structures and collective action can be neatly divided into four categories: international relations and supranational integration, political rights and struggles, entrepreneurship and management, culture, media, and everyday social life. By definition, the realm of everyday social life-worlds is the least institutionalised. The exposition of these four categories with specific reference to German-Turkish spaces in general, and to the case studies that follow in particular, is set within a broader macro-structural and political-economic context focusing on the master processes of European integration.

International Relations and Supranational Integration: The EU, Turkey and Germany

Ever since the then EEC and Turkey signed the Association Agreement (AA), relations between the European Union and Turkey have been crisis-ridden. Initially, and in official statements, both Turkey and the EEC described the Association Agreement, the Additional Protocol (AP), the Customs Union decision of 1995 and later EU applications as significant steps towards 'modernising' Turkey and anchoring it to the 'West'. Indeed, relations did intensify over time. For example, the Association Council (AC) actually foresaw easier access for Turkish workers to jobs in the EU once they had worked in an EU member state for a couple of years (cf. Lichtenberg et al., 1996). Most importantly, the EU and Turkey entered into a Customs Union in 1996. And, despite the fact that the EU denied Turkey's application to the EU in 1987 and did not include Turkey among the next accession candidates in December 1997, the decision made in December 1999 in Helsinki to accept Turkey as a candidate proved to be steps in the right direction – albeit always accompanied by continuing tensions. Turkey and the EU have constantly accused each other of not keeping to the bargains agreed upon regarding trade and economic issues and political development. For example, the EU has demanded 'progress' with respect to Turkey's violation of human rights especially with regard to the Kurdish population, the civilian government's control over the military, and a resolution of the contentious issues in Greco-Turkish relations, but has remained unsatisfied. The Turkish side in turn has usually responded by citing a long list of broken promises. For example, Turkey accused the EU of withholding the right to free movement for Turkish citizens. In sum, the strength and density of relations between the EU and Turkey have increased in the

14 *Transnational Social Spaces*

economic and political realms but have continued to remain highly contentious (cf. Ceylanoğlu, 2000).

One pressing question is whether we can take these reciprocal accusations – such as Europe being a 'Christian Club' or Turkey a semi-authoritarian Oriental state – at face value. Images such as these are in transition, framed and used according to the needs of political actors. One alternative hypothesis is that in the past both the EU and its member states, and Turkey, have misled their respective constituents by declaring a commitment to convergence and integration on the one hand but failing to act accordingly on the other. Both sides seem to have interpreted the legal and policy regulations as they suited their interests best, using a high degree of discretion deriving from the fact that neither party kept its obligations. One the one hand, Turkish governments have until recently persistently deviated from their declared policy and goal of EU orientation, and continued with their control-reliant mode of governance. Moreover, Turkish officials have consistently dragged their feet when carrying out the reforms necessary for convergence towards the EU. The EU, on the other hand, has failed to come up with clear rules governing EU-Turkish relations. The EU's stance has always been vague and non-committal. Having secured a commitment from Turkey for Customs Union, the EU has been rather reluctant in engaging itself in a serious negotiation process for further steps towards full membership. Whereas Turkey's long-term modernisation process provides one strong pillar for future integration, the EU's short-sighted emphasis on the Copenhagen criteria, originally drawn up with the reality of eastern European countries in mind, serves to undermine this very pillar and make future rapprochement all the more difficult. This raises suspicions in Turkey as to whether the EU is actually trying to sabotage the accession process by deliberately helping religious conservatives and ethnic separatists to undermine modernity within Turkey (cf. Özveren, 2000a).

What is remarkable is that during this debate, on the whole actors both in Turkey and the EU have taken recourse to non-divisible policy issues. From research on collective goods (cf. Olson's study, 1966) on the mutually beneficial accession of Turkey to the EU) we know that non-divisible topics such as human rights or ridiculous accusations of the EU being a 'Christian club' are not amenable to package deals. This stands in stark contrast to divisible issues such as tariffs. In emphasizing these political clichés, each side has only derived short-term benefits. The successive Turkish governments were able to uphold 'national pride'. The EU was able to continue and justify a non-committal stand towards Turkey because of its alleged cultural 'otherness', interpreted as backwardness – the EU's form of contemporary Orientalism? (cf. Said, 1979).

It seems necessary to analyse the concrete commitments made on both sides and how they evaded them. It is crucial thereby to look at the explanatory power of culturalist and political-economic approaches. What is more, it is necessary to move beyond research perspectives that one-sidedly emphasise state-centred (intergovernmentalist) or society-centred (functionalist) research (cf. Ugur, 1999). Obviously, among the main actors were not only the supra-state institutions of the

EU and the respective member state governments – but also interest groups, business and trade union networks, etc. In addition, it remains an open question whether the declared acceptance of Turkey as a potential member has overcome a type of prisoner's dilemma, in which the EU's failure to make clear demands on Turkey increases the probability of policy reversals in Turkey, in turn increasing the EU's reluctance to anchor Turkey's convergence towards European standards.

Political Rights and Struggles: Co-operation between Non-State Groups, Networks, Organisations and State Responses

Clearly, a transnational perspective implies that politics is not reduced to affairs of the state. States and supra-state organisations are not the only relevant actors in the public sphere, the realm of life in which discourses, conflicts, and decisions occur and in which, taking equal political liberty as given, all members of a political community may participate. Non-governmental associations whose activities extend beyond the borders of single states are an indication of the potential of how far a civil society can reach across sovereign states and converge with others to build a transnational society. Politics, however, is about contested norms and identities. Seen from a transnational perspective, the point is not so much to emphasise the presence of non-state actors. It is above all a question of the location and the implications of political contention in spaces that cut across nation-states.

Transnational collective political action in the realm of social movements is increasingly translocal. Zeynep Kadirbeyoğlu's analysis of the campaign against Eurogold in rural areas of Western Turkey is thus a useful corrective against the overemphasis of macro-actors in disciplines such as International Relations (Kadirbeyoğlu, chapter 2, this volume). This social movement action was organised on a local level, but with various links to environmentalist experts and activists abroad, and it also addressed the national government. It is obvious that the repertoire of collective action and strategies was adopted from struggles abroad. It seems that there is a sector of the social movement that is at least partially transnationalised. Over the course of time, participants in the Bergama movement, who ranged from peasants in the region to lawyers and other professionals in nearby cities, re-examined their relationship to central government. Not surprisingly, movement entrepreneurs proved crucial in connecting resources from the transnational and national to the local level. Overall, we see a sort of an interlocking mechanism at work, suggesting that not only powerful collective actors such as multinationals are able to organise on a transnational scale. In the particular case of Bergama the fact that Eurogold was a multinational company may have even spurred local resistance. At least, it may have been easier to garner local support against a multinational than against a Turkish company.

In general, the non-governmental sector has become more extensive, as increasing numbers of non-state organisations and actors have entered the public sphere, for example in the fields of human rights, ecology, and business, along with a diffusion of organisations explicitly contending with state power. Over the past decade the growth of organisations registered as transnational associations – so-called International Non-Governmental Organisations (INGOS) – has rocketed. In the period from 1970 to 1994, a total of 544 ethnic organisations registered with the Union of International Organisations. Transnational faith communities have doubled since 1970 to a total of more than 3,000 (Boulding, 1997, p. x). Moreover, there are quite a few associations that are not genuinely of a transboundary kind but nevertheless entertain links with transnational organisations or NGOs in other countries. An example are human rights associations such as *Demokratisches Türkeiforum* (DTV), *İnsan Hakları Derneği* (İHD) or *Türkiye İnsan Hakları Vakfı* (TİHV). Some form transnational networks consisting of genuinely transboundary NGOs (e.g., Amnesty International or Greenpeace) and domestic NGOs such as İHD.

Information exchanges within business and issue-centred networks have intensified over the past years because of the speedy transmission of information through the Internet. It could be hypothesized that the intensification of information exchange has, at times, strengthened co-operation within networks. Ties within non-governmental networks are important for genuinely transnational – in our case here German and Turkish – NGOs. For the – usually less privileged – Turkish NGOs, issue networks provide entry, leverage, information, solidarity and material resources such as money, which are otherwise hard to come by. German and EU-wide NGOs can accumulate credibility as advocates of human and ecological rights and sustain their organisation by mobilising activists (people who are willing to incur significant costs) and sympathetic audiences. Activism in networks and constituent organisations usually does not entail mass mobilisation.

In order to achieve their goals, advocacy networks promote public relations by 'framing' issues to make them comprehensible to large audiences, approaching coalition partners and exerting influence on target actors such as governmental decision-makers. The corresponding repertoire of collective action requires an elaborate infrastructure, reaching across the borders of sovereign states. For genuinely transnational organisations and networks, the EU has come to provide infrastructural support (see above). This is particularly interesting for domestic groups when the channels between them and their governments are blocked, or when such channels are ineffective for resolving demands and conflicts. They may then turn to governments abroad and supra-state actors such as the EU either directly or via organisations and networks (cf. the so-called 'boomerang' model by Keck and Sikkink, 1998).

In terms of institutionalising network co-operation, it is not uncommon for business networks to concatenate into lobby organisations. Usually, the benefits arising out of such networks are clear. The process is more problematic when it comes to advocacy or issue networks. The question here is who are the political entrepreneurs who invest considerable start-up costs for such networks? Often, the political entrepreneurs who become core networkers have gathered experience in earlier campaigns on related issues.

The Border-Crossing Expansion of Social Space

Hanife Aliefendioğlu's study concentrates on a case in which the power asymmetry between the two sides involved is very strong, and the start-up costs for establishing a viable network that can be of practical use are quite high. She starts out from the premise that most Turkish women now in Germany immigrated as dependants of their husbands. In other words, the decision to migrate was in most cases not made by women themselves. Furthermore, these mostly first-generation women have been condemned to housework and confined to solitude within the quasi-extended family of their husbands, cut off from the world outside. Given the fact that they did not speak German, this imprisonment became all the more likely. In this context they found themselves trapped in a 'small' place where they had no access to the space outside. With time such women actually became prisoners in an otherwise transnationalizing world. Whereas their world within the walls of their home was frozen in time, progress made by women's movements in both Germany and Turkey had steadily improved the status of their counterparts (in both countries). Consequently, if anything their losses were compounded as time went by. Whereas transnational social spaces worked to the advantage of many other parties such as male wage-workers and entrepreneurs, after having confined such women to a disadvantageous position, they left their lives untouched. Aliefendioğlu examines whether this vicious circle can be turned into a virtuous one. If only links could be established between such women and women's organisations in Germany as well as Turkey, they would be able to gain access to information concerning their newly acquired rights and social and political strength. However, such links involve set-up costs that require co-operation among women's organisations, both NGOs and others, in Germany and Turkey. Furthermore, such links would need to rely extensively on the use of internet facilities through which information could be shared and diffused. It is no coincidence that Aliefendioğlu's own research has made full use of communication facilities through the internet in order to reach out to such NGOs in both Germany and Turkey. She comes up with an inventory of organisations that have either co-operated or might be willing to co-operate on a project-basis in the future in order to reach out to women handicapped by their disadvantageous position. In her endeavour to develop the means to serve practical ends, Aliefendioğlu nevertheless shows that even in this specific area, where transnational spaces have so far not benefited dependent women, there is enormous potential for future transnational links and thereby the ultimate expansion of such a transnational social space (Aliefendioğlu, chapter 3, this volume).

The impact of NGOs can extend from issue creation and agenda setting to an influence on state behaviour and even policy change. With regard to minority politics and policies, transnational links and resources have certainly helped to draw attention to the dozens of ethnic and religious minorities in Turkey. These minority groups frequently organise campaigns in Turkey with the help of expatriates. An example is the now defunct Alevite *Baris Partisi* founded by activists from Cologne and London. Beyond drawing the attention of the public to new issues, NGOs usually aim to influence state and supra-state behaviour. In this

18   *Transnational Social Spaces*

respect, human rights is a particularly compelling issue because it is concerned with physical harm done to innocent persons, and because it is connected to fundamental rights in a constitutional state (*Rechtsstaat*), which is the necessary, though in itself inadequate basis for liberal democracy. The ultimate goal is to target more powerful actors in governments, bureaucracies and the media and to persuade them to take action. Information must therefore be timely, reliable and dramatic. One of the strategies is accountability politics. State authorities are held accountable for treaties and conventions that they sign. In the Turkish-German case there are manifold difficulties because both the EU and Turkey have continuously avoided making firm policy commitments, engaging instead in seemingly endless mutual accusations and symbolic politics[7] (see above). This makes it all the more difficult to shame target actors.

For example, some Kurdish organisations in Germany approach the German government with respect to the cultural and political rights of Kurds in Turkey. Or, to take an example from Turkey, German women's groups in İstanbui and Ankara lobby both the Turkish and German government to improve the legal status of female German citizens married to Turkish men and living in Turkey. As Bianca Kaiser's study shows, the most important of these groups – Die Brücke – is an example of how Europeanisation, forging ever closer ties between Turkey, Germany and the EU, has opened up a political space for social actors. In their endeavour to improve living conditions for Germans residing in Turkey, *Die Brücke* has not only been active in the educational sector, sponsoring bilingual and bicultural programmes through institutions such as the *Europa Kolleg – Avrupa Koleji*. In Turkey, *Die Brücke* has also been lobbying for legal changes regarding permanent residency, work permits and naturalisation since the mid-1990s. Furthermore, *Die Brücke* successfully lobbied the German government regarding dual nationality. Until recently it was extremely difficult to maintain German nationality when acquiring Turkish citizenship. It was thanks to *Die Brücke* that the new law on citizenship that came into effect in Germany in 2000 includes a stipulation that German 'women living in Muslim countries' are explicitly exempted from the general ruling that prohibits dual nationality. *Die Brücke* also forged ties to the broader 'Network of Foreign Spouses' which has lobbied for years to achieve a liberalization of Turkish Foreigners Law (Kaiser, chapter 4, this volume).

Political parties often serve as transmitters between civil society and the state. Emre Arslan (chapter 5, this volume) deals with a Turkish ultranationalist

---

[7] Symbolic politics means that political actors try to define the terms and images that primarily serve tactical purposes in political competition. Those political actors who are successful in defining issues have more chance of success in the political game. Political actors are thus not only or primarily interested in solving issues and problems that arise from policies: they also strive to be the originators of events. Symbolic politics uses substitutes such as cultural backwardness to address substantive policy problems such as human rights violations, or immigrant competition in labour markets to explain structural unemployment.

The Border-Crossing Expansion of Social Space   19

organisation in Germany, the *ülkücülük*. Their situation seems to be quite puzzling. He observes that for adherents to other ideological currents imported from Turkey, such as socialists and Islamists, there is no fundamental obstacle to changing their primary political focus from Turkey to Germany. Although the *ülkücü* party in Turkey cannot totally dictate the German form, *ülkücüs* in Germany depend very much on their counterparts in Turkey because this radical political movement requires a strict and rigid organizational structure. Viewed from a political point of view, the *ülkücüs* concentrate on building a Turkish lobby in Germany or Europe in order to defend the interests of Turkey. Yet, in sociological terms, they have increasingly become an integral part of the material, cultural and social life in German society.

Economic Realm: Transnational Entrepreneurship and Management

Over the past few decades, the extent and variety of transboundary economic transactions by immigrants has increased; as a rule, these transactions take place within the context of a specific migration system, for example in the USA-Caribbean migration system, and increasingly, in the German-Turkish one. Contemporary studies often deal with transnational economic giants that exert a lot of political and economic influence – so-called 'global players'. The intensity of economic exchange has grown dramatically, also between Germany and Turkey. For example, there has been an increase in the volume of goods and capital exchanged, and the speed of transactions has grown.

One should not jump to the conclusion here that transnational enterprises only include huge corporations like IBM or Daimler-Chrysler. International south-north migration offers chances to establish middle-class businesses (Portes, 1996), for example in the textile industry. International migrants make use of their 'insider advantages' such as kinship ties and knowledge of the language of their or their parents' country of origin. We sometimes find a progressive development of transboundary entrepreneurship from intra-kinship reciprocity and solidarity, complemented at later stages by partial transnational circuits that include families, but also larger groups such as ethnic or national communities. Three forms of transboundary economic exchange tend to develop sequentially: first, remittances of migrants from the immigration countries to transnational households and kinship groups in the emigration countries; second, the inception and growth of immigrant businesses in the immigration countries; and third, transnational production, distribution and sale in economic issue networks and multi-state companies.

In relatively well-developed migration circuits such as that between Turkey and Germany, migrants' savings and remittances from abroad have lost signify-cance in the overall balance of payments. Nevertheless, enterprises established by return migrants still remain relevant. Thus, there is not only the well-documented growth of immigrant business enterprises in immigration countries (see the numerous studies by the Centre for Turkish Studies in Essen). There are also three other important types. First, we find transboundary businesses of former migrants,

20 *Transnational Social Spaces*

such as Öger Tours in tourism or Santex in textiles. Second, there are businesses opened in the emigration country by return migrants. Third, there are joint ventures of German and Turkish companies.

In terms of infrastructure, the transboundary economic ties of business-people are lodged within the overall context of a world market. This does not imply, however, that transnational entrepreneurs are identical with global players. Most economic activities are regionally specific and confined. A large number of relatively privileged, highly skilled migrants come from relatively developed countries in the 'South', such as India and Turkey, and concentrate in a few destination countries of the Pacific rim such as Australia and the USA (cf. Salt, 1997). Others are low-skilled migrants who invest abroad, tapping willing ethnic labour supplies. For example, it is certainly no coincidence that companies such as Yimpaş from Central Anatolia concentrate their economic activities in Germany.

The degree of economic and social informality is, of course, dependent on the degree to which the respective labour market is regulated. For example, it is more strictly regulated in Germany than in France. This means that it is easier for immigrants to gain access to small businesses in garment industries in Paris than in Berlin. In Germany, first-generation immigrants – although they have solid qualifications in tailoring – are not able to set up business as easily. They are still restricted to repairs and alterations because it is relatively easier to get permits in this area than for tailors' shops.

In terms of impact, interesting questions arise with respect to the businesses of return migrants. Very early on in the Turkish-German migration process, a group of social workers suggested to Turkish migrant workers and Turkish authorities that they establish an enterprise in Turkey, financed by the migrants' savings from Germany. A former prime minister, Bülent Ecevit, showed great interest in this idea. With the help of German, Turkish and later also Dutch authorities, so-called people's enterprises, such as Türksan, were established in Turkey; other types of businesses included workers' joint stock companies and workers' co-operatives. Rural co-operatives also emerged through these schemes. These pioneering experiments eventually led to the formation of about 7,000 co-operatives and some 550 industrial companies and service businesses. They constituted part of the popular sector (*halk sektörü*) in the Turkish economy. A few of these experiments were successful, while the majority of companies disappeared or were bought up by private firms. Research has established that workers' remittances were invested in the industrial development process in some econo-mically less developed provinces such as Yozgat, Denizli, Bilecik, or districts in Konya and Kayseri. It would be interesting to find out how the emergence of the 'Anatolian Tigers' (*Anadolu Kaplanları*) is related to these earlier experiments.

In his study of transnational enterpreneurship in Çorum, Cem Dişbudak probes into such questions. Çorum is a small city on the Anatolian plateau that has experienced rapid economic growth over the past two decades, so much so as to qualify it as a second-generation 'Anatolian Tiger'. Deprived of natural resources as well as fertile agriculture and easy access to major domestic markets, Çorum could do little but export labour from the 1960s onwards. Dişbudak investigates what the role of return migrants was in the 'economic miracle' witnessed by Çorum. He identifies 10 firms owned by trans-state entrepreneurs in the city. These owners had previously worked in paid employment in Germany, where they accumulated business know-how and enough savings as well as important business connections. Upon their return, they set up their businesses in Çorum, where where their kinship and confessional community benefited from the employment they offered. The firms involved are not large, yet they are export-oriented, and responsible for a significant and increasing part of the city's exports. By acting as role models to be emulated by local entrepreneurs, they thereby contribute to the spread of new technologies and knowledge of global business conditions. Furthermore, most return-migrant businesses almost exclusively target the German market, where the owners rely on their previously established connections. These entrepreneurs jealously maintain their links in Germany by travelling back and forth regularly; that is, they actively conduct their business in both countries. In this sense, these entrepreneurs never really 'returned' for good, but have capitalised out of their transnational social links only to become trans-state entrepreneurs instead (Dişbudak, chapter 6, this volume).

In Dişbudak's case study we do not find much evidence of the so-called Islamic type of business formation. It is thus plausible to argue that economically successful entrepreneurs can more easily integrate in the respective societies through assimilation (big business or otherwise), whereas less successful entrepreneurs are forced to rely on the support structures of a religious style, for example Islamic business. Whether transboundary economic activities contribute to the integration of immigrants in the country of settlement or the country of return also hinges on the level of discrimination. High levels of rejection prevent entrepreneurs from converting economic capital into social status. Historically, it is clear that xenophobic tendencies have hindered overall economic growth (Landes, 1998, chapter 27 and 28). Migrant entrepreneurs interviewed by Dişbudak assessed their opportunities for business in both Germany and Turkey. Some of them in fact did have small businesses of their own in Germany before finally making the decision to return, depending on such factors as discussed above.

There are also German businesspeople who assess their prospects in Germany and Turkey in much the same way and then decide to work abroad. It is the interaction of such businesspeople with their Turkish counterparts that forms the subject of Marita Lintfert's contribution to this volume. Lintfert focuses on the joint ventures of German and Turkish managers in İstanbul and Ankara in order to explore some of the problems of intercultural interaction and communication. We have known for a long time that, firstly, identity and difference are two sides of the same coin in the constitution of images of 'self' and the 'other', and secondly that the economic realm is embedded in social and cultural structures. Lintfert's study takes a further step towards identifying how success or failure in coping with certain problems of identity and difference pertaining to these structures can help or hinder overall performance in the economic arena. Focusing on eighteen managers and consultants who work for German and Turkish enterprises, Lintfert pinpoints the role of reciprocal perceptions and experiences as impinging upon the local business circumstances of otherwise globally operating businesses. An in-depth study of language and non-verbal communication that reveals the cultural biases, prejudices and misunderstandings of the parties concerned as they manifest themselves in daily patterns of interaction is intended here. Clearly, had there been no transnational social spaces where such problems are actually encountered and negotiated, we would not now be facing such an issue in the first place. Put differently, this very research itself attests to the social and cultural constitution of transnational spaces even within the micro-cosmos of offices. While Lintfert herself dwells upon the possibility of efficient communication across cultures brought into contact through transnational social spaces, her interviews themselves present valuable evidence for future researchers of transnational business with different foci (Lintfert, chapter 7, this volume).

Culture, Media, and Everyday Social Life

Syncretist cultural practices (e.g. music styles, language diffusion and mixing) and identities (e.g. hyphenated ones such as German-Turks or Turkish-German seem to be phenomena that tend to accompany processes of international exchange and migration. Although such phenomena may range from evanescent and temporary to more enduring and stable patterns over time, their observable existence has implications for the self-conception of individuals and groups, and for the definition of these same actors by others. Self-categorisation and categorisation by others in terms of identity and culture are always two sides of the same coin and cannot be separated from each other when analysing cultural trends. This is extremely important because the way groups see themselves often differs from the way they are seen by others, especially when it comes to interactions between majority and minority groups. This also means that the interaction between two groups is always delineated by double boundaries – one constituted by the 'minority' group and one by the 'majority' group.

It is not clear whether the extensity of syncretism has indeed increased in the late 20th century. Prior to the era of modern territorial states, world religions and empires provided the main cultural and institutional means through which long-range communications and cultural interaction could take place, and more settled or embedded, extensive relationships of cultural interaction could be established. For example, the Ottoman Empire provided the venue through which Islam was able to reach South-eastern Europe. What is clear, however, is that in the pre-modern era very few cultural forms lay between villages and great empires. Since the 19th century, cultural diffusion has been 'regulated' by self-declared 'nation-states' that strove to achieve a high degree of cultural autonomy and homogeneity over issues such as language and education. One only needs to think of the Kemalist policies of cultural modernisation in Turkey, or attempts at cultural homogenisation in the German Reich during Bismarck's '*Kulturkampf*'. In the age of transboundary expansion, travel and mass media have again increased the potential for cultural exchange. International migrants and their descendants, in particular, can be seen as prototypical representatives of this trend.

How intensive this trend really is remains a matter of dispute. In principle, the idea of transnational cultural diffusion and syncretism implies the transboundary movement of people, symbols, practices, texts, etc., all of which help to establish a pattern of common cultural belief across borders and patterns of reciprocal transactions between separate places, whereby cultural ideas in one place influence those in another. Various responses are possible to cultural diffusion and exchange in transnational spaces. Possible outcomes include:

- homogenisation and assimilation: the merging of minorities into the 'core majority', i.e. acculturation;
- cultural pluralism: minorities, by and large, maintain their own culture; often transplanted from country of emigration to immigration country, or indigenous minorities maintain a core repertoire of cultural and identity;
- hybridization: mélange or mix of various cultures in a post-modernist sense of each person carrying multiple identities; and
- syncretism (similar to hybridization; but with the additional claim that culture should be analysed both as a relatively stable set of symbolic 'hardware' and changing 'software'). Syncretism allows a dominant culture to co-exist side-by-side with various sub-cultures. Conceptually, this possibility is superior to the first three alternatives. Assimilation and cultural pluralism are concepts that do not consider the impact of transboundary ties upon the formation of identities. And post-modern concepts of hybridization are trivial because they simply acknowledge the multiplicity of self. This is old hat, however, called unitas multiplex by social psychologists (Graumann, 1983), and is always true, regardless of the existence of transboundary social and symbolic ties.

On the collective and institutional level, Islamic organisations in Europe with links back to Turkey offer a particularly pertinent example of syncretism. These associations have undergone significant changes that separate them from patterns of religion found in the emigration countries. The activities of Islamic organisations in countries such as Germany are partly an outgrowth of the re-Islamization of public life in Turkey. For these organisations, Turkish immigrants in Germany were primarily of political interest. Over the course of time, however, these groups lost their monopoly over the shaping of symbolic ties for their German-based clients, if they had ever been able to do so. Since the 1950s Islam has become an extremely contested movement in Turkey, and Islamic groups have tried to gain power in Turkish domestic politics. Since the early 1980s, successive Turkish governments have departed from the Kemalist tradition, at times actively fostering a Turkish-Islamic synthesis (Toprak, 1996, p. 108). In Germany, the branch of the state-controlled Turkish Directorate of Religious Affairs (Diyanet) became very active only after Islamist organisations such the Association of the

New World View in Europe (*Millî Görüş*) had recruited members and built mosques. The Turkish government had every reason to assume that *Millî Görüş* supported the electoral campaigns of the former Islamic Prosperity Party (*Refah*) in Turkey (now the Virtue Party, *Fazilet*). While the activities of Islamic organisations in Turkey and Germany may have strengthened Turkish nationalism and Muslim transnational representations, the messages of the organisations involved have contradictory implications. On the one hand, Islamic propaganda emphasizes in-group social and symbolic ties, and thus segregation from German society. On the other hand, the overwhelming majority of the second and third generations will undoubtedly stay in Germany. While permanent residence in Germany does not necessarily imply increased contact with Germans and vice versa (cf. Hill, 1990), a one-sided orientation towards Turkey gradually transfigures into a bi- or transnational focus. One of the questions is to what extent a Turkey-centred Islamic revival agenda still suffices for the representation of Turkish immigrants in Germany. This would also seem to depend upon the extent to which Islamic organisations in Germany nowadays have to grapple with issues such as dual citizenship, juvenile crime and social work. After all, quite a few Islamic organisations strive to be recognised as quasi-public institutions (*Körperschaften des Öffentlichen Rechts*), for which there are significant incentives, such as the right to give religious instruction in public schools, representation on the boards of public media, and access to 'church taxes'. While it is too early to make any reasonable predictions on prospects for recognition as such, adaptation to immigration country requirements is unmistakably taking place in the public discourse – not disregarding the internal struggles within such organisations.

One final, crucial question can be alluded to only briefly. Even when boundaries between cultural groups may continue to be quite clear-cut, cultural practices may converge. For example, the acculturation tendencies of selected groups among Turkish immigrants in Germany or German immigrants in Turkey – in other words, the adaptation of newcomers to the norms, values and practices of the immigration country – do not mean that the boundaries between the majority and minority cultures dissolve. In short, boundaries on both the 'majority' and 'minority' side can be maintained while the cultural content changes (Barth, 1969). In the German-Turkish context this issue has not yet been explored. It would require a more detailed empirical exploration of actual trends towards assimilation, ethnic pluralism, globalisation and the transboundary expansion of social spaces.

Over the past years, the presence and further spread of Turkish language mass media in Germany has become quite obvious. The Berlin Commissioner for Immigrant Affairs even spoke of the dangers of the 'three Ts', alleging that easier access to Turkish language television, cheaper costs in telecommunication and long-distance travel contribute towards hindering the integration of Turkish immigrants in Germany. While the empirical jury is still out on this claim, dramatic judgements such as these have to be seen in the context of overall developments supporting the adjustment of newcomers. And it is quite telling – depending partly, but not only, on the different group sizes – that the same allegation is not heard about German immigrants in Turkey (estimates range between 30,000 and 50,000 German citizens) watching German-speaking channels such as RTL or SAT1 (cf. Kaiser, chapter 4, this volume). Other phenomena outside the realm of mass media also indicate a more extensive use of foreign languages in the transnational Turkish-German space. In Germany, the children of immigrants, be they of the first or second generation, or born in Turkey and raised both in Germany and Turkey, often speak Turkish at home and among friends, but German in school. And some of them even use slang particular to German Turks, or 'Deutschland-Türken' (Zafer Senocak). This means that there are indications of language mixing. Seen in a wider European-Turkish context, Turkey may also experience immigrants from abroad bringing other languages, and language-mixes, with them. Over the past decade, Turkey has not only been a country of emigration[8] and return migration but has also become a country of immigration and a transit country (İçduygu et al., 2000). Historically, one important phenomenon has been the return migration of people of Turkish descent from the Balkans to Turkey. Beginning after World War One, this privileged form of immigration has continued in ebbs and flows until today. An example is Turks from Bulgaria. Thus these 'Turks' – Muslim Bosniaks, Pomaks, Albanians or Greeks who may 'return' to Turkey without being able to speak one word of Turkish – are in certain respects quite similar to ethnic Germans (*Aussiedler* and *Spätaussiedler*) who have migrated from Eastern and South-eastern Europe to Germany in large, albeit decreasing numbers since the late 1980s. But in contrast to ethnic Germans, this kind of return migration is based on the historical millets (i.e. 'nations', but without the political connotation of claiming sovereign statehood) in the Ottoman Empire. In addition to immigrants, there are also minorities[9] who have been engaging in language construction. A prominent example are Kurdish cultural institutes in major European cities (Berlin, Paris, London) that try to come up with a unified Kurdish language modelled heavily on the *Kurmancı* dialect.

The exact degree of intensity is hard to establish. For example, there are no systematic studies detailing the use of Turkish language media among Turkish immigrants in Germany. A few initial studies identify the content of these media. Various forms of typologies are possible for analysing the content of the media along ideological (e.g. Turkish language newspapers such as *Cumhuriyet* vs.

---

[8] Germany has been the most important immigration country for Turkish citizens for the past four decades. In terms of stocks (not flows which have been much larger!), more than two million Turks have settled in Germany, followed by France and The Netherlands, each with around 300.000 Turkish immigrants.

[9] National minorities are groups with a culture (e.g. language) different from the official culture of the state. These groups were present at the foundation of the state, and sometimes challenge the existing state with demands to self-government or secession (e.g. the Quebecois). Ethnic minorities are groups who came or were formed later, after the foundation. For example, immigrants in a sovereign state may develop into ethnic minorities. In addition, there are all kinds of groups akin to ethnic minorities but with different rallying lines: region, religion, class, etc.

26 *Transnational Social Spaces*

Hüriyet), or religious lines (Kanal 7). The available evidence suggests that many who frequently tune in to Turkish TV channels, for example, also make use of German language TV channels. This preliminary result indicates that languages among consumers and speakers of immigrant or minority origin may be used in a variable-sum game and not in terms of replacing one language by another. Instead, bilingual or multilingual competencies seem to be the rule and not the exception among those living continuously in transnational contexts.

Clearly, the communications infrastructure and public policies matter. This infrastructure has undergone massive expansion, e.g. information carrying capacities have been constantly increasing – from railways, telegraphy, steam-powered shipping and imperial rule in the 19th century to telecommunications via cable, satellite, computer, Internet, radio, television and jet liners in the 20th century. New technologies with the ensuing digitisation of information and images, new cable and fibre-optic technologies have enabled wider audiences to participate in cultural consumerism. When we look at language use in everyday situations, transnational networks matter as much as the local institutions for facilitating or fostering the use of multiple languages. In the long run, none of these telecommunications and other infrastructures could really have facilitated regularised transboundary communications had it not been for the collective representation expressed in shared languages and linguistic competencies.

As to public policies, the mass media is one of the fields in which the 'integration' of immigrants is seen by policymakers as a crucial testing ground. Dominant integration concepts contest the compatibility of integration and continuing transnational ties. In her study of Turkish migrant broadcasting in Berlin, Kira Kosnick shows convincingly that public policies which consciously prioritise 'local' integration over transnational ties, may have unintended consequences. Her contribution can be read as an exploration into the dynamics of cultural transnationalism (Kosnick, chapter 8, this volume). In her study, Kira Kosnick contrasts several broadcasting institutions in Berlin and shows how and what kind of transnational ties have evolved. The 'good guys', *Radio MultiKulti*, upholds multiculturalism and ethnic pluralism as the central tenets of its mission. The message is that multi-culturalism and pluralism must be local and not transnational for integration to work. But there is an irony here. The station has two missions: first, to report on local affairs and second, to maintain the cultural heritage of the ethnic group in question, for example here, the Turkish. Therefore, *Radio MultiKulti* needs journalists with a knowledge of both Germany and Turkey. In particular, the multicultural goal of cultural preservation means that journalists must speak and write *Öztürkce* ('pure Turkish'). This is usually only manageable for those who were socialised in Turkey. In turn, this implies that these journalists have to be imported from Turkey because 'pure Turkish' is seldom found in Germany. Thus, the combination of local orientation and multiculturalism results in increased transnationalism. It is interesting to note that in this case the cultural transfer from Turkey to Germany does not result in syncretism in terms of

The Border-Crossing Expansion of Social Space 27

hybridization but in nurturing one of the chief national projects since the inception of the Turkish Republic in the late 1920s – *Öztürkce*.

According to Kosnick, quite a different relationship between the local and the transnational can be observed in the case of the Open Channel Berlin (OKB). The philosophy of the Open Channel, as espoused by its designers and policy makers, is to imbue it with a local orientation. But as far as Turkish contributions to this channel are concerned, these expectations seem have to gone astray. A large proportion of the airtime is filled by the 'bad guys', such as Turkish and Kurdish nationalists or Islamists. In this case, locally-based multicultural policies provide an avenue for participation in transnational social spaces. In sum, Kosnick's case study indicates that the opposition of the local to the transnational is a misleading conceptual lense.

The institutionalisation of mass media that extend beyond state borders depends on variable market factors and a culturally-bounded constituency. So far, most of the main mass media institutions in the Turkish-German space are based in Turkey. Newspapers such as *Cumhuriyet* and television stations such as the state-run *TRT* channels publish and broadcast from Turkey, with minor subsidiaries such as printing facilities in Germany. In terms of language, institutionalisation depends on educational policies applied in schools and the company policies of employers. In educational institutions in Germany, for example, language policies can be of a more exclusionary or inclusionary nature. For instance, on the one hand there are semi-sovereign states (*Länder*) such as Bavaria, which for a long time ran 'national classes', in which children from major emigration countries were taught almost exclusively in their mother tongue, in the expectation that their parents would eventually return to their country of origin. On the other hand there are states that include immigrant children in regular classes but offer additional 'mother tongue' instruction.

Ultimately, the impact of communication reaching beyond borders and the associated use and mixing of languages concerns issues of cultural diffusion, language politics and policy, and cultural hegemony. It is interesting to see that particular regional spaces such as the German-Turkish one are overlaid by more global diffusion phenomena. Take the use of English as a lingua franca in business, academia (including the Summer Institute in which the authors of this volume all participated) and many other walks of life in both Turkey and Germany. The extent of diffusion also depends on the politico-economic and cultural prowess of the source country, such as Germany or the USA. While the spread of German as a lingua franca and a second language in South-eastern and above all Eastern Europe was sharply curtailed by World War Two and the negative cultural odium associated with this language, English diffused through mechanisms such as international institutions. As to ethnic or national minorities, a certain degree of cultural autonomy is usually very high on the list of demands. This applies to groups such as that which describes itself and is acknowledged by others as Kurdish in both Turkey and Europe. It is debatable to what degree such demands function as a challenge to established cultural hegemonies in sovereign states, and

28   *Transnational Social Spaces*

to what extent this strengthens symbolic ties and social cohesion among the members of minority groups.

On a more down-to-earth note, consuming media and speaking languages pertains to the integration of migrants, travellers, and minority people in the contexts of each particular country and to their life in transnational spaces. One of the questions involved is whether we will find among long-term transnationalists an inter-generational move, as predicted by assimilation theory: a cultural and linguistic melting of immigrants into the core 'majority' by the third generation – or whether an increased transboundary expansion of social spaces and heightened multiculturalism will work towards a longer-term transboundary and multi-linguistic culture (for a detailed discussion, see Faist, 2000b, chapter 9).

All of these findings on mass media in transnational social spaces raise wider issues concerning the connection of the 'local' and the 'transnational' and their mutual constitution in an age of 'glocalization' (Robertson, 1995). Although the terms 'global' and 'transnational' need to be distinguished (cf. Faist, 2003), they may be treated synonymously for the purpose at hand, namely the critique of the thesis that the 'local' is swallowed by the 'transnational' or 'global'. Glocalization shifts the emphasis to an analysis of the ways in which global or transnational phenomena are modified and changed by the particular or local setting that receives them. Rather than perpetuating the dichotomy between the global and the local, the glocalization approach suggests instead that these seemingly incongruous aspects are in fact two dimensions of the same phenomenon. We therefore need analyses of the processes by which global or transnational resources are localised and made relevant to a particular set of socio-cultural practices. This also implies reformulating the term 'local' so that it not only refers to local territory but also to particular practices, or so-called local spaces.

One of the features of transboundary social life that is of great importance is the communal infrastructure. From what we know about international migration from Turkey to Germany, the so-called *hemşerilik* was instrumental for the first generation. *Hemşerilik* can be translated roughly as associations of migrants from the same region Reference to Germany here makes no sense to most native English speakers or anyone without knowledge of German history. They can be described as networks of solidarity, social and symbolic ties based on communal or regional affinities. Many participants liken them to kinship ties, attributing to them a primordial significance, albeit symbolically. The interpretation of the range of *hemşeri* ties varies according to the people using it. Depending on context and usage, the term denotes fellow villagers or people from the same region or province. *Hemşeri* ties proved to be important in helping fellow villagers and townspeople find accommodation, jobs and childcare in the country of immigration. Empirical studies report such ties to be effective in the early stages of immigration (Faist, 2000a, chapter 6). Yet, there is only sparse evidence of its significance with regard to marriage migration in later stages and the second generation.

The Border-Crossing Expansion of Social Space

In the Turkish-German case no veritable 'culture of migration' emerged like there did in Caribbean migration circuits, for example, which are characterised by a permissive transboundary lifestyle. Because of German admission policies that do not stop but curb flows, exogenous opportunities for lifestyle migration did not exist for the hoi polloi (cf. Hunn, 2001). Nonetheless, family reunification accelerated in later stages of the migration process, with an additional push after the recruitment stop in 1973. When family reunification had largely run its course and the supply was exhausted in the mid-1980s, marriage migration gained importance. Often, this type of migration necessitated more generalised and diffuse ties of reciprocity and solidarity. First-generation immigrants tried to arrange the marriage of their offspring – and their daughters in particular. Among other things, they expected a relative to be somewhat more loyal than an unrelated son-in-law or daughter-in-law. Also, kin in rural areas of Turkey often expected their extended and remote family members to search for brides and bridegrooms within the wider kinship group first. A refusal on the part of immigrants in Europe was taken as evidence that they no longer valued kinship ties with home. In a study of a Dutch city in the late 1980s, for example, it turned out that half of the brides and bridegrooms of the second generation came from the same kinship group as their respective spouses-to-be in Turkey (Böcker, 1994).

Understandably, the pressure among families in Turkey to obtain a daughter-in-law in Europe increased after the recruitment stop in 1973. In order to live and work in Europe, marrying the daughter of a migrant was one of the most attractive avenues for young men in their twenties and thirties, who made up the majority of potential migrants. This was not surprising because the demand for migration did not fall during the 1980s. If at all, it probably increased in the 1980s as compared to the previous decade because structural conditions had not changed, that age cohort had increased in numbers, and migrant networks still existed. However, transaction costs had gone up: over time, many second-generation women grew more reluctant to be married to distant relatives from Turkey. They increasingly wanted to choose their own marriage partners. Moreover, kinship and *hemşeri* ties across borders have grown weaker over the years. The latter is a clear instance of the very limited duration of transnational kinship ties.

Nonetheless – and this is of the utmost importance regarding the institutionalisation of transnational social spaces – as Gaby Straßburger points out, marriage choice among the descendants of Turkish migrants in Germany is still heavily geared towards Turkey – albeit for reasons very different from traditional ties (Straßburger, chapter 9, this volume). She focuses on why most second-generation Turks opt for transnational marriage, and concludes that the transnational social space may have changed 'its inner structure and quality' over time. Straßburger's analysis looks at the nature of transnational ties among second-generation Turks living in Germany, using the example of marriage and the ties of transboundary reciprocity and solidarity involved. She discovers that there is indeed a transnational marriage market. It is, however, very different from the practices of so-called first-generation immigrants, who got married in Turkey and often brought along their spouses to eventually settle in Germany. Among the second generation we find truly transnational features. Over time, old transnational ties have lost importance among the second generation. Thus, we see a drop in the proportion of arranged marriages among relatives. However, the ties of second-generation persons to friends, neighbours and members of social groups other than kinship groups in Turkey have increased. It is these circles that increasingly provide opportunities to meet potential spouses. This hunch is borne out by the finding that a decreasing proportion of marriage partners comes from communities of their parents' origin in Turkey, and a growing proportion from other groups in Turkey. We may conclude that the increasing length of residence in Germany has decreased the value of ethnically specific social and cultural capital to be transferred from Turkey to Germany. Yet this does not imply the disappearance of transnational ties for marriage formation. We rather see changing patterns and weak forms of institutionalisation of transnational ties as part of the broader processes of individualisation.

Our Work Site: The German-Turkish Summer Institute as a Transnational Social Space

The two meetings in Bremen in 2000 and İstanbul in 2001 were held with a view to encouraging academic dialogue and the incipient collaboration of young scholars across borders. The discussions and presentations were intended to help the participants to focus and hone their dissertation studies or postgraduate-level research. Also, participants had a chance to engage in small-scale joint projects with other participants. The Turkish-German Summer Institute aimed to enhance academic co-operation and to link selected elements of the respective civil societies in four ways: 1. by contributing towards the development of denser networks between young Turkish and German scholars in their formative period of academic socialisation; 2. by establishing longer-term academic co-operation across the borders of Germany and Turkey; 3. by contributing to concepts aiming at multi-sited research; and, finally, 4. by making a modest contribution of the social sciences to political discourses in public spaces.

1. *Contribution towards the Development of Denser Networks between Turkish and German Scholars*

In the past, co-operation between scholars from Germany and Turkey in the social sciences has been restricted to fleeting and mostly individualized contacts. There have been many initiatives in the past which helped clear some ground for more intensive dialogue. However, none of these efforts addressed the most fundamental requirement for effective and fruitful collaboration across state borders, namely, ties and networks among young scholars at their doctoral and immediate post-doctoral stage. The ultimate long-term goal is to create an 'epistemic community' of scholars from Turkey and Germany who self-consciously engage in the analysis of past, contemporary and future-oriented developments in politics, economics, linguistics and culture. In order to facilitate communication, the common language of the Summer Institute was English. This also helped to situate the Summer Institute within the broader context of building networks of scholars and collaborative research across Europe. And while we initially faced the difficulty of integrating contributions from various disciplines of the social sciences, law and linguistics, this was an asset in forcing us to develop common questions and common concepts right from the beginning.

Eight scholars from each country, either in the process of preparing their doctoral dissertations or conducting postgraduate level research, were offered the opportunity to meet for intense discussions at both Institute sessions. In terms of group composition, gender, university and country background of the participants were mixed. There were participants from various German universities (Universities of Bamberg, Berlin, Bremen, Essen, Freiburg, Hamburg, and Mainz) and Turkish universities (Middle East Technical University, Marmara University, Bogazici University, İstanbul University). What is even more relevant is that the participants represent the 'four worlds' of the Turkish-German space: 1. Germans of 'German' descent; 2. Turks of 'Turkish' descent; 3. children of Turkish immigrant workers in Germany and first-generation Turkish immigrants in Germany; and 4. persons of German background married to Turkish citizens and living in Turkey. This mixed background ensured a plurality of life-world experiences that is partly reflected in the topics and methods chosen in their academic work.

English as a common language served well as a medium of communication. Most of the Turkish participants knew some German and most German contributors knew some Turkish. Since there was no pressure to know the 'other' language perfectly, the participants were able to engage in intensive discussions, and using the global academic lingua franca English as the common language of the Summer Institute removed the pressure from participants to be 'perfect' in the respective languages from the start. Three of the participants from Germany actually took Turkish language courses before the second and final meeting.

2. *Establishing Longer-term Academic Co-operation across State Borders*

The Summer Institute has the potential for more long-term effects than one- or two-shot conferences and shorter meetings. One of the goals of our Summer Institute was that the participants also keep in touch in between workshops, and possibly cooperate in joint projects. In this way, academic collaboration is geared to extend beyond the specific Summer Institute on the 'Transboundary Expansion of Spaces' and lead to more sustainable developments. Our format had the specific competitive advantage of dealing with transboundary issues by both analysing and involving persons, groups, networks, communities and organisations from a EU member state and from a country preparing for accession to the EU. The directors

32 *Transnational Social Spaces*

of the Summer Institute encouraged the doctoral candidates and postgraduate research fellows to form small subgroups on topics of common interest. Several subcommittees have already formed and this may lead to co-authored papers – or at least an intensive exchange of information among the members of subgroups. The subgroups existing at the time of writing are: Identity and Culture, Turkey, the EU and European Integration, and Mass Media and Intercultural Communication.

3. *Making a Contribution to Multi-sited Conceptualisations*

Much has been written about the need to engage in multi-sited research in order to capture processes and mechanisms in transnational social spaces. However, a closer look at the methodological requirements of transnationalism research cautions not to analyse too many sites and ultimately become overwhelmed by them. Rather, the need is to develop research concepts and methodologies that allow us to conceptualise local, regional and national case studies as embedded in a broader realm of glocal or translocal structures (cf. Marcus, 1999, p. 11).

4. *Contributing to Political Discourse in Public Spaces*

The transboundary co-operation initiated at the Turkish-German Summer Institute can help in modest ways to stop the immanent politicisation of issues (such as 'Islam', 'Kurds', etc.) in German-Turkish public spaces. Indeed, there are very few Turkish-German spaces in which dialogue is free of pressure from those who transpose their images of an allegedly more progressive society from one country to another, or those who favour an equally authoritarian 'law and order' perspective, thereby disregarding issues of transnational democracy in both Turkey and Germany. One of the most important goals of the Summer Institute has been to operate with rules and norms that allow an open-minded exchange of viewpoints in our transboundary academic space.

References

Barth, Frederick (ed.) (1969), *Ethnic Groups and Boundaries. The Social Organization of Cultural Difference*, Allen & Unwin, London.

Beisheim, Marianne, Dreher, Sabine, Walter, Gregor, Zangl, Bernhard and Zürn, Michael (1998). *Im Zeitalter der Globalisierung? Thesen und Daten zur gesellschaftlichen und politischen Denationalisierun*, Nomos, Baden-Baden.

Böcker, Anita (1994). 'Chain Migration over Legally Closed Borders. Settled Immigrants as Bridgeheads and Gatekeepers', in *The Netherlands' Journal of Social Sciences*, Vol. 30(2). pp. 87-106.

Ceylanoğlu. Sena (2000). 'At the Origins of Different Relationships: Greece, Turkey and the European Community', in Institute for Intercultural and International Studies (INIIS) (ed.). *German-Turkish Summer Institute Working Papers No. 3/2000*, University of Bremen. Bremen.

The Border-Crossing Expansion of Social Space 33

Engelbrektsson, Ulla-Britt (1978), *The Force of Tradition. Turkish Migrants at Home and Abroad*, Acta Universitatis Gothoburgensis, Göteborg.

Faist, Thomas (1998), 'Transnational social spaces out of international migration: evolution, significance and future prospects', *Archives Européennes de Sociologie*, Vol. 39(2), pp. 213-247.

Faist, Thomas (2000a), *The Volume and Dynamics of International Migration and Transnational Social Spaces*, Oxford University Press, Oxford.

Faist, Thomas (ed.) (2000b), *Transstaatliche Räume. Politik, Wirtschaft und Kultur in und zwischen Deutschland und der Türkei*, transcript Verlag, Bielefeld. (Turkish edition: *Devletaşım Alan: Almanya ve Türkiye Arasında Siyaset, Ticaret ve Kültür*, Bağlam, İstanbul.)

Faist, Thomas (2003), 'The Transnational Turn in Migration Research: Implications for the Study of Politics and Polity', in School of International Migration and Ethnic Relations (IMER) (ed.), *Willy Brandt Working Paper Series No. 4/2003*, Malmö högskola, Malmö.

Faist, Thomas (2004), 'Social Space', in George Ritzer (ed.), *Encyclopedia of Social Theory*, Sage, Beverly Hills.

Freud, Sigmund (1994) [1930], *Das Unbehagen in der Kultur. Und andere kulturtheoretische Schriften*, Fischer, Frankfurt am Main.

Graumann, Carl F. (1983), 'On multiple identities', in *International Social Science Journal*, Vol. 35, pp. 309-329.

Haas, Peter M. (1992), 'Epistemic communities and international policy coordination', in *International Organization*, Vol. 46(1), Winter 1992, pp. 1-36.

Hammar, Tomas (1990), *Democracy and the Nation-State. Aliens, Denizens and Citizens in a World of International Migration*, Gower, Aldershot.

Held, David, McGrew, Anthony, Goldblatt, David and Perraton, Jonathan (1999), *Global Transformations. Politics, Economics and Culture*, Stanford University Press, Stanford, CA.

Hill, Paul B. (1990), 'Kulturelle Inkonsistenz und Streß bei der zweiten Generation', in Hartmut Esser and Jürgen Friedrichs (eds.), *Generation und Identität. Theoretische und empirische Beiträge zur Migrationssoziologie*. Westdeutscher Verlag, Opladen.

Hocker, Reinhard and Liebe-Harkort, Klaus (eds.) (1996), *Zur Kurdenfrage in der Türkei. Dokumente aus der Türkei und aus der Bundesrepublik Deutschland (1980-1995)*, Gewerkschaft Erziehung und Wissenschaft (GEW), Frankfurt am Main.

Hunn, Karin (2001), 'Alamanya, Alamanya, Türk gibi isci bulamanya... Alamanya, Alamanya, Türkten custal bulamanya – Labour Migration from Turkey to Germany 1961-1973', in Institute for Intercultural and International Studies (INIIS) (ed.), *German-Turkish Summer Institute Working Papers No. 4/2001*, University of Bremen, Bremen.

Keck, Margaret and Sikkink, Kathryn (1998), 'Transnational Advocacy Networks in International Politics: Introduction', in Margaret Keck and Kathryn Sikkink, *Activists Beyond Borders: Transnational Advocacy Networks in International Politics*, Cornell University Press, Ithaca, NY.

Landes, David S. (1998), *The Wealth and Poverty of Nations. Why Some Are So Rich and Some So Poor*, Little, Brown and Company, London.

Lichtenberg, Hagen, Linne, Gudrun and Gümrükcü, Harun (eds.) (1996), *Gastarbeiter – Einwanderer – Bürger? Die Rechtsstellung der türkischen Arbeitnehmer in der Europäischen Union*, Nomos, Baden-Baden.

Mandaville, Peter (2001), *Transnational Muslim Politics. Reimaginging the umma*, Routledge, London.

Marcus, George E. (1999), 'What is at stake – and is not – in the idea and practice of multi-sited ethnography', in *Canberra Anthropology*, Vol. 22(2), pp. 6-14.

Marks, Gary (1997), 'A Third Lens: Comparing European Integration and State Building', in Jytte Klausen and Louise Tilly (ed.), *European Integration in Social and Historical Perspective. From 1850 to the Present*, Rowman & Littlefield, Lanham, pp. 23-44.

Olson, Mancur (1965), *The Logic of Collective Action. Public Goods and the Theory of Groups*, Harvard University Press, Cambridge.

Özveren, Eyüp (2000a), 'Modernity with an Elusive Liberal Accent: The Twentieth-Century Turkish Experience', in Institute for Intercultural and International Studies (INIIS) (ed.), *German-Turkish Summer Institute Working Papers No. 2/2000*, University of Bremen, Bremen.

Özveren, Eyüp (2000b), 'The Scope of Turkish Semiperipherality', *Ekonomik Yaklasim*, Vol. 11(36), pp. 1-24.

Risse-Kappen, Thomas (ed.) (1995), 'Bringing transnational relations back', in *Non-state actors, domestic structures and international institutions*, Cambridge University Press, Cambridge, pp. 5-33.

Robertson, Ronald (1995), 'Glocalization: Time-Space and Homogeneity – Heterogeneity', in Mike Featherstone, Scott Lash and Ronald Robertson (eds.), *Global Modernities*, Sage, London, pp. 191-224.

Said, Edward (1995) [1978], *Orientalism: western conceptions of the Orient*, Pantheon Books, New York (1878), Revised Edition, Penguin Books, London.

Toprak, Binnaz (1996), 'Civil Society in Turkey', in Augustus Richard Norton (ed.), *Civil Society in the Middle East*, E.J. Brill, Leiden, pp. 87-118.

Ugur, Mehmet (1999), *The European Union and Turkey: An Anchor/Credibility Dilemma*, Ashgate, Aldershot.

Weber, Max (1988) [1924], 'Der Sozialismus', in *Gesammelte Aufsätze zur Soziologie und Sozialpolitik, 2. Edition*, J.C.B. Mohr (Paul Siebeck), Tübingen, pp. 492-518.

Zlotnik, Hania (1999), 'Trends of International Migration Since 1965: What Existing Data Reveal', in *International Migration*, Vol. 37(1), pp. 21-61.

PART I

RIGHTS AND STRUGGLES

Chapter 2

The Transnational Dimension of the Bergama Campaign Against Eurogold

Zeynep Kadirbeyoğlu

The Latin American literature recurrently recognizes the positive role played in social movements by "outsiders" such as clergy, left wing parties, students, social workers, NGOs and lawyers, teachers and doctors. The outsiders often hold the key to collective action, since they are able to advise on organization, the laws and the political landscape, as well as supporting movements in their negotiations with political authorities (Foweraker, 1995, p. 83).

Introduction

In recent years there has been an increasing interest in issues such as 'global civil society', 'transnational NGOs' and 'issue networks'.[1] Rather than conceptualising globalisation only as the expansion of productive activities and the increased influence of global capital owners, it is also possible to envisage increased supraterritoriality as a means of empowerment of 'global civic networks' (Kaldor, 2000, p. 106). An example of the effectiveness of such networks – whose activities attracted massive public attention – were the demonstrations that took place in Seattle, Washington, Prague and Melbourne (Mittelman, 2000, p. 383). These had an anti-globalist discourse but their contribution, according to Kaldor (2000, p. 106), was to trigger a debate about the nature of the global system.

In addition to such large-scale protests, there are also more localised struggles. One such example is the armed struggle of the Zapatistas that was launched symbolically on the day NAFTA (the North American Free Trade Agreement) was ratified (Morton, 200, p. 3). The Zapatista movement not only organises demonstrations at the national level – like the 'march of the ants' in 1992 when 400 Chol Indians marched to Mexico City – but also has transnational

---

[1] See Lipschutz (1992), Wapner (1995), Tarrow (1996), Keck and Sikkink (1998), Moghadam (2000).

38 *Transnational Social Spaces*

contacts which are strengthened through international meetings (Morton, 2001, pp. 26 and 47). Hence, while a movement may be organised at the national level in order to safeguard indigenous rights, it may still receive support through transnational contacts.

An example where the transnational contacts of a particular movement were essential in changing the course of events was the Bergama Movement's campaigns against the Eurogold Company – an Australian mining multinational that aims to recover gold in the Aegean region of Turkey. This chapter analyses the transnational space that developed around the Bergama Movement. This specific movement is chosen in order to underline the impact of transnational links on the evolution of localised struggles. Furthermore, it should be noted that it is important to examine this movement because it represents one of the only cases of popular mobilisation that was sustained and that achieved some goals in the post-1980 Turkey. The aim of this paper is to uncover the features of the transnational space in the case of the Bergama Movement. In doing so we will concentrate in particular on the space between Turkey and Germany, but also give brief descriptions of the other spaces that developed. Then follows a description of the evolution of the transnational anti-cyanide space, at the same time identifying the features of this space, i.e. analysing it in terms of extensity, intensity, pattern and impact of ties – as identified by Faist (chapter 1, this volume). The main argument is that the anti-Eurogold Movement in Bergama was connected, both implicitly and at times explicitly, to a transnational issue network which attempted to further the interests of the local group.

The Bergama Movement

Gold has signified prosperity and affluence for many civilisations throughout the centuries. It is a precious metal and is used for a variety of purposes including jewellery production, dentistry and plating.[2] It enjoys mass popularity as a valuable asset among the peoples of societies that experience high inflation. However, it has also brought unrest and confusion to the lives of (very many, including) the peasants of the villages around Bergama, a small town in the Aegean region of Turkey, situated at a distance of approximately 120 km from İzmir. Until 10 years ago the town was known for its archaeological ruins that included the glorious altar of Zeus – the Pergamon altar that is now housed in Berlin. The Eurogold Mining Company was established in 1989 and its shareholders were LaSource Compagnie Minière of France – 60 percent of which in turn is owned by Normandy Mining Limited of Australia and 40 percent by BRGM (Bureau de Recherche Geologiques

---

[2] Seventy-five per cent of the annual production of gold is used in jewellery (Karadeniz, 1996). This argument constitutes one of the basic tenets of the resistance camp, which claims there is no need to poison the soil to produce a metal that is already abundant in bank vaults and that is mostly used for ornamentation.

The Transnational Dimension of the Bergama Campaign

et Minières) of France – and Inmet Mining Corporation of Canada (Gökvardar, 1998, p. 137).[3] When the Eurogold Company obtained the mineral exploration license for the land around the Ovacık, Narlıca and Çamköy villages, nobody ever conceived that it would lead to demonstrations, lawsuits and continuous struggle with the company, the state and security forces.

Initially, the peasants and the local elites were enthusiastic, because they believed that gold would bring wealth to their villages, and that the idle youth – or unemployed – would have the chance to be employed by the mine and supplement the agricultural income of their families. However, as information spread about the gold recovery technique, which required the use of cyanide, a debate started in the villages. Since 1996, an endless struggle has continued between the peasants of Bergama and the Eurogold Company and there have been many demonstrations organised by the peasants. The Eurogold Company acted in close alliance with the Turkish state. The aim of the company is to operate the plant that was built at the mining site. The government of Turkey now faces the demands of the peasants on the one hand and pressure from the company on the other.

Legally, the Ovacık plant is not allowed to operate using the 'cyanide leach' method because the High Court has ruled that using such a method entails risks which are not permissible. This decision is based on the rights of people to live in a healthy and safe environment, as laid down in the Constitution of the Republic of Turkey. The government, however, favours the operation of the plant; firstly, because the State of Turkey would have to compensate the company if otherwise, and secondly – perhaps most importantly – because the operation of this first plant would signify a start for the 560 other mining sites for which exploration permission has already been granted. This would send out favourable signals to foreign investors in mining and related sectors who may have hesitated in finalising their decision to invest in Turkey because of the Bergama problem.

Most academic studies and media coverage have focused on the Bergama movement as a local resistance movement. In 1980, Turkey experienced a military take-over followed by state repression of any type of labour, student or political movement (Sunar and Sayarı, 1986, p. 183). This restrictive atmosphere meant that mobilisation for the articulation of one's interests became rather risky. It is for this reason that the local resistance in Bergama represents a special, and – due to its endurance and non-violence – to some extent unique case of mobilisation in Turkey. The peasants were guided and supported by non-locals at both national and transnational level. This paper will concentrate on the external links of the movement, and analyse how the transnational space between Germany and Turkey

---

[3] According to the Mining Journal (1992-01-24), the shareholders of Eurogold in 1989 were Normandy Poseidon (67 per cent) and Metall Mining (33 per cent). However, in 1994, due to changes on the local and global markets, the shares of Normandy Poseidon were divided between Normandy and BRGM and the shares of Metall Mining were handed over to Inmet (Taşkın, 1998, pp. 57-60). Further changes led to the Eurogold Company being owned exclusively by Normandy Mining Ltd. (Orhon, 1999).

40 *Transnational Social Spaces*

affected the evolution of the Bergama movement and how the networks were used by the activists to get their voices heard. Since the campaign began, a network related to the Bergama movement within Turkey has developed, and it is supplemented by external links. The latter includes, among others, links established with two German scientists as well as a German-based NGO, Foodfirst Information & Action Network (FIAN). It is important to analyse the transboundary links that were created for the purposes of anti-cyanide resistance because they strengthened the movement by providing information and support.

The movement's participants and supporters are unanimous with regard to their target: to defeat the Eurogold Company and its project of gold extraction using the cyanide leaching method. However, the motives and guiding forces behind the different sections of the anti-Eurogold movement are varied. It is important to note that not all the peasants of the villages surrounding the mining site are opposed to the company, and especially those who see it as a source of employment and income are in favour of it. The proportion of villagers in favour of the Eurogold Company is highest in Ovacık where, according to several observers, the ratio is 50 percent (Interview, No. 3, 2000-09-17; Interview, No. 10, 2000-09-13 – 2000-09-18). The opinions of the inhabitants of the other villages are more obscure, and it was not possible to discern who was in favour of the mine because it was not always socially acceptable to be so. However, since this study focuses on the resistance aspect, the motivations of those in favour will be left aside.

The research for this paper started in late 1999. The examination of secondary sources was followed by a short period of fieldwork in the area in the summer of 2000. Qualitative research methods were used for gathering the data, since the aim was to uncover the motivations of the movement's participants and their organisational tactics. The movement itself, and the way in which non-locals became involved, is far from formal. Following Kriesi (1992, p. 203) who claims that the more informal a movement's organisation is, the more appropriate it becomes to use qualitative methods, in-depth interviews were conducted with movement organisers and supporters. In order to uncover the motivations and views of the peasants on issues directly and indirectly related to the gold mine, fieldwork was conducted in the villages directly adjacent to it. Interviews with the peasants and movement organisers were undertaken during August and September 2000. The interviews in Germany were carried out during March 2001. Further phone interviews with non-local supporters were conducted during May 2001. A list of all the interviews is given after the references.

This study required the interviewing of both peasants and the supporters of the movement – the individuals belonging to the latter group were not always from the local setting and will be referred to as the Elites. For the Elite interviews, the names associated with the movement were gathered from secondary sources such as books or newspaper clippings. Similar to other social movement research, snowball sampling[4] was used and the interviewees in turn provided new names to be contacted for further research. The sampling of the peasants was more challenging. The reason for this lay in the suspicion a researcher may arouse among the locals because of the ongoing struggle. Accusations of spying are common when conducting research on sensitive topics (Lee, 1993, chapter 1). To overcome this we had to go to the villages with someone the locals knew and trusted. This posed a problem of bias in the sample because the person who accompanied us was in the anti-mine camp. This prevented us from talking to people who might have supported the mine. These biases should be taken into account while reading this paper.

The interviews were semi-structured. This type of interview is also called a focused interview and denotes the situation in which the interviewer has a list of questions for each interviewee (Denzin, 1989, p. 105; Richards, 1996, p. 201). The phrasing and order of the questions was different for each respondent. The interviews took place mostly in the offices or homes of the respondents, and were carried out without a tape recorder. Tape-recording the interviews was not practicable in many cases because it would have made the respondents less forthcoming in answering the questions – again, due to the ongoing conflict. Note-taking during the interviews was possible with the Elite interviewees, but negatively influenced the process with the peasants by either making them reluctant to answer or by making them emphasise and repeat their answers when notes were taken. I therefore took detailed notes during the Elite interviews and short notes during the peasant interviews and supplemented them both afterwards.

The gender of the researcher is usually a very important issue in qualitative studies. If this research had been carried out in a different part of Turkey, access would have been more restricted because of the patriarchal nature of society. In Bergama it was acceptable for me to sit in the village coffee shops – which are exclusively male spaces – and to talk to groups of men.

Furthermore, secondary sources such as government and non-governmental Organisation (NGO) documents and reports, newspaper clippings, company brochures, web sites and publications related to the mining activities in Bergama, are also used as sources of information throughout the study. The articles and clippings from both Turkish and German newspapers are examined to capture the important events of the movement. Other sources include risk assessment reports on the mining activities and some of the official documents obtained through the peasants' lawyer. Participant observation – which can be a useful method for social movement research – has also been employed in addition to the interviews, but there were no protest activities during the fieldwork and hence this method was not used to analyse the movement's events.

---

[4] Snowball sampling refers to the case where the researcher starts with an initial set of contacts and is then passed on by them to others (Lee, 1993, p. 65).

42 *Transnational Social Spaces*

The analysis of the data obtained through the interviews lends itself to five categories under which we can list the motives of the contenders. These categories are not exhaustive, and are ordered as follows so as to facilitate a comprehensive examination of the motivations that were expressed during the interviews:

The Aspiration to Avoid Risk and Defend One's Self-interest by Preserving the Land and Securing the Right to an Adequate Livelihood

The initial motive for the peasants was to preserve their land, and as the following quote highlights, the movement embodies a discourse of risks related to cyanide:

> Our land can be poisoned, animals and crops can be damaged if there is a leak from the pond to the groundwater (Interview, No. 3, 2000-09-17).

The main source of income in the villages of Bergama is agriculture. The major crops of the area include cotton, tobacco, olives and tomatoes. With the appearance of the word 'cyanide' they feared that the water they use for agriculture would be poisoned. Since the main sector is agriculture this would mean a loss of livelihood. The fear proved to be justified when fruits and vegetables they took to the market place to sell were rejected on the grounds that they were allegedly poisoned (Interview, No. 8, 2000-09-18). Taşkın argues that the movement was based on the right of the local people to a livelihood (Elite Interview, No. 2, 2000-08-25). Hence, as the movement progressed, it became possible to identify a trend whereby cyanide became equated with death. The motive of self-interest frequently accompanied the ecological consideration, which constitutes the topic of the next subsection.

Ecological Concerns

The narrow self-interest that sparked the movement in the first half of the 1990s transformed into a more altruistic and wider perspective on the environment and other people. The following quote is an example of this position:

> I am actually not tied to this place, I do not own land here. I can leave any time but one has to live for others too (Interview, No. 4, 2000-09-18).

Over the years, the peasants from Bergama were active in demonstrating against gold-mining projects in other parts of Turkey – such as Gümüşhane – and the nuclear power plant project in Akkuyu (Elite Interview, No. 1, 2000-08-26; Elite Interview, No. 3, 2000-08-25), which also demonstrates a wider concern for the environment.

The Transnational Dimension of the Bergama Campaign 43

I only want the best for my environment and for my land. I am politically aware and I want to assert my rights. But, in this country those who want to defend their rights are accused of forming illegal groups (Interview, No. 3, 2000-09-17).

This quotation, from one of the most active women of the movement, demonstrates the connection between ecological concerns and the discourse of rights adopted by the movement's participants. This type of motivation, which stresses the rights of citizens to take part in decisions concerning themselves, is the subject of the following subsection.

Emphasis on the Rights of Citizens and the Willingness to Have a Say About One's Future

This movement has actually taught us what democracy is. Beforehand we used to curse the workers or civil servants who organised marches. But now we understand that only those who have a problem demonstrate. [...] This mining business has taught us (about) democracy and our rights (Interview, No. 4, 2000-09-18).

Referring to the court decision to ban the use of cyanide, Sefa Taşkın argues that here, for the first time in a country like Turkey, where the democratic tradition is not well established and where the state has a tendency to shepherd its citizens, a group of citizens has won a battle against the state using rules laid down by the state itself.

The campaign for their rights made the peasants aware of international declarations on the environment and human rights such as the Rio Declaration, Principle 10 of which states that environmental issues are best handled with the participation of all concerned citizens (UNEP, 1992).

It can be argued that the insistence of Özay – the lawyer representing the peasants – and other movement supporters on remaining within the boundaries of the law while performing acts of civil disobedience and practising their rights as citizens, transformed the way in which peasants viewed their situation vis-à-vis the central government. It can be said that they became aware that their relation with the state not only consisted of fulfilling certain duties, but also implied the right to object to certain decisions that were taken without their informed consent. The outcry of one of the activists of the movement demonstrates this point of view:

We are the ones who vote but they do not side with us. They should listen to us. I am shouting loud from Bergama that I do not want the law of International Arbitration to erode the power of our judges and empower the foreigners (Interview, No. 9, 2000-09-14).

This last quote brings us to the fourth motivation category that will be analysed in this section: the anti-imperialist independence discourse.

44   *Transnational Social Spaces*

Anti-imperialist Discourse and the Motive to Preserve Turkey's Independence

Many of the slogans that the peasants used in their demonstrations had an anti-imperialist flavour. 'Turkey will not become Africa' or 'Altın'cı Filo Defol' (this slogan was used by the left-wing movement in the late 1960s in order to protest against the visit of the 6th fleet of the American Navy to İstanbul; but the slogan, written thus, actually means 'gold fleet get out') are two such examples. It is not clear why they use Africa, but certain interviewees pointed out that Africa is very poor and that there are also many mining companies there which use environmentally harmful practices (Interview, No. 3, 2000-09-17). The fact that the Company is owned by foreigners, that it will only pay 10 percent of its revenue to the state, and that it would only generate 120 jobs, reinforced the anti-imperialist stance of the movement. They stated:

> Our main goal is to ensure that other people acquire consciousness and become aware like we did. We are shouting out loud that cyanide destroys human life, that foreign firms will enrich themselves and then leave, that they poison the land and, more importantly than anything else, that the territory we secured during the War of Independence is being conquered by them (Interview, No. 9, 2000-09-14).

Self-perpetuating Activism

'They have become experts on demonstrations', was the heading of an article on Bergama that appeared in *Yeni Asır* – a regional daily newspaper (1997-09-29). Over the course of the protest activities the peasants realised that they had the power to resist things with which they did not agree. So a movement that started out 'protecting our land and livelihood' rapidly turned into widespread protest demonstrations all over Turkey. One interviewee pointed out that it was very enjoyable to go to demonstrations because of the opportunity she thus got to travel around Turkey (Interview, No. 2, 2000-09-14). So a combination of the feeling of power which demonstrates itself in the following quote: 'but as long as we resist, this mine will not operate' (Interview, No. 2, 2000-09-14), and the catalytic effect of self-perpetuating collective action, can also be included among the motives.

The participants and supporters do not fall neatly into one or the other category, and their motives can mostly be located at the intersection between two or more of the above mentioned categories.

Transnational Spaces

Transnational spaces refer to 'relatively stable, enduring and dense sets of ties reaching beyond and across the borders of sovereign states' (Faist, chapter 1, this volume). Space is used to denote 'cultural, economic and political practices of individual and collective actors within territories or places' (ibid.). Transnational relations occur mostly without state or government involvement, and according to McGrew (1992, p. 7)[5] they refer to the networks, associations or interactions that create linkages between individuals, groups and organisations within different nation-states. Whereas some of these networks and associations involve economic actors and businesses, there are numerous instances in which they are formed by scientists wishing to influence policy-making or by activists seeking to be heard on a specific issue (Keck and Sikkink, 1999, p. 89). Feminist networks (Moghadam, 2000), environmental activists (Wapner, 1995) and human rights advocates (Sikkink, 1993) have made intensive use of transnational spaces. Generally speaking, the usefulness of these spaces is their ability to provide information and support for members of social movements and activist groups that seek to achieve well-defined goals. This flow of information can work in both directions. Outsiders can provide valuable knowledge to activists in order to increase their effectiveness in defending their interests against opponents – as exemplified by the Bergama case. The activists can also pose an implicit threat to their contenders by disseminating information about the pernicious activities of the latter – most human rights cases fall into this category. As the focal point of this paper is the Bergama Movement against cyanide, we will concentrate here on how transnational networks and spaces are used by the activists in order to further their interests and to gain support.

The transboundary expansion of social spaces is facilitated by the advances made over the past decades in communication and transport technologies. Without falling into the trap of technological determinism, one can safely assert that the intensified use of such spaces is undoubtedly linked to an increased use of the Internet and a fall in costs of long distance communication and travel.

Faist's typology (chapter 1, this volume) categorises transnational spaces according to their potential durability and their degree of formalisation. The degree of formalisation can either be low – as in the case of networks – or it can be high, which would indicate the existence of some form of institutionalised relations. The Bergama Movement is by no means a short-lived one, as will become clear below, which means that we can concentrate on the durable half of the typology at hand and thus reduce the four-quadrant typology to a continuous scale, which runs from issue networks with a low degree of formalisation at the one end, to transnational organisations at the other. We will next discuss the properties of issue networks and transnational organisations in order to situate the transnational anti-cyanide ties on this scale with the help of the empirical material.

A network comprises individual or collective actors and the relations that take place between them. They have an informal level of organisation and possess no formal attributes such as membership lists or hierarchies. Transnational issue networks are formed by actors who are motivated by common values and goals, and work to achieve common objectives (Faist, this volume; Keck and Sikkink,

---

[5] McGrew (1992) uses the term transnational relations, but for the purposes of this paper all the literature will be referred to using the term transnational spaces.

46   *Transnational Social Spaces*

1999, p. 89). According to Keck and Sikkink (1999, p. 89) what is new about these networks is their inclusion of 'non-traditional international actors' who 'mobilise information strategically to help create new issues and categories, and to persuade, pressurise, and gain leverage over much more powerful organisations and governments'.

In contrast to issue networks, transnational organisations are highly formalised and hierarchical. Bull (1977, p. 270) defines them as non-governmental bodies operating 'across national boundaries – sometimes on a global scale, which seek as far as possible to disregard these boundaries – and which serve to establish links between different national societies or sections of those societies'. They can be exemplified by International Non-governmental Organisations (INGOs) – such as Greenpeace or Friends of the Earth, by transnational corporations, such as Unilever, Nestlé or 3M; or by professional associations, such as the International Political Science Association (McGrew, 1992, p. 8). Most INGOs develop from issue networks, but comprise more hierarchical organisation patterns and high levels of labour specialisation in contrast with issue networks. Transnational Social Movement Organisations (TSMOs) are 'INGOs that seek to bring about a change in the status-quo' according to Kriesberg (1997, p. 12). The work of Amnesty International on human rights, for instance, can be categorised as a TSMO. TSMOs bring issues onto the political agenda, draft proposals and monitor governments. They have members in more than two countries, have a formal structure and co-ordinate their strategies through an international secretariat (Smith et al., 1997, p. 61). Their members mostly have professional identities, and this implies more formally structured relationships (Smith, 1997, p. 53).

The external links of the Bergama movement were diverse and had different levels of *extensity*, *intensity* and *impact*. The most important of these links were the following: Minewatch in the UK, the Mineral Policy Center (MPC) in the USA, the Mineral Policy Institute (MPI) and SOS-Pergamon group, Australia, FIAN (FoodFirst Information & Action Network) and Pergamon & Adramytteion (P&A) Association and Professors from Germany. The first foreign link established by the movement was with the Greenpeace boat that visited İzmir in 1992. Taşkın argues that they managed to establish relationships with mining-related NGOs in Australia and the UK through the contacts provided by one of the Greenpeace activists on the boat (Elite Interview, No. 2, 2000-08-25). However, Greenpeace itself made no significant input into the movement, the reason being a lack of expertise on gold mining.

> Minewatch of the UK sent boxes full of documents to us (Elite Interview, No. 2, 2000-08-25).

This quotation from Taşkın illustrates the role that transnational relations played in terms of providing information to the domestic contenders. According to Keck and Sikkink (1998, p. 18) 'information politics', which was widely used in the case of Bergama, is an important component of issue networks, and most of the information exchange is informal, taking the form of telephone calls, e-mails, fax and the circulation of newsletters, pamphlets or bulletins. This, however, is also a feature of transnational organisations, even though the latter keeps a better record of past events and communications. Nevertheless, this feature is not sufficient to classify the anti-cyanide space as an issue network.

The MPC (USA) and MPI were both active in sharing information with Turkish activists. The MPI is based in Australia and pressures that government to force Australian companies to be environmentally responsible. As part of the external links of the Bergama Movement, several citizens of Turkey living in Australia formed the SOS-Pergamon initiative. The group began to attract media attention during the anti-globalist demonstrations in Melbourne in September 2000. Emet Değirmenci and her friends started a petition during the Melbourne demonstrations and sent it to the Federal Parliament of Australia. The collection of 3,000 signatures gave the MPI a basis for directing questions to the government of Australia and demanding an explanation why an Australian company was violating a court decision in Turkey (Elite Interview, No. 7, 2001-05-17).

We thus see companies coming under pressure from increased interaction between people of different locations. This interaction enables information on the specific details of events to be transmitted through networks of activists rather than through the official channel, which has the tendency to withhold information (Keck and Sikkink, 1998, pp. 144-147). TSMOs, as well as issue networks, act in order to provide data pertaining to the compliance of governments with environmental and human rights principles (Kriesberg, 1997, p. 18). In the case of Bergama, both the company and the Turkish government came under pressure as a result of the activities of the peasants and their transnational links. Hence, the area of impact cannot be used as a benchmark in evaluating where a movement can be placed on the continuous scale of transnational spaces between networks and organisations. In what follows we will examine other members of the transnational space and its evolution in order to assert whether it is an issue network or a TSMO.

The transnational space that was created between Germany and Turkey centred around the scientific and individual support that the movement received from the German scientists Prof. Korte and Prof. Müller. Furthermore, the efforts of the FIAN Germany and the P&A Association based in Munich must be taken into consideration.

Prof. Korte is a chemist and established the Institute for Ecological Chemistry at the Technical University of Munich after having worked for a decade in large enterprises such as the Shell Company. He has given lectures all over the world and met the head of the P&A Association during one of these lectures. This person – a citizen of Turkey who lives in Germany during the winter – informed Prof. Korte about the situation concerning the gold mining in Turkey and asked him if he could analyse the issue on the spot. On the invitation of 13 mayors of the Edremit Gulf, headed by Necmi Şengider, the Mayor of Burhaniye, Prof. Korte visited Turkey and met the representatives of the Tüprag Company (owned by the German Preussag), and published his ecotoxicological results in July 1993 on the

48   *Transnational Social Spaces*

basis of this meeting (Elite Interview, No. 5, 2001-03-10). The Tüprag Company had obtained a mining permit at the same time as Eurogold, but whereas the peasants of Bergama had shown no interest in the proposition of the İzmir Bar Lawyers on Environmental Issues to represent them in their struggle with the Company the Küçükdere peasants – from the area where Tüprag was supposed to engage in gold mining using the cyanide leach method – were very enthusiastic about founding initiatives and contacting influential people in order to stop the mining activity from going ahead. This is how the head of the P&A Association came to be informed about the explorations of the multinational mining companies (Elite Interview, No. 4, 2001-03-12).

The Küçükdere peasants who founded the Güzel Edremit Körfezi Bekçileri Initiative (Guardians of the Beautiful Edremit Gulf) were quite effective in voicing their demands. The mayor of Burhaniye asked the German Embassy for asylum for the 30,000 people who live in the area because the mining, according to him, would lead to the loss of livelihood in the Gulf (Özay, 1995, p. 27). The concerned parties organised a meeting in the village of Küçükdere in April 1993, and issued a declaration addressed to the relevant ministries and Parliament, demanding the prevention of what would very likely turn out to be an ecological catastrophe. The result of these efforts was the cancellation of the Küçükdere project licenses by the Minister of the Environment, Doğancan Akyürek, on the 21st May 1993 (Özay, 1995, p. 37).

> When the peasants of Bergama saw what happened in Küçükdere they started to change their minds. The case was brought to the Administrative Court of İzmir, panels were organised to discuss the issue, acts of civil disobedience were perpetrated, and the Bergama case started (Elite Interview, No. 1, 2000-08-26).

The German-Turkish space played a significant role in acquiring relevant, but not public information. The P&A Association established a link to the lawyer Wolfgang von Nostitz, who found out that the project was originally financed by the Dresdner Bank, which – in accordance with UNEP (United Nations Environment Program) – had stipulated that it would not finance any project that would be unacceptable in Germany (Özay, 1995, p. 29). This kind of input was also essential for the work of Prof. Korte, who had published many academic articles on the non-sustainability of the cyanide leach technology (e.g. Korte and Coulston, 1995; Korte and Coulston, 1998; Korte et al., 2000). Prof. Korte had been working in other areas of ecological chemistry and if it had not been for the personal contact established through the P&A Association, he would not have concentrated on the research of gold recovery[6] using the cyanide leaching method (Elite Interview, No. 5, 2001-03-10).

---

[6] Prof. Korte and other opponents of the gold mining stress the fact that this activity should not be labelled as mining, but should in fact be referred to as a chemical industry because of the process they use (Elite Interview, No. 5, 2001-03-10; Elite Interview, No. 4,

The Transnational Dimension of the Bergama Campaign   49

FIAN is an NGO that has members in more than 40 countries, and FIAN Germany has 1200 members; it promotes the human right to food. FIAN informs individuals or groups about their right to feed themselves, and alerts the general public about violations of this right (FIAN, 2001). The link between FIAN and the Bergama Movement was established when Petra Sauerland read an article in the *Tageszeitung* – a German daily newspaper – in April 1993. Through her Turkish husband she established connections with people involved and went on a fact-finding trip to Turkey. Once back in Germany, she presented the information about the gold-mining ventures in Turkey to FIAN members, and they voted in favour of taking the case up (Elite Interview, No. 6, 2001-03-11). Throughout the years of struggle Petra Sauerland has been very active, providing information to the then mayor, Sefa Taşkın, arranging meetings for him with German mayors, and organising urgent calls for action.

In the previous section we saw that what differentiates TSMOs from issue networks is the degree of formalisation. The Bergama resistance movement represents a social movement because it comprises a closely tied group of peasants that was able to launch sustained and unconventional collective action. However, a closer examination of the transnational space concerning Bergama reveals that at the transnational level, rather than having a formal membership, it is an informal, loosely connected and non-hierarchical network. Hence, it does not represent a TSMO. It is therefore appropriate to categorise it as an issue network.

Spatial and Temporal Aspects

This section will analyse the spatial and temporal aspects of the transnational anti-cyanide space in terms of time-space compression, patterns of ties and areas of impact.

Time-Space Compression of Ties: Extensity and Intensity

The transboundary extensity of activities and practices of the Bergama Movement is best illustrated by analysing the localities of the movement's events, media coverage and the variety of actors.

In spatial terms, the events reached from Germany to Australia and even, at certain points, to the European Parliament (EP) meetings, where two resolutions were passed regarding the gold-mining ventures in Turkey. The first of these was passed at a session of the EP on November 17th, 1994; it 'calls on the Turkish

---

2000-09-12). However, they assert, these companies intentionally call it mining in order to subject the process to the regulations pertaining to the mining industry rather than the chemical one. The latter has stricter regulations and according to Prof. Korte they would never be able to use an open system with cyanide under chemical industrial regulations (Elite Interview, No. 5, 2001-03-10).

50 *Transnational Social Spaces*

government to ban the use of substances containing cyanide in mining' (EP, 1994). The second resolution was part of the European Strategy for Turkey and requested the government of Turkey to respect the decisions taken by the highest court in Turkey (EP, 1998).

The activities that took place in Germany include a meeting of the mayors of different towns on the West coast of Turkey with the Dresdner Bank, initiated by Karin Hageman of the Green Party (*Hürriyet*, 1995-11-04). The international meeting on the effects of the use of cyanide in gold recovery processes on ecology and humanity was held in October 2000 and concluded with the issue of the so-called the Berlin Declaration. Participants included Prof. Korte (Munich Technical University), Prof. Müller (University of Saarland), Prof. Duman (İstanbul Technical University), Petra Sauerland (FIAN) and Gila Altman (State Secretary, Ministry of Environment, Germany).

> The declaration states that the 'analysis of the social effects on the people and the humanitarian situation prove that there is no positive effect by [sic!] Gold mining using cyanide process. [...] The public money sanctioned by the governments for the promotion of gold-mining projects should be stopped and where necessary the affected people should receive compensation' (Berlin Declaration, 2000).

The transnational anti-cyanide space was active in the organisation of trips by German scientists to Turkey. There were two meetings organised for the scientific analysis on the effects of gold extraction using cyanide. Prof. Müller (of the Environmental Research Centre, University of Saarland) chaired two meetings in Turkey related to gold mining. The first meeting was held in 1997 at İstanbul Technical University and led to the Pergamon Declaration which stated that, 'based on current evidence, including the technologies involved and knowledge of the natural and cultural environment, the planned extraction of gold in the Bergama region is not acceptable' (Pergamon Declaration, 1997). The second meeting was held in July 1999, and participants included Prof. Korte, Steve D'Esposito (MPC, USA), Senih Özay (lawyer) and Wolfgang von Nostitz (lawyer). This meeting resulted in the Conventus '99 Declaration, in which German and Turkish scientists declared their willingness to continue co-operating in the future in order to preserve the area (Anatolia) as a World Cultural Heritage Site (Conventus, 1999).

Apart from the scientific meetings, the transnational anti-cyanide space also spurred an interest among German environmentalist groups in gold extraction using cyanide. It was after the Bergama case that FIAN Germany became interested in other cases of gold mining and organised urgent action calls about problems related to gold mining in the Philippines, Indonesia and Ghana (Elite Interview, No. 6, 2001-03-11).

The role of the press should not be overlooked, as it is an important actor in the whole process of establishing and maintaining the transnational anti-cyanide space. Both the German and Turkish press have given wide coverage to the activities organised by the parties involved. The press of both countries have

The Transnational Dimension of the Bergama Campaign   51

generally had a positive attitude towards the movement over the last ten years. Most of the demonstrations and most developments reflected a bias in favour of the resistance movement. The German newspapers were also interested in the issue and obtained their information either from their reporters based in Turkey or from the press releases arranged by FIAN.

The urgent action calls organised by FIAN led to 800 letters that were sent by German citizens to the Ministry of the Environment of Turkey in the first half of 1995, demanding a ban on mining activities in an area of such outstanding historical and natural significance.[7]

As can be seen, the spatial distribution of events concentrated in Germany, Turkey and Australia. The actors involved in these events were both Turkish and German and their impact will be analysed in the section *Areas of Impact* in which the extensity of this space to Greece will be examined.

In line with Faist (this volume) the intensity or the magnitude of interconnectedness will be analysed in terms of two sub-fields labelled 1. density of ties, and 2. speed of exchanges. The density of ties, or number of connections and frequency of transboundary exchanges, is an important feature of transnational spaces. The frequency of ties between the actors of the transnational anti-cyanide space was mostly dependent upon the availability of new information concerning the movement, the occurrence of accidents related to gold mining throughout the world or other developments regarding the companies involved. The main tool of communications between the actors was initially the fax machine, but later it was increasingly replaced by e-mail (Elite Interview, No. 1, 2000-08-26; No. 2, 2000-08-25; No. 6, 2001-03-11). The use of the fastest communication technology has facilitated the rapid exchange of information.

The initial involvement of some of the nodes which now constitute important components of this transnational space was random – as witnessed by the way in which Petra Sauerland became involved. However, there are other cases in which people were deliberately drawn into the movement by supporters. Once the links were established and the exchange of information began, the flow was regularised between the main actors of the movement – or, as Prof. Müller put it, 'the Bergama gang was formed' (Elite Interview, No. 8, 2001-05-21). One can therefore attribute a high intensity of ties to the anti-cyanide space, where relations were not random, but highly regularised.

Linkage Patterns

Under this heading we will analyse the infrastructure, institutionalisation and regulation of ties. Infrastructure refers to the modes of transportation, communication and informal norms or procedures. As explained in the previous

---

[7] Only 50 of these letters – whose copies were sent to the lawyers in İzmir – were analysed personally by the present author. The data on the number of letters that were sent is a rough estimate given by Petra Sauerland during the interview (Elite Interview, No. 6, 2001-03-11).

52   *Transnational Social Spaces*

section, correspondence within the transnational anti-cyanide space was mostly carried out by fax and e-mail. Telephone calls were also crucial, but they were not as widely used because of the costs involved and the ease of using a fax or e-mail for transmitting documents in their original format. Another feature of this space that is of interest to the discussion of infrastructure is the language – the main language of communication between the actors was English. The use of English facilitated the transmission of decisions to all parties without involving translations. Hence, the availability of the latest communication technologies and a common language facilitated the development and maintenance of transnational ties. However, it should not be forgotten that it is not the contact provided by advanced technologies that matters, but rather the ability to use the data as knowledge towards specific ends (Lipschutz, 1992, p. 411). Technologically, the actors belonging to the transnational anti-cyanide space are well equipped and have the capacity to use the information acquired through their contacts.

The level of institutionalisation of the transnational anti-cyanide space has always been low, and activities have mostly been the result of networking between the participants. The actors have used their already existing institutional settings – such as FIAN in Petra Sauerland's case – to participate and disseminate information. As far as the regulation aspect of the patterns of ties is concerned, one can say that beyond remaining within the boundaries of the laws, the activities organised by the actors have not been regulated in any way. However, it is certain that the movement's participants, as well as its supporters from Germany, were subject to certain limitations when they endeavoured to access information about the companies involved or the progress of the case at governmental level in Turkey. The peasants have been regulated to a much greater degree than the international exchange of information related to the movement. The simple reason behind this is the ability of the State to regulate and constrain the mass activities of its citizens, but not those transnational actors who establish connections through the Internet or via fax.

Areas of Impact

The areas of impact which will be analysed here can be put into three categories: exchange of information, pressure and spatial expansion. As we have seen earlier, the transnational space created for the purposes of opposing the use of cyanide in gold processing gave rise to a massive exchange of information of many types and in all directions, especially between Germany and Turkey. The information included scientific findings, undisclosed, company-related information and up-to-the-minute news about what was happening in gold-mining industries throughout the world. This information flow contributed to the gathering of evidence to be presented before the High Court of Turkey. The case ended in favour of the local people who demanded a ban on gold mining in Bergama. However, the court's decision to ban the cyanide leach method and to close down the plant built by the Eurogold Company has still not been implemented at the time of writing. In fact, a recent report prepared by TÜBİTAK (The Scientific and Technical Research Council of Turkey), has enabled the Company to obtain all the necessary permission once again and to start the recovery of gold.

Letter campaigns and the European Parliament resolutions supporting the movement and criticising the use of cyanide in gold processing in Bergama may have had no direct impact on the evolution of events, but they certainly played a role in showing the government that international organisations and NGOs were closely following the unfolding of events. The presence of scientists and environmental experts has enabled participants in the movement to counter the company's claims of 'negligible' risk associated with the cyanide leach method.

In Australia, resistance to a gold mine located in Timbarra is also growing. Campaigners there have used the court decision in Turkey that banned the use of cyanide as a precedent and claim that it should also be banned in Australia (Elite Interview, No. 7, 2001-05-17). Hence, we see that the areas of impact of these networks are not restricted to the countries they originally targeted.

The network was also extended to support the anti-gold mine initiatives at Halkidiki, in Greece, where a similar struggle is going on between environmentalists and the gold-mining company. There is also an ongoing court case over a ban on the use of cyanide in the Olympiada Gold Mine, and Prof. Korte was invited to Greece to testify on his findings. The Greek anti-mine movement also contacted Prof. Duman and asked him to prepare a report on the effects of cyanide use in gold extraction. Prof. Duman stated that this report was intended to be used as evidence in the court (*Milliyet*, 2000-09-12). It comes as no surprise to see the same names – Prof. Korte, Prof. Duman, Prof. Müller and Petra Petra Sauerland – at a conference organised by the Thrace Regional Department of the Technical Chamber of Greece in October 2000.[8]

Concluding Remarks

The first section summarised the emergence and the major events of the Bergama Movement. It also included a brief methodological discussion related to the research techniques used for the examination of the movement. The second section dealt with the theoretical framework for the analysis of the case at hand. This framework is based on the notion of transnational spaces and especially on their role in bringing about change through the provision of information. These spaces were shown to be instrumental in providing information and support to the members of the anti-cyanide camp. It was demonstrated that the anti-cyanide space is composed of like-minded individuals who share common values and principles, and who fight for a common purpose through the use of informal relations. Hence, this space has been identified as constituting an issue network. The analysis of the spatial and temporal attributes of the anti-cyanide space demonstrated that its

---

[8] See http://antigoldgreece.tripod.com/en/id91.htm, for details.

extensity, intensity and impact were significant. In this regard it was asserted that the location of the transnational events extended to Germany and Australia, and that the ties between the transnational actors became regularised rather than remaining random. It was shown that the actors employed new technologies for communication purposes and that the area of impact extended well beyond the intended influence on the case of Bergama.

Out of the five categories of motivations outlined earlier, only two are relevant to the involvement of individuals belonging to the external links. These are ecological concerns and citizenship issues, or, in other words, human rights concerns. The motives of self-interest and self-perpetuating activism are simply not relevant because the individuals belonging to the transnational space live elsewhere and they do not participate in the demonstrations. The category of independence and sovereignty of the country does not apply because the supporters are mainly motivated by a combination of environmental and human rights concerns. This is illustrated by the claim of the head of the P&A Association that accepting gold mining with cyanide will bring with it all sorts of other environmentally degrading practices. Once the soil has been poisoned, there will be no reason why toxic or nuclear waste coming from developed countries should not also be stored there (Elite Interview, No. 4, 2000-09-12).

Prof. Müller, for instance, clearly asserts his doubts about the company being able to use a proper detoxification system because of the expenses it entails. He claims that the revenues from gold would not be sufficient to allow an environmentally safe system of production. He is not against gold mining with cyanide but he simply believes that the companies that operate in developing countries do not pay attention to environmental regulations in order to cut costs (Elite Interview, No. 8, 2001-05-21).

Prof. Korte holds a stricter position and believes that this process should not be used because of the risks it brings with it to the environment and thus to human beings (Elite Interview, No. 5, 2001-03-10). Petra Sauerland approaches the matter from a different perspective, and views mining with cyanide as a violation of human rights. As Keck and Sikkink (1998, p. 137) argue, within environmental networks, cases involving loss of livelihood rather than environmental preservation are particularly susceptible to transnational advocacy networking.

When combined, these motives reflect a high degree of distrust towards the company. Nor do the campaigners trust the government's ability to monitor the activities of the companies or to enforce environmentally sound standards. These people are not only concerned about the potential risks of cyanide technologies in Turkey, but they also participate in networks covering many other countries that face similar struggles. Each case involves resistance to multinational companies backed by the governments of each respective country. Had the campaign not been against non-indigenous companies, it would not have received as much support from transnational participants. The reason for this is that campaigners have greater leverage when they can claim that the company is reaping the benefits without contributing much to the community. This in turn is directly related to

The Transnational Dimension of the Bergama Campaign 55

globalization and to the trends in foreign direct investments and multinational activities since the 1980s. If the transnationalization of production had not reached its current levels, and if the expansion of transnational spaces had not intensified over the last two decades, such cooperation would not have been possible. In other words, if the company attempting to mine gold using cyanide had been a Turkish firm, it would not have been possible to contemplate such a transnational support network, and even the movement itself – if it had existed at all – would not have been as influential as it was.

> [O]ne cannot speak *for* the subaltern but only *with* the subaltern
> (Morton, 2001, p. 6).

As this quote suggests, it is important for the transnational and national supporters to speak *with* the peasants rather than voice demands *for* them. In other words, the most important group whose motives and beliefs should be respected and complemented through external links is that of the peasants. In fact, it is important to note that on their own, transnational networks are mostly ineffective – as seen in the example of the transborder democracy network, which did not achieve its goals in Kazakhstan, where local mobilisation for democracy was weak (Scholte, 2000, p. 264). It should therefore be stressed that the transnational level of the Bergama Movement would not have achieved much had it not been in co-ordination with the efforts of the locals.

Another very important aspect of the transnational space that was formed in order to resist the use of cyanide for gold recovery, was the rapidity with which it expanded to provide information and support to other struggles. The clearest case of this expansion was the Greek case, where the organisers of the movement – who were also fighting gold multinationals – established ties with the same activists in Germany and Turkey. The linkage patterns and strategies of the Greek anti-cyanide movement were very similar to those of the Turkish campaign. Of course, the significance of this expansion can be downplayed by pointing to the geographical proximity of Turkey to Greece which facilitated expansion. However, an analysis of the wider anti-cyanide spaces around the world reveals a similar trend. The Timbarra resistance to gold mining in Australia served as an example of this in section *Areas of Impact*. When the court in Turkey decided in 1997 to ban the use of cyanide on the grounds of incompatibility with the interests of the people of Bergama, the movement organisers in Timbarra used this court decision as a tool to apply pressure on the government. This demonstrates that resistance movements are dynamic structures with strategies that are easily transmitted from one area to another through the links that can be established between individuals and groups.

The significance of the transnational space between Turkey and Germany has thus been demonstrated, and it has been asserted that its main function was to disseminate information through several channels. It has also been asserted that transnational spaces and issue networks are ineffective unless there is local support. Finally, the rapid spread of the transnational ties to other countries has

56 *Transnational Social Spaces*

been shown to be an important feature of the dynamic nature of these spaces. Hence, the transboundary expansion of non-governmental ties has been shown to be effective in the case of the Bergama Movement against Eurogold.

References

Bull, H. (1977), *The Anarchical Society*, Macmillan, London.
Conventus (1999), *Konventus 99 – Türkiye; Siyanürle Altın Üretimi, Uluslarası Tahkim* (Conventus 99 – Turkey; Gold Extraction with Cyanide, International Arbitration), Edremit, 21 July.
Denzin, N. K. (1989), *The Research Act: A Theoretical Introduction to Sociological Methods*, Prentice Hall, Englewood Cliffs, N.J..
European Parliament (EP) (1994), *Minutes of the Sitting on Thursday 17 November 1994 – Motion for a Resolution*, Vol. B4-0343/94.
European Parliament (EP) (1998), *Protokoll der Sitzung vom Donnerstag 3. Dezember 1998 – Europäische Strategie für die Türkei* (Minutes of the Sitting on Thursday 3. December 1998 – European Strategy for the Turkey), Vol. A4-0432/98.
FIAN (FoodFirst Information & Action Network) (2001), *About FIAN*, http://www.fian.org, retrieved 2001-02-12.
Foweraker, J. (1995), *Theorizing Social Movements*, Pluto Press, London.
Gökvardar, H. (1998), 'Ovacık Altın Madeni Projesi (The Project of Ovacık Gold Mine)', in A. E. Yüce and G. Önal (eds.), *Altın Madenciliği ve Çevre (Gold Mining and the Environment)*, Yurt Madenciliğini Geliştirme Vakfı Yayınları, Beril Ofset Matbaacılık, İstanbul.
International Meeting on the Effects of the Cyanide Mining Gold Recovery Process on the Ecology and Humanity (2000), *Berlin Declaration*, Berlin, October 27.
Kaldor, M. (2000), '"Civilising Globalisation?" The Implications of the "Battle in Seattle"', in *Journal of International Studies*, Millennium, Vol. 29(1), pp. 105-14.
Karadeniz, M. (1996), *Cevher Zenginleştirme, Tesis Atıkları, Çevreye Etkileri, Önlemler* (Ore Enrichment, Wastes, Effects on the Environment and Precautions), Ofset Basım Yayın, İstanbul.
Keck, M. E. and Sikkink, K. (1998), *Activists Beyond Borders: Advocacy Networks in International Politics*, Cornell University Press, London.
Keck, M. E. and Sikkink, K. (1999), 'Transnational Advocacy Networks in International and Regional Politics', in *International Social Science Journal*, Vol. 51(1), pp. 89-104.
Korte, F. and Coulston, F. (1995), 'Comment: From Single Substance Evaluation to Ecological Process Concept: The Dilemma of Processing Gold with Cyanide', in *Ecotoxicology and Environmental Safety*, Vol. 32, pp. 96-101.
Korte, F. and Coulston, F. (1998), 'Commentary: Some Considerations on the Impact on Ecological Chemical Principles in Practice with Emphasis on Gold Mining and Cyanide', in *Ecotoxicology and Environmental Safety*, Vol. 41, pp. 119-29.
Korte, F., Spiteller, M. and Coulston, F. (2000), 'Commentary: The Cyanide Leaching Gold Recovery Process is a Nonsustainable Technology with Unacceptable Impacts on Ecosystems and Humans: the Disaster in Romania', in *Ecotoxicology and Environmental Safety*, Vol. 46, pp. 241-5.
Kriesberg, L. (1997), 'Social Movements and Global Transformation', in J. Smith, C. Chatfield and R. Pagnucco (eds.), *Transnational Social Movements and Global Politics*, Syracuse University Press, Syracuse.

The Transnational Dimension of the Bergama Campaign   57

Kriesi, H. (1992). 'The Rebellion of the Research "Objects"', in M. Diani and R. Eyerman (eds.). *Studying Collective Action*, SAGE Modern Politics Series, Sage Publications London, Vol. 30.

Lee R. (1993). *Doing Research on Sensitive Topics*, Sage, London.

Lipschutz, R. D. (1992). 'Reconstructing World Politics: The Emergence of Global Civil Society'. in *Journal of International Studies*, Millennium, Vol. 21(3), pp. 389-420.

McGrew, A. G. (1992). 'Conceptualizing Global Politics', in A. G McGrew and P. G. Lewis (eds.). *Global Politics: Globalization and the Nation State*, Polity Press, Cambridge.

Mining Journal (1992), 'More Gold in Turkey', *Mining Journal*, Vol. 318(8157), p. 53.

Mittelman. J. H. (2000). 'Environmental Resistance to Globalization', in *Current History*, Events Pub. Co., New York, Vol. 99(640), pp. 383-8.

Moghadam, V. M. (2000). 'Transnational Feminist Networks: Collective Action in an Era of Globalisation'. in Saïd Amir Arjomad (ed.), *International Sociology* (International Sociological Association). Vol. 15(1), pp. 57-85.

Morton, A. D. (2001). '"La Resurreccion del Maiz": Some Aspects of Globalisation, Resistance and the Zapatista Question', Paper presented at the *42nd Annual Convention of the International Studies Association*, Chicago, 20-24 February.

Orhon, D. (1999). 'Ovacık Altın Madeni Isletmelerinin Çevresel Özelliklerinin Tespiti ve Risk Belirlenmesi' (Environmental Properties and Risk Determination of the Ovacık Gold Mine), in TUBITAK, *Eurogold Ovacık Altın Madeni: TÜBİTAK-YDABCAG Komisyon Değerlendirme Raporu.*

Özay, S. (1995). '"İnsanlığın Ortak Orospusu" Altın' (Gold: the Common Prostitute of Humankind). SOS Akdeniz Derneği Yayınları, İzmir.

Pergamon Declaration (1997), *Scientific Aspects of Gold Extraction Using Cyanide*, Symposium organized by İstanbul Technical University, Faculty of Mining Sciences, İstanbul. June 26-27.

Richards, D. (1996). 'Elite Interviewing: Approaches and Pitfalls', *Politics*, Vol. 16(3), pp. 199-204.

Scholte, J. A. (2000). *Globalisation: A Critical Introduction*, Macmillan, London.

Sikkink, K. (1993), 'Human Rights, Principled Issue-Networks and Sovereignty in Latin America'. *International Organization*, Vol. 47(3), pp. 411-41.

Smith, J. (1997). 'Characteristics of the Modern Transnational Social Movement Sector', in J. Smith. C. Chatfield and R. Pagnucco (eds.), *Transnational Social Movements and Global Politics*, Syracuse University Press, Syracuse.

Smith, J., Pagnucco. R. and Chatfield. C. (1997), 'Social Movements and World Politics: A Theoretical Framework'. in J. Smith, C. Chatfield and R. Pagnucco (eds.), *Transnational Social Movements and Global Politics*, Syracuse University Press, Syracuse.

Sunar, I. and Sayarı. S. (1986), 'Democracy in Turkey: Problems and Prospects', in G. O'Donnell. P. C. Schmitter and L. Whitehead (eds.), *Transitions from Authoritarian Rule: Southern Europe*, Johns Hopkins University Press, London.

Tarrow, S. (1996). 'Fishnets, Internets and Catnets: Globalization and Transnational Collective Action'. *Working Paper*, Centro de Estudios Avanzados en Ciencias Sociales, Vol. 1996/78.

Taşkın, S. (1998). *Siyanürcü Ahtapot* (Octopus that Employs Cyanide), Sel Yayıncılık, İstanbul.

UNEP (United Nations Environment Program) (1992), *Rio Declaration on Environment and Development.* http://www.unep.org. retrieved 2001-03-20.

Wapner, P. (1995). 'Politics Beyond the State. Environmental Activism and World Civic Politics'. *World Politics*. Vol. 47, pp. 311-40.

58 *Transnational Social Spaces*

List of Interviews

Elite Interviews

No. 1:   Senih Özay. 2000-08-26.
No. 2:   Sefa Taşkın. 2000-08-25 and 2000-09-16.
No. 3:   Oktay Konyar. 2000-08-25.
No. 4:   Informant No. 1. 2000-09-12 and 2001-03-12.
No. 5:   Prof. Friedhelm Korte. 2001-03-10.
No. 6:   Petra Sauerland. 2001-03-11.
No. 7:   Emet Değirmenci. 2001-05-17.
No. 8:   Prof. Paul Müller. 2001-05-21.
No. 9:   Murat Arsel. 2001-03-20.
          (Murat Arsel is a PhD candidate in Cambridge University and works on the same social movement. Some of the information was gathered from his fieldwork and will be referred to as Elite Interview, No. 9.)
No.10:   Vojtech Kotecky. 2001-05-20.

Interviews

No. 1:   A female villager, 2000-09-13.
No. 2:   A female villager, 2000-09-14.
No. 3:   A female villager, 2000-09-17.
No. 4:   A male villager. 2000-09-18.
No. 5:   A male villager. 2000-09-17.
No. 6:   A family from Tepeköy, 2000-09-13.
No. 7:   Owner of a local paper in Bergama, 2000-09-18.
No. 8:   Interviews on the cotton field, 2000-09-18.
No. 9:   A male villager. 2000-09-14.
No.10:   A male villager and our guide in the villages, 2000-08-25 and 2000-09-13 – 2000-09-18.

List of Newspapers

Hürriyet – Nationwide daily newspaper, Turkey.
Milliyet – Nationwide daily newspaper, Turkey.
Yeni Asır – Local (Aegean Region) daily newspaper, Turkey.

Chapter 3

Transnational Space Between Women's NGOs in Germany and Turkey: Current Situation and Future Expectations

Hanife Aliefendioğlu

Introduction

One of the most important social phenomena to occur over the last 50 years is that of international migration. In 1961, Turkish workers began to migrate to Germany in accordance with the bilateral agreement between Turkey and Germany.[1] In 1975, 80 percent of the Turkish migrants living in Europe had emigrated to Germany (Kadıoğlu, 1997, p. 538; Çağlar, 1995, p. 309). Turkish migrants now make up 28 percent of the foreign population in Germany, and are thus the largest group of foreigners living in that country (FGCFI, 2000, p. 7). According to information from the German Ministry of Employment, the total Turkish immigrant population in Germany is 2,110,223 (1,145,057 of whom are men, whilst 965,166 are women). The largest subgroup consists of people between the ages of 15 and 29 (316,073 women and 365,643 men) (ÇYGB, 2000, p. 9). 400,174 men and 170,474 women are in paid employment (ÇYGB, 2000, p. 12). In 1960, the number of migrant female workers was just 173, however by 1974, the number had increased to 159,984 (SPO, 1994, p. 106).

Labour migration from Turkey to Germany, as well as other European countries, is not just a simple matter of financial gain like saving money and buying property. A new country means a new and very different life for the immigrants themselves. It is also a means of obtaining a livelihood from different production and service sectors besides the traditional economic pursuits associated with agriculture (Kıray, 1986, p. 88). The impacts of immigration on women reflect the gendered aspects of international migration. This experience has created a long-lasting transnational space between the two countries at both official and unofficial levels.

---

[1] Workers from Turkey have also migrated in significant numbers to Austria, Belgium and the Netherlands since 1964, to France since 1967 and to Australia since 1968.

60   *Transnational Social Spaces*

In most cases, the decision to migrate to another country is not made by women. Most women migrate as dependants of their husbands. According to one study, in 82 percent of cases it was the husbands who ultimately made the decision to migrate (AAK, 1996, p. 45). Initially, only single men left for Germany on their own. By the late 1960s, single women had also begun to join that group. After 1975, as a result of family unification, women and children were given residence permits as the dependants of men. Some women joined the workforce as dependants of their husbands and fathers. This fact prompts us to consider the more multi-faceted dimensions of the immigration process (Kadıoğlu, 1997, p. 538) and the enlargement of transnational space over time. Generally, women of this generation have been perceived as a relatively unimportant group, since they are dependants of their husbands and do not participate in paid employment (Köksal, 1993, p. 112).

Immigration does not always result in immigrant women's interaction with Western culture and their emancipation. Some first-generation migrant women who went to Germany along with their husbands had no opportunity to work outside the home. This was due to the patriarchal nature of traditional Turkish society, especially in rural areas. This ideology tends to project women first and foremost as housewives and mothers. In fact, these ideologies are reflected in all societies, whether the women are migrants or not. Employers, on the other hand, tend to view migrant women as a source of cheap labour due to their status as 'dependants' (Köksal, 1993, p. 113). Migrant women not only face discrimination within the family and the labour market of host societies, but also as members of marginal ethnic or racial groups (Kadıoğlu, 1997, p. 538).

During the early years of migration from Turkey to Germany, when women were given the status of dependants of their husbands, they usually had to work illegally, at least during the early stages of migration, until they legally obtained a work permit. They entered working life at the lowest levels, taking on jobs as domestic cleaners, babysitters, waitresses etc. In short, the only opportunity they had was to work in the black economy (Kadıoğlu, 1997, p. 539). In 1961 the ratio of employed to non-employed women among the Turkish migrant community was one in three. By early 1971 this ratio had increased to two in three. The percentage of working women has increased in direct correlation with those leaving to return to their home country. Some women actually migrated to Western countries as workers before their husbands. These women lost their economic and social independence as soon as their husbands joined them. Nevertheless, although it seems that migration occurs for individual reasons, it should be noted that chronic economic instability and the patriarchal character of Turkish society also have significant impacts on this issue (SPO, 1994, p. 106).

Most migrant women lose the traditional network of social support that they had in their home country. They lose the status associated with being a member of an extended family as well as childcare support within this family. Moreover, they encounter a drastic change in value systems. They are still faced with performing their reproductive and domestic roles as housewives and mothers (Kadıoğlu, 1997, pp. 543-44). Or: While still faced with performing their reproductive and domestic roles as housewives and mothers (Kadıoğlu, 1997, pp. 543-44), however, they nevertheless encounter a drastic change in value systems. Moreover, working within the public sphere and earning an income does not necessarily or automatically lead to the emancipation of migrant women. Their right to make important decisions concerning their own lives remains limited within the context of patriarchal ideology in the Turkish family.

Another motivation for migration is marriage. When the admission of guest workers ceased in 1973, marriage to a Turkish girl living in Germany became the most attractive way of staying and working in Germany for Turkish men. On the other hand, women who immigrated to Germany from Turkey through marriage to a relative or another man, form another subgroup which has its own problems and necessities. In 1996, over half of the second-generation Turkish people born in Germany married residents of Turkey. In 1996, 10,387 men entered Germany as non-German husbands of Turkish women, whilst 7,275 women entered Germany to join Turkish men as non-German wives (Straßburger, chapter 9, this volume).

This multidimensional problem has some effects at the institutional level. In Turkey, the Ad Hoc Committee on Women, Family and Children of the State Planning Organisation has tense set up a working group to research into Turkish women living abroad in preparation for its Seventh Five-Year Development Plan. A report from this working group underlines the need to divide the Turkish working women in Germany into three groups: those in skilled employment, those in semi-skilled employment, and those in unskilled employment. The report highlights that after the 1967 economic crisis in Germany, migrant women only had the opportunity to work in extremely low-paid, low-prestige occupations in Germany. The report stressed that it was vital to provide support for Turkish migrant women who are either working or seeking a job, by providing training programmes to show them how to gain access to welfare support in Germany, encouraging migrant women to become involved in trade unions and non-governmental organisations (NGO), and opening a women's advice centre affiliated to the Turkish Consulate in Germany. However, it should be stressed here that the report focused on Turkish migrant women mostly as members or potential members of the labour force, rather than viewing them more holistically as a disadvantaged group in almost every respect in Germany.

The pioneer studies on migrant workers were carried out by Abadan-Unat. There are not many studies on Turkish women immigrants living in Germany. One of the most recent studies on this issue concerns women facing domestic violence in Germany (İlkkaracan, 1996, p. 1). The research work was carried out by a group called Women for Women's Human Rights with a view to collecting information on the family life of Turkish immigrant women living in Berlin, their experience of domestic violence and their strategies for combating it.

It should be stressed that migrant women from Turkey who now live in Germany do not constitute a homogeneous group. Among them there are those who are in paid employment and those who stay at home, those with rural and

62 *Transnational Social Spaces*

urban origins, those who face violence, and those who don't (Toksöz, 1993). Turkish women living in Germany can be divided into several subcategories with respect to such criteria as ethnicity and language. A variety of distinctions can made, for instance, between those who speak German and those who do not, Turkish-Kurdish or Sunni-Alevi women, those in paid employment and those who are not, those who have adopted German citizenship and those who are not, as well as between the first, second and third generation. Those of them who work outside the home are in a minority; as a group they are relatively advantaged and emancipated compared to the rest. In this study, it is assumed that this latter group is more involved than any other in organisations that actively participate in civil society. This gives flexibility to transnational space, adding complexity to the conceptions of fields and actors.

Immigration has forced the German and Turkish governments to take precautions and implement measures specifically relating to migrants. The Turkish government has employment, educational, and religious attachés affiliated to the embassy and the consulates. There is a Turkish secretary of state in Berlin, and employment attachés in 13 other provinces in Germany.[2] However, no welfare support has ever been provided to the immigrant workers and their families working in Germany, even for the first years of immigration. According to the Turkish government, it was more appropriate to send religious and educational attachés to Germany than to establish and develop welfare institutions. The same problem still exists today. The advisory centres (*Türk-Danış*) are affiliated bodies of the Worker's Welfare Organisation (*Arbeiterwohlfahrt*) in Germany. They are structured in such a way that there is only one social worker for every 3,000 clients.[3] *Türk-Danış* is the first organisation to offer services to Turkish migrants; it was founded by the German government. After recruitment stopped in 1973, special courses were offered for women in such subjects as reading and writing, language learning and handicrafts. These were separate from the services offered to youths and single migrant workers or children. After the 1980s, more and more social workers – mostly women – started to work for *Türk-Danış*, adding to the curriculum new and more diverse services such as informing migrants preparing to return to their home country. *Türk-Danış* provides services to various Muslim groups, of which immigrants from Turkey compose the largest group.

The patriarchal patterns experienced by women from Turkey tend to be duplicated in subsequent generations, perpetuating the disadvantaged life situation of Turkish women as a whole. Second and third-generation women face various forms of coercion and violence such as early marriage, dropping out of school early, early pregnancy and motherhood, forced marriage with someone from the homeland, and domestic violence. These women are generally not aware of their

---

[2] These provinces are Berlin. Frankfurt/Main, Mainz, Hanover, Hamburg, Düsseldorf, Karlsruhe, Essen, Nuremburg. Stuttgart, Munich, and Cologne (ÇYGB, 1999, pp. 374-75).

[3] Interview with Fuat Boztepe. Ministry of Labour, Head of Department of Immigrant Worker's Social Services. Ankara.

Transnational Space Between Women's NGOs

legal rights. A reform of the welfare services provided for women is therefore urgently needed.

The development of transnational ties, both official and unofficial, between Germany and Turkey, was both unpredicted and unintended. For this reason the development of linkages in terms of professional, institutionalised organisations has been difficult. The first alliances between Turkey and Germany in terms of civil organisations were established after the approval of Turkey's full candidacy for accession to the European Union. This is a very recent development. However, neither the German nor the Turkish government can provide enough welfare services to encompass such a heterogeneous client group of migrant women from Turkey with such a diversity of reasons for immigration, provenance, and educational background.

Women's Share in Civil Movements

As a concept, civil society has spread since the 1960s. Civil society is characterised by pressure and protests against the state administration and decision makers (Sallan-Aksu, 1997, p. 490-91). Particularly in European countries, the women's movement has generally participated in discussions on civil society as well.

With time, migrant women also gradually began to establish their own organisations. However, unemployed immigrant women from the first generation, in particular those who do not speak German, do not have the potential to establish their own organisation. The participation of immigrant women within organisations in the public sphere as a whole is of secondary significance, as the ethnic or religious-based organisations established by immigrants from Turkey do not regard women's issues to be of primary concern. Although this situation heightens the need for women's organisations with the aim of consciousness raising and offering mutual assistance, most of the first-generation women have no information about such organisations. Mosques, for example, are public spaces from which only men benefit. As Turan (1997, p. 105) states, only 19 percent of immigrants from Turkey belong to any form of association, and these associations are generally mosques or fellow-townsmen's (*hemşerilik*, cf. Faist, this volume, chapter 1) organisations. The characteristics of transnational space have changed for the first, second and third generations in Germany. Different generations need different kinds of transnational networks because needs differ from one generation to the next.

The civil organisations associated with the immigrant population from Turkey developed predominantly after it became acknowledged that immigrant workers in Germany were no longer guests, and were now able to stay in Germany permanently (Kastoryano, 2000, p. 120). The self-organisation of immigrant groups may be a reflection of the lack of interest on the part of non-governmental and governmental organisations in the social problems suffered by the immigrant population. Since the 1990s, social issues relating to foreign women have steadily gained importance in the women's movement in Germany (İlkkaracan, 1996). Groups of foreign women have developed their own, specific agendas within the

64 *Transnational Social Spaces*

context of the women's movement in the host country. This development has resulted in the self-organisation of immigrant women to deal with their own problems (Köksal, 1993, p. 115). The number of studies carried out by second-generation Turkish women researchers has also increased (Straßburger, 2001, p. 10).

First-generation migrant women generally only have personal relationships or contact with other first-generation migrant women. Therefore, they generally have no information on civil organisations, nor do they take part in their activities. However, since they operate exclusively in small-scale minority communities and 'traditional' solidarity networks, they do not find it imperative to speak the language of the host country. These women rarely venture outside their home neighbourhood. They therefore often cannot speak the language and find it difficult to participate in public space. Women from the first generation do not have a history of belonging to associations, but of course they do maintain transnational ties with their own country. They also invest a great deal of energy into maintaining these ties. Only after the traditional forms of social solidarity had either collapsed or fulfilled their function – and the second generation began to write their own stories and do their own research – did women's organisations begin to be established. This is the second step in the establishment of transnational ties. When we look at women's organisations active in Germany in the 1990s, we can see that these organisations work in a wide range of areas. They concentrate on various female groups and focus on specific problems (see the section on *Findings and Discussions*).

Why Study Transnational Spaces?

Given this background, it must come as no surprise that women from Turkey who reside in Germany, especially the first generation, live in relatively closed milieus in comparison to men. They cannot participate in the public sphere for a number of reasons. The first one is that they do not speak the language. Second, they lack social support and welfare assistance, at least in the early stages of immigration. These two factors have been influential in determining their living conditions in the host country. As Faist (chapter 1, this volume) states, since they live in close physical proximity to the people they know, especially their relatives, neither language problems nor their non-participation in public space were vital issues in their lives.[4] Subsequent generations, however, tend both to join existing organisations and form their own.

---

[4] Relations with relatives are more stable, safe, long-term when compared to other ones. They may be evaluated as social capital since they are flexible and multi dimensional at the same time (See Nauck, 1999, p. 202). According to a study made in 1982, ⅔ of Turkish people living in Germany reside in the same neighbourhood, and ¼ of them reside in the same house with their relatives. 99 percent of immigrant people mentioned that they have

Links between women's organisations are a good example of transboundary interactions between non-state actors. The focus of this study is on transboundary exchanges and transactions in networks; in particular, on the interaction between women's organisations as non-state actors in Turkey and Germany. The main aim of this research is therefore to analyse information exchanged between women's organisations in Turkey and Germany, to understand their needs and thus contribute towards strengthening existing transnational ties. Within this framework, it is envisaged that in practical terms we will eventually be able to supply the necessary information to women from Turkey living in Germany concerning legal and social supports available to them by reaching women's NGOs in Germany. To this end I hope to build upon and greatly improve information exchange mechanisms that maintain and cultivate the transnational space between German and Turkish organisations. This research is an endeavour to inform migrant women from Turkey (as well as German women's organisations in general) about governmental and non-governmental organisations in Turkey. In addition, through an analysis of the current situation, it seeks to understand and improve the exchange of contacts and information between women's organisations in both Turkey and Germany.

This study will investigate how Turkish women's organisations relate to, and collaborate with, German women's organisations and migrant women in Germany. The answers will be sought from various organisations both in Turkey and Germany. In terms of methodology, the study will rely mostly on questionnaires. An additional source of information consists of interviews with other people who deal with, or study this subject area.

Content of Research and Collecting Data

As already mentioned, for this research I have contacted and co-operated with women's associations in Germany and Turkey in order to explore their past, current, and potential contacts with each other. It is important, to initially contact women's organisations in Germany which were either established by German women or by women from both countries (Turkey and Germany). It was not possible to find a booklet publishing the list of such organisations in Germany. Women's organisations in Germany had to be contacted through personal recommendations or their web sites.[5] I also expected to reach some organisations in German cities with a high concentration of Turkish residents by mail. Most of the contacts were made by mail and e-mail. Some of the NGOs assisted me in contacting other organisations, and by giving basic information in their answers to

---

relatives residing in Germany. Almost all of them expressed that they visit their relatives regularly whereas 34 percent of them mentioned that they visit their relatives less frequently (Nauck, 1999, p. 200).

[5] http://www.euronet.nl/~fullmoon/womlist/womlist.html.

66 *Transnational Social Spaces*

my questionnaire. As an example, the ZIF sent my inquiry to 120 autonomous women's shelters. Between October 2000 and June 2001, I continued to correspond by e-mail and mail with NGOs in Germany and Turkey. In Germany I primarily contacted organisations that work with, or that I believed might possibly work with women from Turkey. It was important for this study to contact NGOs that had a large Turkish membership, or that were established by women of Turkish origin (contradicts statement made in this paragraph above). However, only eight of them responded (*Akarsu, ISI Bacım, Papatya, Hinbun, Uğrak, Elişi Evi, TIO* and *Türkische Frauen*). The organisations that were contacted in Germany provide advisory services to women, make publications, run archives and conduct research. I assumed that these sorts of women's organisations would be more likely to co-operate, exchange information, and share experiences to create effective transnational links. Organisations with similar qualifications were chosen in Turkey. Academic organisations, such as graduate programmes and women's research and implementation centres in universities were not included in this study. Other organisations like the Foundation for the Development of Human Resources, the Turkish Family Planning Association, the Federal Working Committee of Immigrant Associations in the FRG (*Bundesarbeitsgemeinschaft der Immigrantenverbände in der Bundesrepublik*) and the German Federal Commissioner for Foreign Nationals (*Beauftragte der Bundesregierung für Ausländerfragen*), which have women's divisions or which study women's issues were included in this research, despite the fact that they are not solely organisations for women.

The difficulties encountered when contacting the organisations in this study may be perceived as a reflection of the difficulties that NGOs face when they endeavour to co-operate with each other. This was especially the case with regard to those organisations in Germany that were contacted through personal reference. These contacts were made through friends living in Germany, the results of my own Internet research, the addresses of organisations listed in the questionnaires filled out by NGOs, and participants of the German-Turkish Summer Institute that I attended in July 2000 and August 2001. Clearly, then, various creative ways were used to reach these organisations, using many resources that are not readily available to migrant women. Since I have participated in many women's studies projects in Turkey, it was much easier for me to reach women's organisations there. Again, however, it is highly likely that it would be quite difficult for a foreigner to reach these organisations in the same manner. There are no published booklets listing women's organisations in Turkey. The second stage of this project highlighted the difficulties in gaining answers and information from these NGOs and posing new questions. Unfortunately, most of the organisations did not reply to my initial request for information, whilst some of them gave very brief and often quite late responses.

The limited number of staff and irregular working hours at the organisations' offices, I assume, were the cause of problems in written communication. This is at least partly a result of ineffective transnational ties between NGOs. There were also organisations and potential interviewees who could not be contacted by e-mail. Many simply did not reply to the messages. Limited resources and volunteer staff weaken the organisational structures and exacerbate the difficulties of co-operation.

The data collecting techniques used were questionnaires in conjunction with a literature survey. The questionnaire was eventually sent to 35 German and 27 Turkish organisations. The questions were open-ended, and related to co-operation and the exchange of information (See Appendix). The answers were generally short, but some organisations gave quite detailed responses, such as *Bora Frauenberatung* (Germany), the Womens' Solidarity Foundation (Turkey), the Contemporary Women and Youth Foundation (Turkey), Lara (Germany), Capital Women's Platform (Turkey), Antalya Women's City Council (Turkey). All the organisations from Turkey and Germany saw the need for both continuous communication and project-based co-operation.

Infrastructure of Transnational Ties: the Women's Movement in Turkey in the 1990s

Improvements achieved for women, and the current situation of women's organisations, help to make the conditions of co-operation clear. The women's movements in Turkey have voiced their demands, and put them on the social agenda, in a country like Turkey that is in essence patriarchal. In line with the modernisation ideology during the rise of the Republic, women's organisations have two basic approaches that target the disadvantages of women. The first concerns the private sphere; the second concerns women's empowerment in the public sphere by raising their levels of education (Sallan-Aksu, 1997, p. 501). Women's organisations that had worked prior to the 1980s acted mostly in the capacity of a charity. By the early 1980s, the women's movement in Turkey had become well known through campaigns and street demonstrations. The most favoured organisational forms in the Turkish women's movement during that time were consciousness-raising groups and non-hierarchical initiatives. Through the development of feminist discourse emphasising equality in the 1980s, new organisations found a channel, and the existing ones changed their perspective. Since 1984, the feminist movement has been organised in a variety of forms; associations, foundations and non-profit organizations. The ideologically inspired actions of the 1980s were transformed into co-operation on research projects, and developing relationships with local governments and state institutions in the 1990s (Esin, 2000, pp. 63-64). Studies show that women's organisations are aware of the importance of being completely independent from the state. Women's organisations in Turkey are not subsidised on a systematic basis; however, they would want no intervention should any support be provided (Sallan-Aksu, 1997, p. 503).

The number of issue-based organisations in the women's movement increased in the 1990s. Tekeli (1993, p. 35) states that in the decade following the Military Coup in 1980, the women's movement, with its decentralised and participant-based organisational form, was the pioneer civil society movement in Turkey. It should be stressed here that the women's movement in Turkey is comprised of organisations with a vast range of different ideologies, perspectives and approaches to women's problems, and the feminist point of view, for instance, differs greatly from the point of view of women's charities.

By the early 1990s, women's organisations in Turkey were more widespread. Their aims are to combat violence against women (the Women's Solidarity Foundation and Purple Roof); promote the participation of women in political decision-making processes (the Association for Training and Supporting Women Candidates), develop communication and collaboration among women's organisations (Flying Broom), fund documents created by and on women (Women's Library), and promote women's rights (Women for Women's Human Rights). Women's organisations also took part in civil society debates that have in turn gained impetus throughout the 1990s. These organisations played an important role in establishing co-operation between civil society organisations for various actions. Therefore women's organisations in Turkey seem the most appropriate organisations for transforming policies because they have a potential to develop. Having thus proven their capabilities and potential in specific issue areas and at the local level, a logical consequence is to demand that they should also be involved in policy-making processes at the regional, national and international level.

Women's Studies programmes and Research Centres established at universities can also be considered here as 'follow-up mechanisms', since they have been instrumental in organising seminars and activities, and producing various articles and documents. The Middle East Technical University, Ankara University, Ege University, and İstanbul University have become well known for their training programmes and publications, as well as their graduate programmes on consciousness-raising for different women's groups. These four universities offer multidisciplinary masters degree programmes within their graduate programmes.

The women's movement in Turkey has demonstrated various forms of struggle to the immigrant women in Germany (Tekeli, 1993, p. 17). A meeting held in Germany and the book (Neusel, Tekeli and Akkent, 1991) published after a symposium on women and migration created an interest in further developing the women's movement in Turkey. This constituted one of the first co-operative initiatives between women's groups in two countries. There is no women's organisation in Turkey that studies female migrants, or investigates research projects carried out in Germany. The Association of Solidarity with Asylum Seekers is an association that aims to assist migrants and refugees in Turkey, and it is supported by the United Nations High Commissioner for Refugees.

More than 200 women's organisations or women's branches of various organisations are still working to improve the status of women in social, legal, economic and cultural contexts. Most of the women's organisations focus on literacy training, women's health, or reproductive health. Recently, women have started discussions exploring the opportunities to become organised in a participatory, horizontal, flexible and creative manner. There are only few national or small-scale networks that would enable different groups to keep in touch; women's magazines generally don't offer a forum for broad discussions on 'doing something together'. Platforms are quite new experiences in Turkey. Some women's organisations have been coming together in platforms and groups to deal with specific issues of women's movements, like the İstanbul and Adana Women's Organisations' Union, the Rainbow Women's Platform, Capital Women's Platform and the NGO Advocacy Network for Women (Esin, 2000, pp. 95-97).

Women's Achievements at the Legal and Administrative Level in Turkey

The commitment of the Turkish government to implementing the necessary policies and allocating a budget to enable women to be active in public spaces is a very recent development. There are two state institutions in Turkey that provide public services for women: the Directorate General on the Status and Problems of Women (*DGSPW*) and the Social Services and Child Protection Organisation (*SSCPO*). The DGSPW is one of the main actors to set up a gender mainstreaming approach. The second is a social service organisation that provides services for the most vulnerable groups. The SSCPO has a division for women's affairs, and seven women's guest-houses which offer counselling and accommodation for women (and their children) who have been victims of violence. Community Centres are affiliated to the SSCPO and also offer their services to women and their families.

The Directorate General on the Status and Problem of Women (DGSPW) was established in 1990 in order to improve women's status in the social, economic, cultural and political fields in an environment of equality. The Directorate General, constituting the first and only official governmental body, currently operates as a unit of the State Ministry responsible for women's issues. The goals and responsibilities of the Directorate are to ensure that women gain equal access to education and training, to enhance women's contribution in various economic sectors, to provide proper health and social insurance coverage, to gather and disseminate studies on women's issues, to co-ordinate co-operation between organisations which undertake responsibilities concerning the status of women, and to support voluntary organisations active in this field (DGSPW, 1997).

As one of aims of the organisation is to support volunteer organisations and to co-ordinate co-operation between the NGOs, the Directorate acts in liaison with NGOs, the Ministries of Education, Health, Justice, Employment and other public and private organisations, and helps other bodies carry out strategies and take appropriate measures for the implementation of gender mainstreaming in their organisations. The objectives of the UNDP project, implemented by the Directory General in co-operation with the United Nations and Development Programme (UNDP), are to establish a fully operational national WID (women in

70 *Transnational Social Spaces*

development) policy and programme, and to strengthen the co-ordination and collaboration between the government and NGOs. In line with this project some small-scale women's projects have been supported financially or technically for over six years.

The State Ministry responsible for Turkish citizens residing abroad established the Consulting Committee for Turkish Citizens Residing Abroad in 1998. The Committee has come together three times so far and drawn up a work schedule with eight sub-committees. The DGSPW is the co-ordinator of one of these eight sub-committees, called the Committee for Women and Family. As co-ordinator of this sub-committee, the DGSPW establishes contact with women's organisations in Germany (and Holland, Austria, France, USA and Australia) and exchanges information and documents with them on women's issues. The Women and Family sub-committee decided to prepare consciousness-raising projects, to establish women's centres in Germany and to collect statistical data about Turkish citizens in Germany. However this effort is also at an initial stage and has yet to succeed in paving the way for effective co-operation.

The Family Protection Law – a law that women's organisations had been working for so as to create a lobby to voice public opinion – was adopted in January 1998 by the TGNA and put into force. With this Law, the issue of domestic violence was addressed for the first time in Turkey. The Law grants third parties the right to file complaints of domestic violence and makes it possible for judges to impose restraining orders on a family member who has used violence at home, thereby ensuring that the perpetrator is kept away from the victims (DGSPW, 1999, p. 4).

The Turkish Civil Code, adopted in 1924, also had to be amended in line with the contemporary needs of society. The women's movement played an important role in setting the agenda here, and after many long discussions, the Justice Commission of the TGNA accepted the new amendments to the Civil Code in terms of the representation of the family etc. One of the articles on property separation led to an immense debate within the Commission. Finally, the amendment included the right of women to an equal share of any investment holding and possessions acquired after the marriage has been contracted, excluding any properties gained before the marriage and personal property in the case of divorce. The new Law has been in force since 1st January 2002 with the approval of the TGNA.

In Turkey, women's organisations can meet for any number of reasons. They work co-operatively, for instance, the report for the Women's Conference in Beijing was prepared at a meeting organised by the Flying Broom in February 2000 with the participation of several women's organisations. This meeting contributed to women's organisations being able to understand each other's approach and their capacity for co-operation. The Flying Broom also held a meeting on improving collaboration among women's NGOs in February 1998. Several other national and international meetings have been held for the same purpose. Before the approval of statutes relating to women's status and family by the Justice Commission of the TGNA, women's organisations all around the country organised a campaign by visiting deputies, making press releases and distributing purple ribbons in public places. An electronic discussion forum was established following the Third Meeting of Women's Shelters in Turkey, enabling the participation of women's organisations from every corner of the country.

The United Nations' special session on Gender Equality, Development and Peace for the 21st Century was organised with the aim of discussing issues such as the complete implementation of the Beijing Platform for Action. These include the achievements made in the last five-year period, the influences of the developments of the last five years on the women's agenda, and action for the future. A preparatory meeting was held in April 2000 by the DGSPW with the participation of all related organisations, mostly including women's organisations and individual women, in order to discuss the draft report that would be submitted during the special session.

Specialised expert committees on Health, Education, Employment and Law were established in 1997, under the auspices of the DGSPW. These special commissions (expert committees) bring together related non-governmental organisations and function as consultative bodies for the implementation of the National Plan of Action. Through these four commissions, NGOs have the opportunity of setting the gender equality agenda and advocating women's issues (DGSPW, 1999, pp. 11-12). This is one of the main accomplishments of the NGOs in co-operation with the state for changes at policy-making level.

Findings and Discussions

The women's movement is not a movement that has mushroomed overnight. There is no local individual leader, but there may be some more 'experienced' women's organisations within the movement. The women's movement paved the way for joint co-operation under the slogan *private is political.* This challenges the transnational level consensus. During the last decade, at the regional, national and global levels of the public sphere, there has been a proliferation of civil society movements. The NGOs have generated new political formations and pressured governments into questioning their policies. The establishment of networks of information and co-operation with other NGOs has increased the effectiveness of individual NGOs. Some women's organisations define for themselves an ideological aim, and while some of the organisations aim for the wholesale transformation of society, others merely seek to implement grass-roots developmental changes (Gordenker and Weiss, 1995, p. 548).

As a non-governmental initiative, the women's movement has taken its place within this framework. Among its accomplishments at the international level, we can cite the placing of women's human rights on the agenda, the pressure brought to bear on governments to raise the status of women and the establishment of service organisations focusing on women's issues, and the benefits provided by

72   *Transnational Social Spaces*

the sharing of experience and information through continuous communication via the Internet. Of course, this requires a large number of staff, volunteers and resources. Women's organisations still face the problem of understaffing and limited resources – a problem faced by most NGOs all over the world. Those organisations both in Turkey and Germany that participated in this project confirmed that 'we lack not only financial but also personnel power'.[6]

Civil society movements seem to have a flexible and dynamic structure, and thus tends to encourage democracy in particular countries and throughout the world. These bodies are also suitable for establishing an effective transnational space between two countries that have independent civil structures. NGOs gain power and effectiveness by working regionally, and by knowing their grass roots well. Women's organisations, in line with the civil society movements, left their mark from the beginning through their activities either in support of the state in areas where the state is strong, or as an alternative to the state. Regional women's movements also have this advantage. However, they often lack sustainability unless they receive outside support.

Paradoxically, sustainability leads to institutionalisation that goes hand-in-hand with co-operation with government and international organisations. As a result, professional organisations necessitate new resources and staff. Co-operation seems to be possible only within a network, and without disrupting the autonomous structure of the organisations. As a result of the rapid dissemination of information, the formation of issue-based networks has become easier. Regional and national organisations tend to prefer to be part of such networks. They recently started to talk about the waste of time and energy that results from a duplication of work done at different places. Women's organisations have come to favour issue-based alliances, and the research done for this paper indicates that women in Germany and Turkey also define these kinds of connections as real 'co-operation'. These examples show that the differences, as much as the similarities, in these encounters drive the NGOs – which aim to conduct studies efficiently and voice themselves effectively – towards more self-reflection and assessment in terms of connecting with the networks.

According to replies from women's organisations from both countries, it seems that they prefer an active form of co-operation based on working together to a constant flow of communication. This occupies an important place on the agenda of the women's movement. Women's organisations prefer active local and transnational co-operation over a particular issue that can be re-activated when necessary. As will be explained later, the organisations that were contacted tend to

---

[6] It was established in 1978 as a free institution and offers archive and library services. It has scholarly and popular works on feminist movements, like women's biographies, around 700 German and foreign feminist periodicals, personal papers. It files women's initiatives, associations, clubs and federations etc. also provides counselling on archival matters, supporting to campaign, network are lobbying.

Transnational Space Between Women's NGOs

prefer this option. It should be remembered that the most important problem they face is a lack of resources, especially in terms of money and personnel:

> Generally it would be very interesting to work collaboratively with Turkish NGOs which are related to women issues, but altogether we have little time for any sort of public work. It depends on the concrete plans and aims as to what might be possible (*Türkisher Frauenverein*, Germany).

> In Germany Turkish-German women collaboration can only be established arbitrarily. Because as we do not see this sort of collaboration between two societies there is no reflection of it in women's projects. It does not seem realistic today, but what is realistic is to bring migrant women who are foreign citizens together under the umbrella of a common project (Uğrak, Germany).[7]

Reports on the situation of women in Turkey, highlighting some of the main achievements at the legal, administrative and social level were sent to organisations in Germany (*Lolapress*,[8] *Lara*,[9] FFBIZ, The Federal Government's Commissioner for Foreign Citizens) in order to let them know about the current situation and recent achievements in Turkey, and also to bring them up-to-date with the activities of women's organisations in Turkey, their specific fields of concern and the public perception of those activities. Almost all of the women's organisations (Turkish and German) showed an interest in these documents, showing improvements in the women's movement in Turkey. *Ban-Ying*, *Lola Press*, *Lara* and *Bora Frauenberatung* stated that the documents containing information regarding the women's movement would be useful, especially for the organisations in Germany that Turkish migrant women themselves established. BIG[10] also stressed that 'it is important to have a document about the situation of Turkish women in Berlin and in Germany'. But they underlined that they are also interested 'in the legal developments in the fields of domestic violence in Turkey' (BIG, Germany).

---

[7] It was established in 1981 as a women project that serves to migrant women form Turkey. First it defined the migrant women's problems and than started to provide some services such as language courses and consciousness raising workshops. Today it is financed by German Senate and has a permanent team including two Turkish and one German staff.

[8] It is an international bilingual (English and Spanish) feminist magazine which has international editorial board from Latin America, Africa and Europe.

[9] It is a rape crisis hotline and counselling centre in Berlin aiming to support women who have suffered sexual violence. They offer training sessions for individuals and professional groups such as police, medical staff and schools.

[10] Berlin Intervention Project Against Domestic Violence. It is a collaborative project that is supported by German Federal Ministry of Women Affairs and Berlin State Ministry of Women Affairs. It is a stake-holder of intervention projects networks for inter-agency and community cooperation with other organizations. Currently it conducts a project on domestic violence in Germany.

74 *Transnational Social Spaces*

Existing Communication, Co-operation and Joint Projects

The second question of my inquiry was: 'Have you, or your organisation, undertaken research or compiled publications that relate to Turkish women residing in Germany? Do you have plans to do so in the future?' The organisations that were contacted stated that they have never conducted research or attempted a publication together. The only Turkish women's organisation that carries on work related to the women from Turkey in Germany is women for the Women's Human Rights Project[11] (see p. 4). Other women's organisations that responded from Germany stated that they have no research related to immigrant women from Turkey. But they have some publications in Turkish, including basic information on their organisations and services that they provide for women. Two of these organisations are *Berliner Initiative Gegen Gewalt Gegen Frauen* (BIG) and *Cocon e. V.* Turkish women's organisations such as the Women's Solidarity Foundation[12] did not express any interest in a research or publication project related to Turkish immigrant women in Germany.

> The Women's Solidarity Foundation has no specific projects or programmes concerning women from Turkey who live in Germany. It has no future plan in line with this theme [...]. We need project knowledge and co-operation with German organisations and other EU member countries. It's not easy to conduct a joint project with independent women's shelters in Germany, due to their structure and characteristics on the subject of violence against women (WSF, Turkey).

The most common collaborative efforts between the organisations are information exchange and mutual visits. For women's NGOs in Turkey and Germany, the exchange of information is a natural and form of creating a linkage between organisations when it is needed. When necessary, the information exchange has been transformed into co-operation, but this linkage does not usually last. Women's organisations in Turkey tend to establish ties either at the stage of their formation, or later, in order to solve specific problems. They have tended to prefer co-operation that ends when the issue is dealt with, but that can be re-activated if and when necessary. The Women's Library,[13] Women for Women's

---

[11] Founded in 1993 aiming of working collaboratively with the International Network of Women Living Under Muslim Laws (WLUML). It aims to provide women empowerment programs linked to action-oriented research technique.

[12] Established in 1990 and opened its shelter in 1993 as a first independent women's shelter in the country. It provides legal, psychological counselling and conduct research on violence against women.

[13] Established in 1990 as the first women's library in the country with the aim of gathering knowledge about history of women. It has books, magazines, grey materials and serves both academic and non-academic and readers.

Human Rights, Mother and Child Education Foundation,[14] the Contemporary Women and Youth Foundation,[15] the Women's Solidarity Foundation stated that they visited and were being visited in the framework of exchange of information and experiences.

As a powerful member of the European Union, Germany can be said to be the outward link for both women from Turkey who live in Germany and who are involved in women's organisations, and for the women's movement in Turkey. Various contacts in Turkey have indicated that all the organisations that provide services for women (such as the Women's Solidarity Foundation (WSF), Purple Roof,[16] and the Women's Centre[17]) established connections with women's organisations in Germany while they were setting up their organisations, or during various steps of their projects. The WSF stated that through one of their endeavours to contact new women's organisations in Germany they aim to receive new funding via transnational ties. Their communication has generally been based on the need to benefit from the experiences of older organisations, and to consult them on their models of organisation and operation. Their contacts have mostly been women from Turkey who are members or workers of organisations in Germany.

Turkish organisations have connections with various German organisations, however, these connections do not represent intense, institutionalised forms of transnational co-operation. In other words, the density and speed of ties are generally low. They are connections that are activated as required, on the basis of particular issues. When there are continuing connections between two organisations, this is usually due to a personal connection with a Turkish member of the German organisation. In some organisations, Turkish volunteers and members who have lived in Germany for some time provide the links. These ties make it easier for Turkish women's organisations to reach women's organisations in Germany. It should be stressed that most of the actors of these transnational ties already have transnational connections, like returning migrants with ties in Germany or migrants in Germany with ties in Turkey.

---

[14] Established in 1993 with the aim of educating adults with different programmes such as mother-child education, father support programme and literacy courses.

[15] Established in 1994 aiming to contribute to the development and socialisation of people who have been socially isolated due to rapid urbanisation and social development. The foundation has a Community Centre serving women training and counselling.

[16] Established in 1990 by a group of feminist women with the aim of providing shelters and counselling services for women who subjected violence. It also organises meetings, conferences, seminars and 'get togethers' to inform women.

[17] Established in 1997 in Diyarbakır with a group of women who believe in power and necessity of autonomous women's movement. It aims to increase women's solidarity and support women who face violence and provides consciousness raising programmes.

76   *Transnational Social Spaces*

> Despite the fact that we are close geographically to Europe our relations with them are not close, we have contacts with different NGOs in USA [...]. However there are no contacts with European NGOs. A lack of infrastructure makes it difficult to establish relations (Capital Women's Platform, Turkey).

There seem to be two fundamental reasons why Turkish women's organisations are willing to cooperate with women's organisations in Germany. The first is the wish to carry out work beyond national borders, to ensure the openness and participatory qualities of the women's movement. In this respect, Germany is currently the easiest country to reach for Turkish women NGOs. The second reason is the desire to gain access to the resources and the pool of experience available in the countries of the European Union. Some women's organisations in Turkey, like the WSF and Antalya Women's City Council, consider themselves fortunate to being able to reach Turkish women who work in German organisations and who know them.

Thus, global networks have become actors beyond nation-states. The process of globalisation has created as much a common space for NGOs as for other institutions (Lenz, 1999, pp. 64-65). But cultural differences and differences in infrastructure may create obstacles to gaining access to transnational networks, once again, bringing inequality into the picture. The rise of international social movements, emerging concepts of social civil rights and global gender democracy affects and pushes women's movements to set up new, long-term networks.

> They have still integration problem. Most of them migrated to Germany before they had even seen a city in their own country. This reality creates problems for them and the Turkish and German governments. Then political, ethnic and religious organisations had some privileges. This led to the failure of Turkish NGOs in Germany. Mutual visits between organisations helps co-operation (Federation of Women's Associations,[18] Turkey).

The expansion of social spaces across borders is greatly facilitated by the improvements in new communication technologies. Globalisation and communication technologies have made a major, effective contribution to transnational space. As spelled out in this paper, we can safely assume that women's organisations do not possess adequate opportunities to make the most of the information technologies. Many of them do not yet have electronic mail or web sites. E-mail contact was established with a total of 20 Turkish and 10 German organisations. It has been seen that a total of 18 organisations have web sites. And this amounts to 23 percent of the organisations that were reached. We can therefore conclude that some of the organisations in Germany have no e-mail connections or web sites. This can be interpreted as an indication of insufficient economic resources and difficulties in gaining access to information technologies, and this

---

[18] Interview with head of Federation.

fact might hinder electronic co-operation and communication between women's organisations in the two countries. This factor affects the intensity of transnational space – in terms of speed of the exchange of knowledge – among women's organisations in Turkey and Germany. Under these circumstances, neither institutional or transnational level co-operation nor non-institutional transnational ties are likely to be prevalent.

The following list includes some of the current joint ventures of women's organisations:

- Publication of Turkish booklets and newsletters by German NGOs (*Cocon e. V.*, B.I.G).
- Short-term bilateral workshops and reciprocal visits between individual organisations or representative groups of different women's organisations (Women's Library, WSF and ACEV).
- Consulting models and benefiting from experiences of the older organisation in Germany.
- Contacting German women's NGOs during the initial stage of establishing shelters.
- Liaison work by Turkish women activists between Turkish and German NGOs (from Turkish to German NGOs or vice versa).
- Publication of a book entitled Domestic Violence and Family Life as Experienced by Turkish Immigrants.

Areas for New Co-operation

There have been co-operative ventures between Turkish and German NGOs, though they were very rare and short-lived. For instance, the annual Interdisciplinary Women's Symposium on Women and Migration held in the early 1980's showed the demand for such co-operation. The İstanbul Bar Women's Rights Implementation Centre shared its experiences with German colleagues at a meeting on legal developments for women in Turkey. Purple Roof's members have stated that they co-operated with a German organisation in the early 1990s when they first set up their shelter.

Violence against women is a concrete area where co-operation between the two countries' women's organisations would be extremely beneficial. The most important project for which Turkish women's organisations consulted German organisations was related to the founding and running of a women's shelter. Organisations that are currently either planning or establishing women's shelters (the Women's Solidarity Foundation, Purple Roof, Antalya Women's Council) all say that they have benefited from information on the experiences, administrative models and division of labour at German shelters. The women's organisations in Turkey have profited immensely from the experiences of the German women's organisations on the issue of violence against women. For example, the WSF stated that they were given financial support from the first women's house founded in

78   *Transnational Social Spaces*

Berlin and they used German women's organisations' experience on the subject as a model for their financial organisation and management. The foundation is also hoping to find funding for research work. Purple Roof stated that their organisation is visited every year by 10-15 women's organisations from all over Europe including Germany.

Purple Roof has been organising self-defence courses for women with the support of German women's activists. Sharing experience and getting support from German women's NGOs in the development of strategies and strategic management is the general context of transnational ties between women's NGOs in the two countries.

> No matter how different a country or culture is, violence against women shows the same characteristics all around the world. Things can become easier by taking steps to combat violence all around the world by adopting a women's point of view (Women's Centre, Turkey).

> Every year 10-15 women from different European countries visit us for the exchange of information (Purple Roof, Turkey).

Co-operation between the women's organisations in Germany and Turkey can also be useful from the point of view of providing an orientation guide for immigrant women who plan to return to Turkey. In other words, before returning to Turkey, immigrant women can obtain information on Turkish women's organisations where they can find support or even be able to work. The Women's Solidarity Foundation confirmed that Turkish women returning from Germany were able to reach them thanks to the organisations in Germany, and other organisations mentioned similar cases. Another noteworthy dimension of this kind of co-operation is that German organisations know about organisations and services that may be more useful to women returning to Turkey than women living in Germany.

> In the case of deportation, women either consult us themselves or via women's organisations (Purple Roof, Turkey).

Work in the area of immigrants and immigration has mostly been carried out by academics. Womens' organisations joint projects tend to focus on meetings, conferences, and mutual visits rather than long-term research and publications. This has been the experience of most of the women's organisations (such as Capital Women's Platform,[19] the Women's Solidarity Foundation, Turkey) that

---

[19] Established in 1995 with the participation of women from different associations and foundations to discuss and identify present position of women and to produce some alternative views and practical solutions. The platform gives importance to women-to-women dialog.

responded to the questions posed in this paper. Their contacts are generally based on an exchange of information on shared experiences and practices between the Turkish and German organisations working in similar areas.

Co-operation has not always only been between women's organisations. The Turkish Family Planning Association has received financial support from the Organisation of German Technical Co-operation. The work carried out by the Turkish Family Planning Association in three cities between 1998 and 1999 focused on reproductive and sexual health. The Women's Solidarity Foundation mentioned that the German Embassy supported them. Another organisation, the Mother & Child Training Foundation, carries out its programme of supporting mothers, *Migranten e.V.* works with the Turkish immigrant families in Bremen. The Bremen Girls' Organisation (*BDP Mädchenkulturhaus*) implemented an exchange programme in co-operation with Flying Broom and the Contemporary Women and Youth Foundation. Moreover, some international German organisations like the Friedrich Naumann and Heinrich Böll Foundations are known to be very supportive of the women's movement and civil society in Turkey.

Common themes with German and Turkish women's organisations with the potential to create transnational ties can be summarised as follows:

- helping migrant women adapt to the new culture in Germany and participate in the public sphere, especially in working life,
- making them aware of German legislation on employment, civic life, social support etc. and helping them benefit from these laws and regulations,
- preventing violence among migrants like domestic violence, 'honour killing', social pressures etc., often stemming from traditional sub-cultures,
- acting together with local authorities on combating domestic and all kinds of violence,
- sharing impressions of lessons learnt and best practice (i.e. organising study tours),
- providing migrant women with the opportunity to participate in local policy-making processes,
- helping migrant women to enlarge their scope of freedom,
- creating working conditions for migrant women that enable them to undertake paid employment, putting pressure on local governments to provide social support such as child-care,
- encouraging the involvement of migrant women in local organisations such as municipalities, environmental organisations, schools etc.,
- organising parental training,
- carrying out socio-anthropological research on migration patterns and culture and the social life they left behind,
- working on the re-writing of the social history of immigration from women's points of view,

80 *Transnational Social Spaces*

- planning programmes and co-operative action on the subject of informing Turkish women about EU regulations concerning gender equality (e.g. supporting women's enterprises in line with EU regulations, EU funds),
- developing joint projects and programmes together with women's organisations or providing training in reproductive health and family planning,
- carrying out comparative cultural research in provinces where large numbers of the people emigrated to Germany in order to explore the cultural changes after emigration,
- preparing women planning to migrate to Germany for the new culture (although this group is gradually getting smaller it should still be taken into consideration),
- encouraging returning women to set up business with their savings and acquired skills, thus encouraging them to participate in working life,
- informing and supporting returning women on the subject of possible conflicts with traditional (home) culture.

Future Expectations on Co-operation

Whether they have actively co-operated or not in the past, both Turkish and German women's organisations tend to favour co-operation. However, the range of their expectations and circumstances varies greatly. Organisations in both countries believe that communication, co-operation and the mutual exchange of information would be valuable, but the areas where they expect benefits are different. Some of the women's organisations in Turkey, such as the Women's Solidarity Foundation and the Turkish Family Planning Association, the Mother & Child Training Foundation expect to benefit from the past experiences of German organisations and they also expect financial support and co-operation.

On the other hand, the women's movement in Germany recognises the women's movement in Turkey and also help to smooth the way for Turkish women both while they live in Germany and when they return to their country of origin. For example, while some German women wanted to know about the status of women in Turkey, the development of the women's movement, women's NGOs and gains made at governmental level, and expressed a need for such information, the women's organisations in Turkey focused on individual women's organisations, their resources and experiences. It should be stressed here that unlike civil organisations in Turkey, NGOs in Germany are often supported by the German government.

An examination of the responses concerning plans for the future reveals that themes of co-operation have been suggested even if there is no concrete plan of action. Women's organisations in Germany have stepped up their efforts to approach women's organisations in Turkey by making a decision to support a project to be defined by them. While one organisation (Capital Women's Platform) states that it can work with German organisations on the subject of human rights, the Turkish Family Planning Association says it would be eager to cooperate in the area of reproductive health. The organisation named *Anakültür* (Turkey)[20] that carries out consciousness-raising and applied projects in the Eastern and South-eastern regions of Anatolia states that it would be valuable to work with a German organisation that focuses its work on the needs of first and second-generation women immigrants from Eastern and South-Eastern Anatolia. The Women's Library foundation stated that by putting their documents on-line, German women's NGOs could reach across borders, giving the opportunity to Turkish researchers to access documents from the German women's movement. The foundation also stated they have documents belonging to just four women's organisations in Germany (the Women's Library, Turkey). One German organisation (*Lara*) that focuses on the issue of sexual violence against women suggests building a European Network of Organisations Working in the Field of Sexual Violence, which would also include Turkish organisations.

It is clear that a great deal more co-operation is necessary for the growth, increased power, public recognition, effectiveness and reputation of the women's movement. As the struggle to develop and transform women's lives continues, and as efforts to reveal sexism gain strength, both national gains and the process of transnational co-operation between women's organisations will increase. New contacts and better communication between the women's movement in Turkey and in Germany might provide a better social and political context for that process.

Bilateral and mutual co-operation needs to be strengthened, both between Turkish and German NGOs and also among NGOs and governmental and international organisations. There are enough infrastructures to establish an effective and encouraging, institutionalised transnational space. The process of labour migration from Turkey to Germany that has continued for 40 years has prepared the ground for co-operation in various areas. It is expected that improved contacts, better and effective information exchange and communication between the women's movements in Turkey and Germany will contribute towards the establishment of a political context in which the issues of women from Turkey will be viewed sympathetically and with tolerance in Germany.

In Turkey, there is a general sensitivity on the issue of migration. Voluntary and forced migration within the country are factors that have contributed to the development of this sensitivity. In fact, there are similarities between migration from the village to the city, and from Turkey to Germany, both in terms of both the trauma experienced and the adaptation required. This common ground may increase interest in work directed towards Turkish immigrant women in Germany. Having experienced inter-regional migration, i.e. the process of migration from the village to the city, women of Turkey have experienced a similar loss of values and known a similar need for solidarity to that experienced by women migrating to Germany from Turkey (see Ilkkaracan and Ilkkaracan, 1998).

---

[20] Founded in 1997 with the aims of reaching all sections of the community to encourage community life by organizing cultural activities, carrying out educational projects and arranging cultural tours.

The main weaknesses of women's organisations are their lack of assertiveness, inconsistencies in pursuing their agenda. It seems that these deficiencies can be overcome through new local and transnational ties and spaces that will give these organisations the power for joint action. However, the increase in the number and variety of areas of activity of women's organisations, makes the establishment of such co-operation more difficult. The movement needs new organisations to work on improving communication and co-operation between organisations. Yet communication and collaboration are in themselves different projects, and should be taken seriously by those who have a stake in women's movements, civil society, and transnational space.

Appendix

Questions

Germany

1. Can you provide some general information about your organisation? (For example: Can you briefly outline the range of issues and problems your organisation deals with? Can you provide me with your organisation's date of establishment, the number of current members, and the cost of the membership fee?)
2. Have you, or your organisation, undertaken research or compiled publications that relate to Turkish women residing in Germany? Do you have plans to do so in the future?
3. Have you participated jointly with women's organisations in Turkey on research projects concerning migrant women from Turkey? Do you believe that, if undertaken, joint projects of this kind have the potential to be successful? What are the conditions which would favour (or hinder) such a collaborative effort?
4. What is your opinion on the possibility of working collaboratively with any Turkish NGOs which are related to women's issues?
5. Do you think it would be useful for your organisation to have documents which;
   - Describe the current situation of women in Turkey?
   - Set forth the legal and administrative developments for women in Turkey?

Turkey

1. Have you, or your organisation, undertaken research or compiled publications that relate to Turkish women who are residing in Germany? Do you have plans to do so in the future?
2. Does your organisation have any contact with any women's organisations, associations or initiatives in Germany? Please clarify.
3. Have you participated in any joint ventures with women's organisations in Germany? Do you believe joint ventures with women's organisations in Germany established by Turkish or German women are feasible? If so, what are the pre-conditions for this collaboration?

84　　　*Transnational Social Spaces*

Tables

Table 3.1 Organisations to which the questionnaires were sent in Germany

Organisation	Address	Phone	Fax / e-mail / website
AKARSU e.V.	Oranienstr. 25 10999 Berlin Germany	+49 (0)30 - 616769 - 30/31	akarsu1987@yahoo.de
Emma-Frauenverlag GmbH	Alteburger Str. 2 50678 Köln Germany		
I.S.I. e.V. (Initiative Selbständiger Immigrantinnen e.V.)	Schlesische Str. 32 10997 Berlin Germany	+49 (0)30 - 6113336	info@isi-ev.de
Archiv der Deutschen Frauenbewegung - Bibliothek & Studienzentrum	Gottschalkstr. 57 34127 Kassel Germany	+49 (0)561 - 9893670	+49 (0)561 - 9893672 frau-bib@hrz.uni-kassel.de http://www.uni-kassel.de/frau-bib/
VIVID Comunication with Women in their Cultures	Schamhorststr. 11 36037 Fulda Germany	+49 (0)661 - 64125	+49 (0)661 - 606851
Schwarze Witwe Autonome Frauenforschungs-stelle Münster e.V.	Achtermannstr. 10-12 48143 Münster Germany	+49 (0)251 - 511195	+49 (0)251 - 518876 schwarzewitwe@ connecta.woman.de http://www.woman.de/ frauimnetz/index.html
Die Media, Frauen Information Online	Marienplatz 4 50676 Köln Germany	+49 (0)221 - 2408675	+49 221 - 2408676 die.media@edina.xnc.com http://www.diemedia.de
Marie-Schlei-Verein e.V.	Dr. J. Hoffmann-Str. 15 55278 Hahnheim Germany	+49 (0)6737 - 9181	+49 (0)6737 - 9498 Marie-Schlei-Verein@t-online.de
Frauenpunkt Courage e.V.	Wartenbegerstr 24, Haus 2 13053 Berlin Germany		+49 (0)30 - 98622189
* GOLDRAUSCH Frauennetzwerk Berlin e.V.	Postdamer Str. 139 10783 Berlin-Schöneberg Germany	+49 (0)30 - 2157554	
Lila Archiv e.V.	Choriner Str. 9 10119 Berlin Germany		+49 (0)30 - 4485713

Transnational Space Between Women's NGOs

Organisation	Address	Phone	Fax / e-mail / website
Hinbun	Jagowstr 19 13585 Berlin- Spandau Germany	+49 (0)30 - 336662	
DF Deutscher Frauenrat - Lobby der Frauen (German Women's Council)	Simrockstrasse 5 53113 Bonn Germany	+49 (0)228 - 223008	+49 (0)228 - 218810, +49 (0)228 - 218819 DFrauenrat@aol.com www.deutscher-frauenrat.de
Frau und Beruf e.V. Frauenselbsthilfe- verein für erwerbs- lose Frauen	Glogauerstr. 22 10999 Berlin Germany		+49 (0)30 - 6189066
* GOLDNETZ	Dircksentstr 47 10179 Berlin Germany		+49 (0)30 - 2832777
Frauenhausberatungs stelle	Alt-Moabit 55 10555 Berlin- Tiergarten Germany		
* LARA Krisen- und Beratungszentrum für vergewaltigte Frauen und Mädchen	Tempelhofer Ufer 14 10963 Berlin- Kreuzberg Germany		
* Frauenberatung Bora	Berliner Allee 130 13088 Berlin- Weißensee Germany		Bora-Frauenberatung @web.de
Frauen gegen Gewalt an Frauen e. V.	Postfach 200757 13517 Berlin Germany		
* Ban Ying e. V. Koordinationsstelle	Anklamer Str. 38 10115 Berlin-Mitte Germany		ban-ying@ipn-b. comlink.apc.org www.ban-ying.org
* BDP Mädchenkulturhaus	Heinrichstr 21 28203 Bremen Germany	+49 (0)421 - 328798	
* BIG – Koordinierungsstelle Berliner Initiative gegen häusliche Gewalt	Paul-Lincke-Ufer 7d 10999 Berlin Germany	+49 (0)30 - 61709100	
Cocon e. V.	Auguststr 71 10117 Berlin Urbanstr 115 10967 Berlin Germany	+49 (0)30 - 91611836	

Transnational Social Spaces

Organisation	Address	Phone	Fax / e-mail / website
Uğrak	Weisestr 36 12049 Berlin Germany	+49 (0)30 - 6211037/ - 6212873	
Bacim	Oldenburgerstr 22 10551 Berlin Germany	+49 (0)30 - 3953037/ - 3953055	
Wildwasser Frauenselbsthilfe	Friesenstr. 6 10965 Berlin-Kreuzberg Germany		
* LOLApress Lolapress International Feminist Magazine	Friedrichstr. 165 10117 Berlin Germany	+49 (0)30 - 20450240	+49 (0)30 - 20450241 lolapress@ipn-b. comlink.apc.org, LOLApress@ipn-b.de www.chasque.apc.org/ lola
Zentrale Informationsstelle autonomer Frauenhäuser	ZIF Postfach 101103 34011 Kassel Germany		info@ZIF-Frauen.de www.zif-frauen.de
Elişi Evi	Skalitzer Str. 50/51 10997 Berlin-Kreuzberg Germany	+49 (0)30 - 6187383	
Kontaktbüro für Frauen in Gewaltsituationen	Immanualkirchstr 10 10405 Berlin Germany		
* FFBIZ Frauenforschungs, -bildungs und -informationszentrum	Danckelmannstrasse 47 or 15 (gallery) 14059 Berlin-Charlottenburg, Germany		+49 (0)30 - 3221035
** Beauftragte der Bundesregierung für Ausländerfragen	Lengsdorfer Hauptstr. 78-82 53127 Bonn Germany		www.bundesausländer beauftragte.de
** Bundesarbeits-gemeinschaft der Immigranten-verbände in der Bundesrepublik Deutschland e.V.	Baumschulallee 2a 53115 Bonn Germany		
Frauenhaus Koordinierungsstelle		+49 (0)69 - 6706252	
Türkischer Frauen-verein	Urbanstr. 115 10967 Berlin Germany	+49 (0)30 - 6923956	

Transnational Space Between Women's NGOs 87

Organisation	Address	Phone	Fax / e-mail / website
Frauenzimmer e. V.	Ebersstr 32 10827 Berlin- Schöneberg Germany		

* Organisations that responded to the inquiry
** Governmental organisations

Table 3.2 Organisations to which the questionnaires were sent in Turkey

Organisation	Address	Phone	Fax / e-mail / website
* Mother & Child Training Foundation (Anne-Çocuk Eğitim Vakfı Ankara)	Itri Dede Sok. 39/8 81030 Kızıltoprak / İstanbul Ahmet Rasim Sok. 10/1 Çankaya / Ankara Turkey	+90 (0)216 - 3365793/ - 3455254 + 90 (0)312 -4413548	+90 (0)216 - 3475340, +90 (0)312 - 4413548 www.annevebebek.org
* Capital Women Platform (Başkent Kadın Platformu)	Mediha Eldem Sok. 41/12 Kızılay / Ankara Turkey	+ 90 (0)312 - 4341225/ - 3528024	+ 90 (0)312 - 4341225
Association of Women for Republic (Cumhuriyet Kadınları Derneği)	Necatibey Cad. No:27/11 Sıhhiye /Ankara Meşrutiyet Cad. No: 20/3 Kızılay/Ankara Turkey	+ 90 (0)312 - 2299371/ - 4255732	+ 90 (0)312 - 2307860, + 90 (0)312 - 4253899
* The Contemporary Women and Youth Foundation (Çağdaş Kadın ve Gençlik Vakfı)	Tıp Fakültesi Cad. No:243 Tuzluçayır/Ankara Turkey	+ 90 (0)312 - 3673516/ - 3645348	+ 90 (0)312 - 3646743
Association of Research on Women's Social Life (Kadının Sosyal Hayatını Araştırma ve İnceleme Derneği)	Dede Korkut Sok. 4/2 A. Ayrancı/Ankara Turkey	+ 90 (0)312 - 4404204/ - 4407166/ - 4407188	+ 90 (0)312 - 4400622 kasaid@ superonline.com
Association for Training and Supporting of Women Canditates (KA-DER)	İrfan Başbuğ Sok. Yuva apt. No:11 80280 Esentepe/ İstanbul Turkey	+90 (0)212 - 2732535	+90 (0)212 - 2732536 kader@net.tr

88 *Transnational Social Spaces*

Organisation	Address	Phone	Fax / e-mail / website
Women's Human Rights Information Center (Kadının İnsan Hakları Bilgi Belge Merkezi)	Arjantin Cad. 22/10 06700 Kavaklıdere / Ankara Turkey	+ 90 (0)312 - 4671337	+ 90 (0)312 - 4681833 info@kadin2000.gen.tr www.kadin2000.gen.tr
* Association for Supporting Contemporary Life (Çağdaş Yaşamı Destekleme Derneği)	Konur II Sok. 51/6 Kızılay/Ankara Turkey	+ 90 (0)312 - 4257433	+ 90 (0)312 - 4257433
Association of Women's Politicians (Kadın Siyasetçiler Derneği – KASİDE)	Tahran Cad. No:22/2 G.O.P/Ankara Turkey	+ 90 (0)312 - 4263269	+ 90 (0)312 - 4263269
* Flying Broom (Uçan Süpürge)	Bestekar Sok. 80/6 Kavaklıdere/Ankara Turkey	+90 (0)312 - 4270020	+90 (0)312 - 4269712 ucansupurge@ucan. supurge.org www.ucansupurge.org
* Women's Solidarity Foundation (Kadın Dayanışma Vakfı)	Mithat Paşa Cad. Apt. No:10 6. kat Sıhhiye/Ankara Turkey	+90 (0)312 - 4350070	+90 (0)312 - 4350070
* Family Planning Association of Turkey (Türkiye Aile Planlaması Derneği)	Ataç Sok. No:73/2-3 06420 Kocatepe/ Ankara Turkey	+90 (0)312 - 4318355/ - 4311878	+90 (0)312 - 4342946 tapd@ada.net.tr
* Federation of Women's Associations (Türkiye Kadın Dernekleri Federasyonu)	Akay Cad. No:15/2 06660 Küçükesat/ Ankara Turkey	+90 (0)312 - 4172604/ - 3051095/ - 3243849	+90 (0)312 - 4172604, +90 (0)312 - 4260668
* Foundation for the Development of Human Resources (İnsan Kaynağını Geliştirme Vakfı)	Yeni Çarşı Cad. 54 Beyoğlu/İstanbul, Turkey	+ 90 (0)212 - 2931605	+90 (0)212 - 2931009 ikgv@ikgv.org www.ikgv.org
* Roza Women's Magazine (Roza Kürt Kadın Dergisi)	Sıraselviler Cad. Aslanyatağı sok. 6 Taksim/İstanbul, Turkey		Roza96@hotmail.com

* Organisations that responded to inquiry

** Governmental organisations

References

Aile Araştırma Kurumu (Family Research Institution) (1996), *Yurt dışına İşçi Göçü ve Parcalanmış Aile*, AAK Yay. Ankara.

Akkent, Meral (1993), Gerekli Bir Düzeltme Kadın Bakış Açısından 1980ler Türkiye'sinde Kadın, İletişim Yayınları, İstanbul.

Çağlar, Ş. Ayşe (1995), 'German Turks in Berlin: Social Exclusion and Strategies for Social Mobility', in *New Community*, Vol. 15, pp. 309-23.

Çalışma ve Sosyal Güvenlik Bakanlığı (ÇSGB) (Ministry of Labour and Social Security) (2000), *Yılı Raporu: Yurtdışındaki Vatandaşlarımıza İlişkin Gelişmeler ve Sayısal Bilgiler*, ÇSGB Dış İlişkiler ve Yurtdışı İşçi Hizmetleri Genel Müdürlüğü, Ankara.

Devlet Planlama Teşkilatı (State Planning Organization) (1994), *Kadın, Çocuk ve Gençlik Özel İhtisas Komisyonu, Kadın Alt Komisyonu Raporu*, DPT Yay, Ankara.

DGSPW (Directorate General on the Status and Problems of Women) (1997), *National Action Plan of Turkey* (Implementation and Follow-Up the Conclusion of the UN 4th WCW), DGSPW, Ankara, unpublished report.

DGSPW (1997), *Combined 2nd and 3rd Periodic Country Report of Turkey to CEDAW*, DGSPW Publications, Ankara.

DGSPW (1999), *Response of the Republic of Turkey to the Questionnaire on Implementation of Beijing Platform for Action*, DGSPW, Ankara, unpublished report.

Esin, Çigdem (2000), *Feminism Women Movement(s) and Women's Organization in Turkey*, Department of Gender and Women's Studies, Middle East Technical University, Ankara, unpublished MS Dissertation.

Federal Government's Commissioner for Foreigners' Issues (eds.) (2000), *Facts and Figures on the Situation of Foreigners in the Federal Republic of Germany*, Federal Government's Commissioner for Foreigners' Issues (FGCFI), Berlin and Bonn.

Gordenker and Weiss (1995), 'NGO Participation in the International Policy Process', in *Third World Quarterly*, Vol. 16(3), pp. 543-55.

İlkkaracan, Pınar (1996), 'Domestic Violence and Family Life as Experienced by Turkish Immigrant Women in Germany', *Women for Women's Human Rights Reports*, İstanbul.

İlkkaracan, İ. and İlkkaracan, P. (1998) 'Kuldan Yurttaşa: Kadınlar Neresinde', in *Bilanço 98*, Yılda Tebaadan Yurttaşa Doğru, İş Bankası, İMKB, Tarih Vakfı Yayınları, İstanbul, p. 75.

Kadıoğlu, Ayşe (1997), 'Migration Experiences of Turkish Women: Notes From a Research Diary', in *International Migration*, Vol. 35(4), pp. 537-56.

Kastoryano, Riva (2000), *Kimlik Pazarlığı: Fransa ve Almanya'da Devlet ve Göçmen İlişkileri*, İletişim Yayınları, İstanbul.

Kıray, Mübeccel B. (1986), 'The Family of the Immigrant Worker', in F. Özbay (ed.), *The Study of Women: An Anthology*, UNESCO and Turkish Social Science Association, Ankara.

Köksal, Sema Erder (1993), 'Uluslararası Göç Sürecinde Kadının Gündeme Gelişi ve 'Getto'da Kadın', in *Kadın Araştırmaları Dergisi*, KAUM Yay, İstanbul, Vol. 1, pp. 110-25.

Lenz, Ilse (1999), 'Globalisation, Networks and Organizations: New Issues for Gender Equality', in M. Goldmann (ed.), *Rationalisation, Organization, Gender*, Proceedings of the International Conference October 1998, Dortmund, pp. 64-71.

90 Transnational Social Spaces

Nauck, Bernard (1999). 'Kinship as Social Capital', in R. Richter and S. Supper, *New Qualities in the Lifecourse: Intercultural Aspects*, Ergon Publisher, Würzburg, pp. 199-218.

Neusel, A.. Tekeli. Ş. and Akkent, M. (eds.) (1991), Aufstand im Haus der Frauen, Orlado Frauenverlag. Berlin.

Sallan-Gül. S and Aksu-Coşkun. Z. (1997), '1980lerin Sivil Toplum Kuruluşu Anlayışı ve Gönüllü Kadın Kuruluşları Üzerine Bir Çalışma', in *Yüzyılın Sonunda Kadınlar ve Gelecek*. TODAİE Yay, Ankara, Vol. 20, pp. 489-503.

Straßburger. Gaby (2001). 'Transnational Ties of the Second Generation: Marriages of Turks in Germany', in Institute for Intercultural and International Studies (INIIS) (ed.). *German-Turkish Summer Institute Working Papers No. 7/2001*, University of Bremen. Bremen.

Tekeli, Şirin (1993). *Kadın Bakış Açısından 1980ler Türkiyesi'nde Kadın*, İletişim Yayınları. İstanbul.

TODAİE (Türkiye Orta Doğu Amme İdaresi Enstitüsü) (1997), *Yüzyılın Sonunda Kadınlar ve Gelecek*. TODAIE Yay, Ankara, Vol. 20.

Toksöz, Gülay (1993), 'Almanya'da Türkiyeli Kadınlar, 'Kızkardeşleri' ve Etnomerkezcilik'. *Birikim*, Vol. June, pp. 35-42.

Turan, Kadir (1997). *Almanya'da Türk Olmak*, Başbakanlık Aile Araştırma Kurumu Yay, Ankara.

Chapter 4

German Migrants in Turkey:
The 'Other Side' of the Turkish-German
Transnational Space

Bianca Kaiser

Introduction

Today, there are about 3.3 million residents of Turkish origin in the European Union, with approximately 2.5 million of them living in Germany. Conversely, an estimated 100,000 citizens of EU origin living in Turkey, among them some 60,000 German citizens. These figures explain why research has hitherto largely focused on Turkish migrants in Germany; in fact, research on the life-worlds of German migrants in Turkey is very scarce. Yet, the last two decades have observed a marked increase in migration flows from Germany to Turkey.

There are three major reasons for this increase. Firstly, Turkey's increasing political and economic liberalization during the 1980s has made it a more attractive destination for migrants than before. Secondly, due to this increased liberalization, Turkey has become a very attractive tourist destination since the mid-1980s. And, finally, there is Turkey's bid for full membership of the European Union. In 1987, the formal application for membership was submitted to the European Commission. In 1996, the Customs Union between Turkey and the European Union was established. At the Helsinki Summit in 1999, Turkey was declared a formal candidate for full membership.

All of these factors have contributed significantly to an intensification of ties between Turkey and the EU; specifically, there has been a marked increase in German migrants in Turkey. Germany is the most important trading partner of Turkey in the European Union. German investments rank at the top among foreign investors in Turkey. As a consequence, German companies are sending managerial staff and their families to Turkey for limited periods of time. Furthermore, there has been a steady increase in Turkish-German marriages, amounting to several thousand each year: whereas in 1996 they amounted to 6,000 marriages, numbers

92 *Transnational Social Spaces*

rose to some 90,000 by 2001.[1] Many of these bi-national families have decided to set up home in Turkey. Lastly, increasing numbers of Germans who visited Turkey initially as tourists, decide to migrate to Turkey on a permanent basis.

Research on German migrants in Turkey is very limited. Many studies have concentrated on the long-established group of German migrants, the *Bosphorus Germans*, whose roots of immigration go back to the Ottoman Empire (Dietrich, 1987; Kuran-Burçoğlu, 2002). Few studies have analysed the dynamics of contemporary migration from Germany to Turkey. Some, however, have looked into the legal situation of EU migrants and other foreigners in Turkey (Gümrükçü, 1997; Erbaş, 1997; Tekinalp, 2002). This contribution attempts to further close this research gap by describing some aspects of the social life-worlds of German migrants in Turkey. A further dimension is added by placing this description within the context of transnational spaces between Turkey and Germany (Faist, 2000a; Faist, 2000b).

The descriptive part of this contribution comprises three sections that are in part based on a study on the concept of freedom of movement for EU migrants in Turkey (Kaiser-Pehlivanoğlu et al., 2001). These sections are on: 1. the legal situation; 2. citizenship; 3. the classification of migrant groups and reasons for migration; 4. networking activities. The last part seeks to establish the nature of transnational links between German migrants in Turkey according to the threefold-typology of the dimensions of transborder expansion of social spaces established by Faist (2000a, pp. 4-8): the temporal and spatial compression of ties; linkage patterns; and the impact of these ties.

The Legal Situation of German Migrants in Turkey

The legal situation of German migrants in Turkey is a useful starting point for determining the scope and nature of transnational ties and organisational structures of this community. Generally, all foreigners in Turkey are subject to the *Turkish Law on Foreigners* (Law No. 5683 of July 15, 1950).[2] In some cases, however, bilateral agreements between Turkey and other individual states accord a special status to citizens of these states with regard to visa regulations on entering Turkey and their duration of residence in Turkey, in which case no permit is required. German citizens may enter the country with a valid passport; they do not need to obtain a visa prior to entry, and they may stay in Turkey for up to three months without a residence permit. Regulations regarding the acquisition of property, for

---

[1] These figures were announced by the Director of the Turkish Research Center, Faruk Şen, and quoted in the online edition of *Turkish Daily News*, accessed on August 08, 2002. It must be taken into account, however, that this figure does not even yet include Turkish-German marriages made outside Germany.

[2] For more information see the new website for foreigners constructed by the Turkish Ministry of the Interior at: http://www.egm.gov.tr/yabancilar/birincisf.htm.

instance, depend on bilateral agreements.[3] Known exceptions to the usual provisions relating to access to the labour market and residence permits concern migrants from countries with ethnic Turkish minorities (like Northern Cyprus, Bulgaria, the Turkic Central Asian Republics), and so-called pink-card holders[4] (*pembe kağıdı*). These groups enjoy preferential treatment over other migrant groups. The following gives a brief overview of legal provisions applying to German migrants.

Residence Permit

One of the most prominent characteristics of the *Turkish Law on Foreigners* is that it does not recognise the *right to residence* for migrants. That is to say, independent of the amount of time that a migrant has spent in Turkey, or of their purpose of stay (for instance, marriage to a Turkish citizen), he is never entitled to unlimited residence. Residence permits can be issued for periods of between six months and five years. Up until 1998, the maximum duration was two years only; unrestricted residence is still unknown. *Denizenship* is a concept first used by Hammar (1990) in the context of modern migration research. It is a normative category designating foreign nationals residing in another country, who have obtained a secure position within the receiving society without being a formal member of it. The decision to permission to reside in Turkey lies with the Foreigners' Department of the Security Forces. Officials may decide at their own discretion whether any of the five different grounds listed in Article 7 of the *Law on Foreigners* on which a foreign national may be denied residence obtains or not.

Administrative fees for a residence permit often change due to high inflation in Turkey. In January 2001, it amounted to TL 250,000,000 for a five-year permit. At that time, this was the equivalent of about 400 Euro, or about 1.5 times the average minimum monthly salary in Turkey.[5] Slow administrative practice – although this is said to have improved in the large cities – may sometimes cause hardships.

Access to the Labour Market

Under Turkish law, work permits for foreigners are issued independently of the residence permit. Regardless of duration of residence in Turkey, free access to the

---

[3] For further information on acquisition of property, inheritance rights, burial etc. see Kaiser-Pehlivanoğlu, 2001.

[4] Turkish citizens are required to relinquish their Turkish citizenship when they adopt German citizenship. 'Pink cards' are a form of compensation for this group, abolishing restrictions for them which apply to other foreigners in Turkey. These include work and residence permits, inheritance rights, acquisition of property rights etc.

[5] For comparison: around the same time, administrative fees for residence permits in Germany amounted to DM 80,- for the first permit, DM 40,- for each renewal, and around DM 100,- for an unlimited residence permit.

94 *Transnational Social Spaces*

labour market does not exist under any circumstance. Furthermore, a work permit is not given to the migrant who has applied for it, but rather to the institution or firm he works for. This leaves the migrant in a conceivably weak and vulnerable position vis-à-vis the employer. Foreigners are denied access to a large number of – in fact most – professions. The *Law on Activities and Professions in Turkey Reserved for Turkish Citizens* of June 16, 1932 (Law No. 2007) provides a long list of professions that are exclusively reserved for Turkish citizens, among them almost all activities in the services sector. These include professions such as photography, tourist guiding, transporting persons, acting, singing, waitressing, interpreting, and all other employment in the production sector.[6]

There are also several other laws concerning different professions such as the medical professions, employment in television and broadcasting, the veterinarian profession, judges, public prosecutors and public notaries, engineers and the like, which also exclude foreigners on principle. Some stipulations, however, allow for exemption if a foreign citizen is able to pass a state examination in the field in question. Yet, reportedly, this seems to be extremely difficult, if not impossible. Allegedly, this is due to the fact that state examinations for foreigners are different and more difficult than examinations for Turkish citizens.

The number of illegally employed migrants in Turkey is sharply on the rise. In early 2001, the *Turkish Daily News* reported that the Turkish Labour and Social Security Minister, Yaşar Okuyan, estimated that around one million foreigners were working illegally in Turkey at that time. Specifically, the percentage is reported to be particularly high in the textile sector. Turkey's problem with illegal immigration, as a major country of destination for migrants, has been highlighted by Kirişçi (2002). It figured especially prominently in public debate in 2002 due to an increased fear of immigration within EU countries and discussions surrounding the EU Summit at Seville. At that Summit, it was debated whether Turkey and other countries accused of not taking appropriate measures to prevent illegal migration to the EU from their territory – both as sending and transit countries – should be sanctioned. This plan was, ultimately, not put into practice but political pressure on Turkey has increased substantially.[7]

Meanwhile, a new law for foreigners has been drafted, and is still awaiting approval by the Turkish Parliament. In a statement by the Turkish Labour Minister in April 2001 on the occasion of a visit by the German Employment Minister to Turkey, it was announced that the new law would be passed by the end of 2001; yet, to date this has not happened. An attempt to include the law in the historic reform package of August 3, 2002, was also unsuccessful.[8] The draft law provides

---

[6] For further information on this issue see Gülören Tekinalp, 2001.

[7] See also *Migration und Bevölkerung*, July 2002, Vol. 6, pp. 4-5. Further details about the Seville Summit at: http://ue.eu.int/pressData/de/ec/71213.pdf.

[8] Interview with Can Ünver, Director-General, Turkish Labour and Social Affairs Ministry, on September 6, 2002.

that under certain circumstances an unlimited work permit may be issued.[9] The issue of unlimited residence permits is not included, nor does a draft law concerning residence permits yet exist.

The issue of free movement of persons in Turkey has received little attention from the European Union so far. Yet, as has been mentioned above, since the first Regular Report on Turkey of 1997 this issue has been brought up every year in subsequent regular reports. Whereas Turkish residents in member states of the European Union have been able to improve their legal situation by taking legal recourse at national courts within the EU or at the European Court of Justice, this has not been the case with EU migrants, including German migrants, in Turkey. There have been about 16 cases before the European Court of Justice involving Turkish migrants in the European Union. Turkish law professors have argued that EU residents in Turkey have not been able to take their cases to the European Court of Justice because they live outside the scope of jurisdiction of that court, that is to say outside the territory of the European Union. Interviews conducted by the author have revealed that a lack of confidence in the Turkish legal system on the part of EU migrants in Turkey, and the fear of getting into trouble with Turkish authorities, have prevented them from taking cases related to access to the labour market to the courts. An exception to this is a case concerning the recent prohibition of foreign educators at Turkish pre-school institutions.[10] The Turkish Court of Appeal ruled on August 25th, 2002 that this prohibition was introduced by decree. This contravenes the law, which does not provide for discretionary powers regarding the enlargement of the list of professions from which foreigners are excluded. Exclusion from certain professions can only be determined by law. Nonetheless, this example shows that far from shortening the list of professions from which foreigners are excluded, endeavours are even being made to enlarge it.

Insurance Coverage

Apart from the above-mentioned obstacles regarding access to the Turkish labour market, German migrants face further difficulties with respect to insurance coverage. The Turkish state insurance system is divided into three categories:

1. *Sosyal Sigorta Kurumu* (*SSK*) for employees in the state sectors: This insurance also covers foreigners. There have, however, been reports of problems concerning pension rights and unemployment benefits – the latter only having been introduced in October 2001 in Turkey. This insurance covers only the

---

[9] For details, see the draft law by the Labour and Social Security Ministry (T.C. Çalışma ve Sosyal Güvenlik Bakanliği, 2001, pp. 1-16). For an evaluation of the situation of foreigners in Turkey by the Labour and Social Security Ministry see: T.C. Çalışma ve Sosyal Güvenlik Bakanliği, 2002, pp. 37-38.

[10] Dr. Mehmet Köksal, a long-standing board member and legal advisor of *Die Brücke*, was the legal representative for this case.

96   *Transnational Social Spaces*

most basic social benefits at the state hospitals (excluding university hospitals), which is usually of rather a low standard.

2. *Emekli Sandiği* for civil servants: This insurance is much more comprehensive than the SSK insurance, but excludes foreigners as they cannot become civil servants. They may only benefit from this insurance as the spouse of a Turkish civil servant, but not in their own right. Problems have also been reported regarding old-age pensions from this insurance for surviving foreign spouses.

3. *Bağ-Kur* for the self-employed: This insurance does not cover self-employed foreigners if they own the company, which understandably limits the number of foreigners willing to set up their own business. In this respect, it must be mentioned that until recently, foreign residents faced severe difficulties if they intended to open their own business. One requirement was to deposit US \$50,000 with the Turkish state. This restriction has now been lifted, as the relevant authorities have confirmed, in the case of foreigners who have legally resided in Turkey for at least three years. In practice, however, difficulties are reported to have continued.

In principle, German migrants are only discriminated against with respect to *Bağ-Kur* insurance. Apart from that, they have to cope with the same difficulties arising out of an insufficient social security system as Turkish citizens. Private insurance companies provide an alternative to the state insurance system, and these have mushroomed since the mid-1990s in Turkey. Despite the fact that they usually admit foreigners on a non-discriminatory basis, it is an alternative that only few foreigners opt for. It has been reported that the main reason for this is the high cost of insurance contributions. Fees have in some cases been raised arbitrarily from one year to the next, purportedly due to high inflation, and the private insurance sector is insufficiently regulated or monitored. Within the context of adapting Turkey's legislation on the free movement of services to EU legislation, however, some progress has been made and is expected to continue.[11]

Citizenship

The definition of 'citizen' can vary from country to country. The condition for citizenship can be based on the principle of *jus sanguinis* (parentage and blood relations) or on the principle of *jus soli* (birthplace). Examples of both principles can be found within the European Union. Both Turkey and Germany basically apply the *jus sanguinis* principle. However, elements of the *jus soli* principle were incorporated into the new German citizenship law which came into effect in 2000. At the heart of this change was the long-overdue political recognition that

---

[11] See the Regular Progress Reports on Turkey by the European Commission at the website of the EU's Representation in Turkey: http://www.deltur.cec.eu.int/englisch/main-e.html.

German Migrants in Turkey: The 'Other Side' 97

Germany is *de facto* a country of immigration. Increased international migration brought about by globalisation processes and *de facto* transnational spaces, in which increasing numbers of people live today, have forced Germany and other countries to reconsider the definition of 'citizenship'. An extensity of political, social and cultural rights has also been observed. This is increasingly applied to foreign nationals residing within the boundaries of nation-states whose formal membership – citizenship through naturalisation – they have have not obtained. The elimination of certain obstacles to obtaining formal membership are a further measure.

This development represents a rapprochement between two seemingly opposed basic political principles. One is the democratic idea of representative government, based on the principle of general suffrage. The other is the principle of the nation-state, which proclaims that only formal members can participate in political affairs. The increasingly obvious and unsatisfactory situation of migrants being bound by obligations (e.g. abiding by the law, paying taxes) in the receiving countries without having any rights (e.g. the right to vote for political representatives who decide upon the obligations they have to fulfil) has led to a shift in attitudes. It appears that increasing globalisation and expanding transnational spaces will warrant further changes in the future.

Turkish politics is based upon, and revolves around, the idea of nationalism and integrity of the nation-state. Responses to new international developments have been sluggish. Hence, laws regulating the residence of foreigners in Turkey and their access to the labour market have not been changed for decades. Furthermore, Turkish law does not recognise the right to unlimited residence or full access to the labour market even for foreign citizens who have resided for long periods of time in Turkey. As already outlined above, residence permits are valid for no more than five years at the most.

The normative category of 'denizen', first rediscovered by Hammar (1990) for migration research, designates a foreign national residing in another country, who has obtained a secure position within the receiving society without being a formal member of it (OED: foreigner admitted to residence and certain rights). This category, however, does not exist in Turkey. The concept of citizenship in Turkey centres on the idea of the unitary state. The Congress of the Republican People's Party in 1931 adopted six principles – nationalism, secularism, populism, republicanism, statism and revolutionism – that framed this concept of citizenship. In 1937, these principles were defined as constitutional obligations (Kramer, 2000, pp. 1-92). The official understanding of the concept of citizenship is based on the notion of obligations rather than on rights. The aim of these obligations is to strive for the common good as defined by official state ideology, rather than to realise the demands and rights of individual citizens. This understanding implies state intervention in the private life of the individual, family life and religious as well as pastime activities (Kadıoğlu, 1999, pp. 54-65). All this can clearly be observed in the status of German migrants in Turkey. Access to the labour market is very limited and restricted to narrow areas of employment where there is a shortage

98   *Transnational Social Spaces*

(usually in education and at managerial level) of Turkish employees. Such provisions are, of course, present in other European countries as well, but hardly to such an extent as to exclude foreign nationals from almost every profession.

On the other hand, in contrast to the numerous difficulties foreign nationals face in obtaining residence and work permits, formal citizenship may be obtained with relative ease when marrying a Turkish citizen. Here, the threshold is much lower than in the EU. Citizenship can be applied for directly during the formal marriage procedure, or within 45 days if the marriage takes place outside Turkey. However, such an option is open only to foreign women. Foreign male spouses are, in this context, subject to discrimination. To them, such an option is not available. Yet, in the process of modifying the *Turkish Law on Foreigners* a new bill has been proposed to the effect that foreign female spouses no longer have the automatic right to obtain Turkish citizenship upon marriage. Just like male foreign spouses they shall gain this right only after five years of marriage to a Turkish citizen. This new law was expected to be passed by the end of 2001, but has not yet been approved. Until 1979, foreign women marrying a Turkish citizen automatically received Turkish citizenship. This is why, in the case of German women, dual citizenship was accepted by the German state. However, when the adoption of Turkish citizenship became an option in 1979, German women lost their German citizenship if they adopted Turkish citizenship.

As already stated, the acquisition of citizenship in Turkey is based upon the *jus sanguinis* principle. The Constitution provides for the *jus solis* principle only in exceptional cases, for instance, if a child born on Turkish soil would otherwise be stateless, if a foreign child is adopted by Turkish parents or, as mentioned above, in the case of marriage (for female foreign spouses only). The conditions for naturalisation are a minimum of five years of uninterrupted residence in Turkey, an indication of the intention to live in Turkey (marriage to a Turkish citizen or the acquisition of property, for instance), good conduct and a minimum knowledge of the Turkish language (Aybay, 1991, pp. 35-48).

Moreover, the naturalisation trend in Turkey among EU citizens appears to have declined in recent years. As the Turkish daily *Milliyet* reported in 1999, for unknown – but speculatively political – reasons, not one foreigner was naturalised in the two years preceding the year 1999 (Baydar, 1999). Interviews conducted for this research also revealed that naturalisation procedures have come to a halt. The *Network of Foreign Spouses* has reported cases in which five or eight years after formal application by the foreign spouse for Turkish citizenship, still no official reply has been received as to the progress of the procedure.

Categories of German Migrants in Turkey and Reasons for Migration[12]

In legal terms, German migrants in Turkey are equally affected by the above-mentioned conditions for residence and access to labour market. Yet, depending on their personal circumstances and individual length of stay in Turkey they may be affected to differing degrees. In order to identify these differences, German migrants[13] are categorized into different groups according to their reasons for migration:

Groups of German Migrants

1. *Posted personnel and their families*:   These are managerial staff in German businesses or Turkish-German joint ventures, teachers at German-language schools or universities, personnel of cultural institutions, research centres, and diplomatic and economic missions. Most of them are male with single German citizenship; consequently, accompanying spouses are predominantly female. Usually, these migrants come to Turkey on limited work contracts (2-3 years, renewable once or twice) and residence permits. Under the strict entry regulations, accompanying spouses are often denied access to the labour market. This affects mainly women, and often restricts them to the role of homemaker.

2. *EU spouses of Turkish citizens*:   More than 95 percent of these are women; yet the number of male EU spouses is rising as growing numbers of Turkish women study and work abroad. A large proportion of this group has established their official place of residence in Turkey and is heavily affected by the restrictive legal regime on foreigners. Problems are gender-related. On the one hand, German women are largely confined to the role of homemaker and are therefore financially dependent on their Turkish husbands. In the case of divorce or death of the Turkish spouse, problems may increase if the German wife intends to stay in Turkey but is denied access to the labour market. Extensity of a residence permit is no legal right (especially before the 1998 hardship cases were reported), but current practice is to grant extensity if the migrant has lived in Turkey for a long time, the marriage has lasted at least three years, and the presence of under-age children is documented.[14] Male German spouses of Turkish wives may equally experience substantial difficulties, especially if they are trying to fulfil the traditional role of family

---

[12] The findings of this part are based on a series of semi-structured interviews conducted for an earlier study in Kaiser-Pehlivanoğlu, 2001. For a detailed list of interview partners see footnote 3, p. 47. Interview partners included representatives from all groups of migrants enumerated here.

[13] This classification is a modified and extended version of Suzan Erbaş's classification (Erbaş, 1997).

[14] Interview with the Head of the Foreigners' Department at the Headquarters of the Turkish National Security Forces in İstanbul on November 23, 2001.

100   *Transnational Social Spaces*

breadwinner but are denied access to the labour market on the grounds of being a foreigner.

3. *Descendants of EU spouses of Turkish citizens*: Most foreigners in this category have dual citizenship and therefore do not face the same legal problems as other migrants. However, dual citizenship may be a hindrance if they try to take up a professional career in law-enforcement, the military or politics. There is now a second generation, and even an emerging third generation of EU migrants.

4. *Retired EU citizens*: Increasing numbers of retired EU citizens are buying property and settling along the Turkish sunbelt-coast (Bodrum, Marmaris, Antalya, Alanya). They have reported substantial problems with residence permits. Many of them leave the country every three months and then return a short while later in order to circumvent this problem.

5. *Alternative life-style seekers*: Members of this group tend to settle along the Turkish sunbelt-coast, or in large urban areas, especially in İstanbul. They often aim to make a new start in life, and generally belong to the age group of 40 to 50 year-olds. Many of them set up or are employed in small businesses in the tourist sector, or pursue free-lance artistic occupations. Most of them leave and re-enter the country every three months.

6. *EU citizens of Turkish origin*: Many of these are 'pink card' (*pembe kağıt*) holders, which allow them basically the same rights as Turkish citizens with respect to residence, access to the labour market, inheritance etc. They are, however, exempted from political rights, that is to say they cannot stand for election or vote.

7. *Bosphorus Germans*:[15] These are descendants of tradespeople, military personnel and academics who came to Turkey during the Ottoman Empire.[16] During World War II, several thousand refugees (Jews and political activists) fled there from Germany. Many of those who stayed on after the war later adopted Turkish citizenship. Yet some are reported to have dwelled in Turkey for generations as migrants without formal citizenship, experiencing the same problems as other migrants.

---

[15] For a detailed description of German refugees in Turkey during World War II see: Nedret Kuran-Burçoğlu, 2002, and Anne Dietrich, 1987.

[16] One of the main symbols of this immigration group is the foundation of the German society *Teutonia* in 1847 in İstanbul, which continues to exist today. In 1897, the society moved to a building that is still called *Teutonia* today and which celebrated its 155th anniversary in November 2002 in its newly renovated facilities. The building continues to serve cultural exchange activities, mainly by the *Goethe Institute*.

Reasons for Migration

1. Push and pull migrational factors from Germany to Turkey:
1.1 *Push factors*:
   - Rising unemployment in Germany, specifically after unification.
   - Increased xenophobia and an escalation in the number of acts of violence against foreigners in Germany during the 1990s. This has especially affected bi-national Turkish-German families.

1.2 *Pull factors*:
   - Perceived increase in employment opportunities in Turkey, especially after completion of the Customs Union between Turkey and the EU in 1996.
   - Mediterranean climate and mentality in Turkey, often acknowledged after a tourist visit.
   - Comparatively low living expenses in Turkey.

2. Push and pull factors of migration from Turkey to Germany:
2.1 *Push factors*:
   - Occurrence of two major earthquakes in Turkey in 1999.
   - Perceived increased political instability in Turkey.
   - Ongoing financial crisis in Turkey.

2.2 *Pull factors*:
   - Cheaper and better education opportunities for children in Germany.
   - Better social security in Germany.
   - New citizenship law in Germany.

Networking Activities: *Die Brücke*

The number of German migrants in Turkey multiplied throughout the 1980s and especially in the 1990s. Likewise, an increase in networking and cultural activities has been observed in the large cities, along the Turkish sunbelt-coast and, to a lesser degree, along the Black Sea coast. These increased activities are basically due to the synergizing effect of the following three factors:

- rising numbers of migrants, especially throughout the 1990s,
- increased activities of the Protestant and Catholic church in the large cities (particularly in İstanbul), the *Goethe Institutes*, the German Embassy and Consulates, political foundations (Friedrich Ebert Foundation, Konrad-Adenauer Foundation, Friedrich Naumann Foundation and Heinrich Böll Foundation), trade delegations and other research institutions,

102   *Transnational Social Spaces*

- foundation of the interest group *Die Brücke e.V. – Deutscher Kultur- und Wohltätigkeitsverein* ('Bridge – German Cultural and Charity Association'),[17] which has association status under Turkish law.

Die Brücke has succeeded in establishing a network for the exchange of information and active lobbyism not only among German and German-speaking residents (including Turkish remigrants from Germany as well as Austrian and Swiss citizens) in İstanbul, but also among various German migrant groups that have formed in other areas of Turkey (Ankara, Izmir, Alanya, Antalya, Marmaris, Zonguldak), as well as among German remigrants in Germany (Munich, Hamburg and Berlin). There are contact partners in all of these cities, in some of them more than one. In İstanbul alone, there are around 15 contact partners, one in almost every large city district. Members of the association number around 800 and are contacted through a monthly newsletter. Most German residents in İstanbul and other urban areas appear to be aware of the existence of this association, even though they may not be members. An increasing number of German citizens already made contact with it before migrating to Turkey, thus receiving practical information on how to get settled in Turkey.

Die Brücke was formed at its constitutive meeting on January 23, 1990, with 90 persons present. The first newsletter was immediately published at the end of that month. By February 1990 there were already 300 members. In May 1992, *Die Brücke* gained status as a registered Turkish association. The overall goal of the association, in the words of its president Uschi Akın, is 'to help improve and lobby for a better legal situation of German residents in Turkey'. Other goals include:

- bringing together German-speaking people;
- formation of a Turkish-German lobby;
- promotion of bi-lingual education for children from bi-national families;
- providing help for the acculturation process in Turkey;
- planning of cultural events;
- planning social and charity projects.

During the formative years of the association, close cooperation between the Consulate General in İstanbul and *Die Brücke* played an important role. The Consulate General, for instance, helped to inform all German citizens registered at the Consulate in İstanbul of the formation of this association. Furthermore, many events organised by *Die Brücke* have been carried out under the patronage of the General Consulate. The original idea of forming an association actually stems from the former German Chancellor Helmut Kohl. During an official visit to Turkey he was approached by the president-to-be of *Die Brücke* and lobbied to help improve the restrictive legal situation of German residents in Turkey. Helmut Kohl, then

---

[17] For more information see *Die Brücke's* website at: http://www.bruecke-İstanbul.org.

reportedly suggested forming an interest group, out of which eventually the present association developed.

In terms of membership of *Die Brücke*, it is worth noting that women outnumber men by far, and that the association is principally run by female German spouses of Turkish citizens. Yet other groups of migrants are also represented: male spouses of Turkish citizens, posted employees and their families, German-speaking Turkish citizens with and without German citizenship, single German residents in Turkey, as well as German and Turkish citizens living in Germany. Recently, *Die Brücke* has started its own research on the re-adaptation of German remigrants who move back to Germany from Turkey. This research is still in the fact-finding stage and no results have been produced so far. Regarding the age of association members, it has been ascertained that the youngest are 13 and the eldest 94. In 2001, a new group was formed within *Die Brücke*, which consists of young people aged from 13 to 26, most of whom come from bi-national families and hold dual citizenship. This group of youngsters feels the need to share experiences and feelings with one another and discuss problems arising out of their specific situation.

To sum up it can be said that the membership of *Die Brücke* reflects the different groups of German residents in Turkey, with proportionate over-representation of female German spouses of Turkish residents. This fact can be explained by the insecure legal situation that is particularly felt by this group. Another explanatory factor is that most members of this group have children and are very concerned about German language education and the cultural socialisation of their children within the receiving society, of which they represent a minority. Furthermore, few women of this group have been able to obtain work permits due to the restrictive laws described above, although most of them are professionally qualified. This is also true of the predominantly female spouses of German personnel posted to Turkey. Due to the fact that under Turkish law many of them are not allowed to work, or choose to take up the occupation of homemaker, there is a certain potential of energy and time available which increasingly appears to flow into the organisation of cultural events. These cultural events and their preparation are seen as a means of spending time with other German-speaking people while at the same time providing an opportunity for cultural formation and the acquisition of language skills (i.e. German) for the children.

The list of activities of *Die Brücke* is a long one. It ranges from coffee mornings to children's play groups, from family outings to Christmas and Easter events, from extensive help in the aftermath of the devastating earthquakes in 1999 to supporting individuals (of both Turkish and German nationality) in need of medical, social or financial support, from monthly dinners for working women to bowling events, weekly discussion rounds and football matches for men, from organising tickets for concerts and the theatre to gymnastics, from meetings for Bosphorus Germans to weekly boat trips to the Black Sea during the summer. In early 2002, *Die Brücke* started to co-host seminars and conferences on Turkish-German issues together with the Konrad Adenauer Foundation. The two most

104   *Transnational Social Spaces*

prominent conferences so far hosted a leading German CDU politician, Jürgen Rüttgers, and Bassam Tibi of Göttingen University. Main topics were the integration of Turkish and German migrants in Germany and Turkey respectively, as well as the co-existence of cultures and the phenomenon of Islamism. In this way, the association has attracted further media attention and gained political lobbying weight.

The major achievement of the association so far, however, has been the opening of *Avrupa Koleji – Europa Kolleg* ('European College') in İstanbul in September 1998. Born out of the long-acknowledged lack of adequate schooling for Turkish-German bi-lingual and bi-cultural children, this is the first school in Turkey to offer bi-lingual education in Turkish and German from pre-school to high school. It is a private Turkish school under the jurisdiction of the Turkish Education Ministry, established on the initiative of *Die Brücke*, which had long sought a suitable school. *Die Brücke* has official advisory status in this school, especially with respect to methodological approaches in education, the development of curricula for German language instruction and the selection of teachers. In September 2002, the Turkish Education Minister participated in a conference at the school on reforms in the Turkish education system, where he was introduced to the education philosophy of the school.

The goal of the school is not only to provide bi-lingual education, but also to form a synthesis of the Turkish and German education systems. German cultural events such as Christmas, Easter and Carnival etc. are integrated into the school curriculum. For instance, on St. Martin's Day in November 2001, some 250 people participated in an organised and authorised procession in the İstanbul district of Bakırköy, where the mayor had arranged for the closing down of some of the major roads during the early-evening rush hour. Policemen amiably escorted pre-schoolers and first-year pupils of the school and their families (of Turkish and German origin alike) along the roads as they sang traditional St. Martin's songs with self-made lanterns in their hands. The school aims specifically to enrol children from bi-national and remigrant Turkish families, facilitating access to both societies and cultures. Currently, they represent about 60 out of 600 pupils. Ultimately, *Avrupa Koleji – Europa Kolleg* strives to offer its pupils a Turkish high-school diploma as well as a German high-school diploma (*Abitur*). In 1999 the school gained official acknowledgement by a visit of the German Ambassador to Turkey, and it continues to benefit from official German state funding. Building upon the experience of *Avrupa Koleji – Europa Kolleg*, a similar school was opened in Izmir by the local branch office of *Die Brücke* in September 2001.

Another, albeit less spectacular success of *Die Brücke*, has been achieved with regard to citizenship. The only way out of the restrictive legal regime for foreigners residing in Turkey is the adoption of Turkish citizenship. Thus, while on the one hand Turkish laws have determined the situation of German migrants, German laws on the other did not allow these migrants to adopt a second – that is to say Turkish citizenship, have equally determined it. Thus, while on the one hand German migrants have been oppressed by Turkish laws, they have on the other been equally afflicted by German law, which did not allow them to adopt a second citizenship. *Die Brücke*'s lobbying efforts produced some results to ameliorate this situation in 2000. Prior to that date, the adoption of a second citizenship resulted in most cases in the loss of German citizenship for German citizens living abroad (this did not apply to their children).[18] In autumn 1993, *Die Brücke* started a petitioning campaign for dual citizenship. In 1994, a petition was handed over to the German *Bundestag* in Bonn demanding dual citizenship for German women living in Turkey. This led to an enquiry by the oppositional Social Democrat Party (*Kleine Anfrage der SPD*) of the coalition government of CDU/CSU and FDP in 1995. Intensive lobbying continued, including talks with the former Vice-President of the German *Bundestag*, Dr. Burckhard Hirsch, and later with several Members of Parliament from the Green and Social Democrat Parties.

The coalition government of Social Democrats and Greens, which came into power in 1998, introduced a new law on citizenship, which came into effect in January 2000. A new stipulation regarding permission to maintain German citizenship while adopting a new one was introduced specifically as a result of the lobbying efforts of *Die Brücke*. The law explicitly refers to German 'women living in Muslim countries'. *Die Brücke* is not quite happy with this formulation, as Turkey is a secular country in which jurisdiction is not based on religion, although the formulation in the new law could be interpreted to imply just that.

Parallel to lobbying German lawmakers, *Die Brücke* also intensified its efforts to bring about changes in the *Turkish Law on Foreigners*. In 1993, a petition to that effect was handed over to the Turkish Interior Ministry, and later also to German Chancellor Helmut Kohl. In 1996, in cooperation with *Die Brücke's* legal advisor, Dr. Mehmet Köksal, a draft proposal for the reform of the *Turkish Law on Foreigners* was drawn up and submitted to the Turkish authorities. The German translation of the draft proposal was also presented to the former Vice-President of the German *Bundestag*, Dr. Burckhard Hirsch.

In 1998, *Die Brücke* lent a helping hand in the formation of the *Network of Foreign Spouses*, which campaigns for the same agenda as its German counterpart, namely the improvement of the legal status of foreigners in Turkey. This association conceives itself as an umbrella organisation for individual national groups and cultural associations. It also publishes a monthly newsletter and was especially active during the year 2000/2001 in lobbying for reforms of the *Turkish Law on Foreigners*, which are currently pending before the Turkish Parliament. In March 1998 and November 2001, in cooperation with the *Goethe Institute*, *Die Brücke* participated in an international symposium on the situation of EU citizens in Turkey held at Yildiz Technical University in İstanbul.

It is noteworthy that leading members of *Die Brücke*, and particularly members of the executive board, have been able to establish good contacts with

---

[18] The option of obtaining a special permission for obtaining a second citizenship was available at that time already. Yet, lengthy administrative procedures were discouraging, and even if not results were almost always negative.

106   *Transnational Social Spaces*

politicians in Ankara and Berlin. Sometimes these contacts stemmed from personal ties and connections and were used to the benefit of the association. Individual members of the association covered the start-up costs for these lobbying efforts, including travel and other expenses. Many of the active members come from middle or upper middle-class families, which facilitated funding the necessary lobbying efforts. Such voluntary commitments to improving the situation not only of German residents, but all foreigners living in Turkey, can also be observed among members of the executive board of the *Network of Foreign Spouses*. All of them are dual-citizenship holders, most of them originally from the United States and Canada, that is to say, countries that allow dual citizenship. These people have no need to improve the situation of foreigners living in Turkey for their own benefit, as they do not face any legal discrimination. However, most *Network* members interviewed believe that an improvement in the legal status of foreigners in Turkey will positively contribute to economic, political, social and cultural development in Turkey. In this way Turkey will, in their view, become a better place to live in, both for Turkish citizens and for migrants from Germany, the European Union and elsewhere.

Conclusion: German Migrants in Turkey as Part of the Turkish-German Transnational Space

The situation of German migrants in Turkey outlined above represents only a small fragment of their social life-worlds. The following section comprises an analysis of the nature of transnational ties, as defined by Thomas Faist (2000a), thereby focussing mainly on *Die Brücke*. It is evident that the main agenda of this association – and at the same time its motivation for action and activities – was borne out of the restrictive legal space to which German migrants had been confined in Turkey. This legal space, on the other hand, is a transnational space in itself, determined as it is by Turkish laws (residence, access to labour market, citizenship) and by German laws (citizenship). In this context, another dimension has become increasingly important, that is, the European dimension. As Turkey intends to become a full member of the European Union, it has started to place increasing emphasis on adopting the EU's *acquis communautaire* (i.e. the whole set of common norms, values, rules and procedures applied throughout the EU).[19] It has also come under pressure through the European Commission's annual progress reports on Turkey with respect to the application of the Association Agreement between Turkey and the European Community of 1963 (commonly

---

[19] One indication is the above-mentioned court decision on banning foreign pre-school teachers from Turkish institutions. In its decision, the court has for the first time recognized the European Agreement on Settlement as part of Turkish national law. Turkey had ratified the Agreement in 1989.

German Migrants in Turkey: The 'Other Side' 107

known as the *Ankara Agreement*), and subsequent decisions by the Association Council.[20]

In Turkey, a new awareness has begun to set in regarding the different sets of rights for citizens (civil, political, social, cultural and economic). This has not least been due to the political pressure exercised by the European Union, which insists that Turkey must strictly enforce the Copenhagen Criteria before it can start any serious accession negotiations. This awareness has now gradually begun to develop among foreign nationals residing in Turkey. Three modifications were already made in 1998 to the *Law on Foreigners*, facilitating the issue of residence permits, and a complete overhaul of the law is purportedly due to be passed by the Turkish Parliament soon, although very little detail is known about this proposal as yet. According to rumour, it will apparently still not be possible for anyone to obtain an unlimited residence permit. Under certain circumstances, however, unlimited work permits may be issued. With regard to work permits, Article 33 of the draft law states that Law No. 2007 dating back to June 11, 1932, which restricts access to the labour market for foreigners, will be invalidated (T.C. Çalışma ve Sosyal Güvenlik Bakanliği, 2001). This is intended to bring Turkish law more in line with European Union law as part of the process of adopting the *acquis communautaire* of the EU.

Some minor steps have been taken to address the problem of the legal status of EU migrants in Turkey. The Regular Report for the year 2000 by the Commission on Turkey's Progress towards Accession, which was issued in November 2000, acknowledges the problem. The chapter on the free movement of persons in this report, which is one of the 29 chapters of the *acquis communautaire* that constitute Turkey's basis to assume membership obligations, is part of the so-called four freedoms which form the cornerstone of the internal market. The other three freedoms are the free movement of goods, freedom to provide services and free movement of capital. While these are assessed to be more or less satisfactory, or at least some progress has been reported, the freedom of persons is the only area in which Turkey has made 'no progress' according to the Commission. In response to this, the Turkish National Programme of April 2001 mentions increased liberalization of the freedom of movement for persons (i.e. EU citizens in Turkey) among its medium-term goals.

Activities carried out by *Die Brücke* take place predominantly in Turkey, but to a minor degree also in Germany. This is true of political lobbying work in Ankara and Berlin, as well as interviews and contributions on radio and television programmes both in Turkey and Germany.[21] Cultural activities, on the other hand,

---

[20] Notably decision 2/76 of December 20, 1976 (esp. Arts. 2 and 3); decision 1/80 of September 19, 1980 (esp. Art. 6); decision 3/80 of September 1980 (esp. Art. 4). The full text of all is reprinted in Bülent Çiçekli, 1998. For further evaluation see also Harun Gümrükçü, 1997.

[21] An example of the transnational nature of these activities is my own contribution on that subject in a TV program (*Çözüme Doğru*) on April 14, 2001, with Turkish and German

108   *Transnational Social Spaces*

take place almost exclusively in Turkey, yet sometimes with participants from Germany who are invited to Turkey especially for that purpose. As already outlined, activities cover all aspects of life, including education, religion, politics, economics and law. The spatial compression of time has gradually intensified, both in terms of volume and speed of transactions. This is due to overall forces of globalisation, including increased and faster travel, as well as the increased speed with which information can be distributed through the internet. This is manifested in increased communication among members of the community, as well as the previously mentioned appearance of *Die Brücke's* website.

As for linkage patterns, it can safely be asserted that German migrants in Turkey have built up dense information structures. It has already been mentioned that *Die Brücke* has a widespread network of contact partners all over Turkey, as well as Germany. The same holds true for the German-speaking Protestant and Catholic religious communities in Turkey, although for reasons of space this has not been discussed here. These two churches co-operate closely with each other on an ecumenical basis to reach as many members of their communities as possible. They achieve this through newsletters, internet sites, telephone hotlines and, more traditionally, by organised visits to more remote parts of Turkey. All this hints at efficient organisation and an increasing degree of institutionalisation. *Die Brücke*, for instance, has a number of regional subgroups as well as age-specific groups (e.g. the young people's branch for 13-26 year-olds mentioned above).

An outstanding example of the areas of impact of these transnational ties is the effect of lobbying on citizenship outlined above. *Die Brücke* has in fact brought about a change, or rather an addendum to the new German citizenship law, facilitating access to formal membership in Turkey for its constituency. Another important area of influence is the educational sector. Here, a factual synthesis of the German and Turkish educational systems and philosophies has been attempted. In fact, the *Avrupa Koleji – Europa Kolleg* is a genuinely transnational idea. It seeks to adapt the German integration model in the field of education to the Turkish experience. The *Avrupa Koleji – Europa Kolleg* itself is modelled and named after German schools bearing the same name and educational philosophy in Kassel and Berlin. In fact, a partnership has already been established with the *Europa-Kolleg* in Kassel. Again, what is striking here is that, as with the legal space, the German-Turkish transnational space is enlarged by the notion of 'Europe'. This is a documentation of Turkey's and Germany's Europeanization (Kaiser-Pehlivanoğlu, 2002) as well as the Europeanization of the Turkish-German transnational space. Increasing numbers of German migrants in Turkey will continue to reinforce and expand the structure of the community, lending it increased permanency. Growing links and ties between Turkey and Germany will

---

participants of a conference on Turkish-German relations held in İstanbul on April 11-13, 2001. *TRT International* broadcasted the TV program both in Turkey and Germany. The *Goethe Institute* in İstanbul provided for simultaneous translation facilities during the course of the program.

German Migrants in Turkey: The 'Other Side' 109

further enlarge the existing transnational space; while at the same time an increased prominence of the European dimension is also expected.

References

Aybay, R. (1991). *Yurtaşlık Hukuku*, Aybay Hukuk Araştırmaları Vakfı, İstanbul.

Baydar, Yavuz (1999), 'İki Yıldır Kimse Vatandaş Yapılmıyor', in *Milliyet*, July 23, 1999.

Çiçekli, Bülent (1998), *The Legal Position of Turkish Immigrants in the European Union*, Karmap. Ankara.

Dietrich, Anne (1987), *Deutschsein in İstanbul*, Leske + Budrich, Berlin.

Erbaş, Suzan (1997), 'EU-Bürger in der Türkei: Stand und Perspektiven – Unter besonderer Berücksichtigung der Situation der deutschen Staatsbürger', in Harun Gümrükçü, Ursula Neumann and Wolf-Rüdiger Felsch (eds.), *ITES-Jahrbuch 1997-1998: Bikulturalität – staatliches Handeln – Mensch*, Schriften des Instituts für Türkisch-Europäische Studien, Vol. 7, pp. 119-34.

Faist, Thomas (2000a), 'The Border-Crossing Expansion of Spaces: Common Questions, Concepts and Topics', in Institute for Intercultural and International Studies (INIIS) (ed.). University of Bremen and Faculty of Economic and Administrative Sciences, Middle East Technical University, Ankara, *Summer Institute Working Paper No. 1/2000*, Bremen and Ankara.

Faist, Thomas (2000b), *Transstaatliche Räume: Politik, Wirtschaft und Kultur in und zwischen Deutschland und der Türkei*, transcript Verlag, Bielefeld.

Gümrükçü, Harun (1997), 'EU-Bürger in der Türkei: Die noch ausstehende Auseinandersetzung um ihren Assoziationsstatus', in Harun Gümrükçü, Ursula Neumann and Wolf-Rüdiger Felsch (eds.), *ITES-Jahrbuch 1997-1998: Bikulturalität – staatliches Handeln – Mensch*, Schriften des Instituts für Türkisch-Europäische Studien, Vol. 7, pp. 87-118.

Hammar, Tomas (1990), *Democracy and the Nation State: Aliens, Denizens and Citizens in a World of International Migration*, Avebury, Aldershot.

Kadıoğlu, Ayşe (1999), *Cumhuriyet İradesi Demokrasi Muhakemesi*, Metis, İstanbul.

Kaiser-Pehlivanoğlu, Bianca (2002), 'Germany's European Policy: Some Implications for Turkey'. in *International Quarterly Review of Turkish Industrialists' and Businessmen's Association*, Vol. Special Issue 'German-Turks', pp. 50-6.

Kaiser-Pehlivanoğlu, Bianca, Armağan E. Çakır and Mutlu, E. İlker (2001), 'The Concept of "Free Movement of Persons" and Turkey's Full Membership in the European Union'. in *Final Project Report for the Research Fund of Marmara University*, Marmara University, Marmara, Vol. 2000/SOB-5.

Kirişçi, Kemal (2002). 'Immigration and Asylum Issues in EU-Turkish Relations: Assessing EU's Impact on Turkish Policy and Practice', in S. Lavenex and E. Uarer (eds.), *Migration and the Externalities of European Integration*, Lexington Books, Lanham.

Kramer, Heinz (2000), *A Changing Turkey: The Challenge to Europe and the United States*, Brookings Institution Press, Washington (D.C.).

Kuran-Burçoğlu. Nedret (2002), 'Historischer Überblick über die kulturellen Beziehungen zwichen der Türkei und Deutschland', in Hagen Lichtenberg, Muzaffer Dartan and Ali Eliş (eds.). *Das Deutsch-Türkische Verhältnis: Auswirkungen auf den Beitrittsprozeß der Türkei zur Europäischen Union*, Jean Monnet Lehrstuhl für Europarecht. University of Bremen, pp. 239-88.

Migration und Bevölkerung (2002), Newsletter of the Institute for Population Sciences at Humboldt University in Berlin, Humboldt University, Berlin, Vol. 6, July 2002.

110 *Transnational Social Spaces*

T.C. Çalışma ve Sosyal Güvenlik Bakanliği (Ministry of Labour and Social Security) (2001), 'Yabancıların Çalışma İzinleri Hakkında Kanun Tasarısı', unpublished document, Ankara, July 5, 2001.

T.C. Çalışma ve Sosyal Güvenlik Bakanliği (Ministry of Labour and Social Security) (2002), *Yeniden Yapılma ve Yeni Atılımlar: Çalışma ve Sosyal Güvenlik Bakanlığı Faaliyet Raporu*, Second edition, Ankara.

Tekinalp, Gülören (2002), 'Aspekte des Niederlassungs- und Dienstleistungsverkehrs', in Hagen Lichtenberg, Muzaffer Dartan and Ali Eliş (eds.), *Das Deutsch-Türkische Verhältnis: Auswirkungen auf den Beitrittsprozess der Türkei zur Europäischen Union*. Jean Monnet Lehrstuhl für Europarecht, University of Bremen, pp. 129-44.

Websites

Conclusions of the Seville Summit in June 2002 at:
  http://ue.eu.int/pressData/de/ec/71213.pdf.
Turkish Daily News online at:
  http://www.turkishdailynews.com.
Die Brücke online at:
  http://www.bruecke-istanbul.org.
Website for foreigners of the Turkish Ministry of the Interior at:
  http://www.egm.gov.tr/yabancilar/birincisf.htm.
Website of the European Union's Representation in Turkey at:
  http://www.deltur.cec.eu.int/englisch/main-e.html.

Chapter 5

Turkish Ultra-nationalism in Germany: Its Transnational Dimensions

Emre Arslan

Introduction

Turkish immigrants have been living in Germany now for more than forty years. One might expect that any nationalist feelings Turkish immigrants might have towards their homeland would weaken over the years. Among Turkish people in Germany, however, there are still many who tend towards ultra-nationalist views. Throughout the generations, the extensity and the intensity of the relationship between the Nationalist Action Party (MHP) in Turkey and Turks in Germany has not declined. In this paper, I will focus on the effect of the *ülkücü*[1] movement on the construction of a transnational space between Germany and Turkey. Transnational space, as Thomas Faist puts it, denotes 'relatively stable, enduring and dense sets of ties reaching beyond and across the borders of sovereign states' (Faist, 2000, p. 4). The *ülkücü* movement in Germany should not be seen as a loose and short-lived network of Turkish people. Since it is an institutionalised and long-standing movement, it can be included in the category of political communities and organisations.[2]

For an ultra-nationalist ideology and movement, the situation of *ülkücülük* in Germany seems quite paradoxical. As in all other forms of ultra-nationalism (or: all other ultra-nationalist organisations), *ülkücüs* exalt their own state and nation. In accordance with this ideology, their politics mainly depends on a reverence for the Turkish nation. Although most of the *ülkücüs* have resolved to live in Germany, the German nation-state or territory is not the main objective or space for their politics. They live in a territory that can be ignored, or at least bears secondary importance from their political point of view. In other words, their political imagination transcends the territory in which they live. In fact, such an affinity to their homeland may also be valid for other Turkish political organisations in Germany. But the *ülkücü* case has a distinctive feature. For other

---

[1] While *ülkücü* literally means 'idealist', *ülkücülük* implies idealism. Both of these terms are adopted by Turkish Ultra-nationalists.

[2] Communities and organizations should have a long-lived and institutional character. For their place within types of transnational space in a clear description see Faist, 2000, p. 8.

112   *Transnational Social Spaces*

ideologies (socialists, Islamists and liberals), there is no ontological or definitive obstacle to changing their political projections from Turkey to Germany. Ultranationalists, however, should by definition feel alien within the boundaries of another nation.

One could assume that the longer people stay in a new country, the more they will identify with it. However, this is the case only at a certain level of abstraction. In reality, the number of people who are in favour of the *ülkücü* movement is on the increase in Germany. How can we connect the ideological demands of Turkish ultra-nationalism at a certain level of abstraction and the rise in the appeal of *ülkücülük* to Turkish immigrants in Germany? Is the concept of *ülkücü* in Germany just a name that no longer implies ultranationalism? In order to get an idea of the real character of the *ülkücülük* in Germany, I shall compare it with the *ülkücülük* in Turkey. With this comparison, I shall endeavour to establish an understanding of the ideological nature of *ülkücülük* in both contexts by focusing on some revealing characteristics of fascist ideologies. The research presented includes participant observation in some *Ülkü Ocağı*[3] in different towns in Germany, group discussions with young ülkücüs, and biographical interviews with members and officers of the *Ülkü Ocakları*. Other sources of the work are internet pages of the *Ülkü Ocakları* in Europe, as well as books, newspapers and magazines of the *ülkücüs* themselves and other critical works about them.

Revealing Characteristics of a Typical Fascist Ideology

Here, fascism is defined as a socio-political phenomenon that indicates the phase or the situation of capitalist crisis in which ultra-nationalist ideology becomes widespread and mobilises the masses. In this sense, the concept can be used for defining the MHP movement, since it signifies the mobilisation of ultra-nationalist ideology in a relatively developed capitalist country. The term ultra-nationalism reveals the ideological core of fascism. One can delineate ultra-nationalism in three steps. First, ultra-nationalist ideology conceives of history as the struggle between nations. In other words, the *nation* is the unit of analysis from the ultra-nationalist point of view. Secondly, ultra-nationalists identify the nation with the state. For ultra-nationalists both nation and state have mythical connotations. In their view, state and nation are inseparable and constitute a homogeneous entity. Finally, they see themselves as the real representatives. Since they always exalt the nation or nation-state without question, they believe that they love their own country the most, which means they are the real protectors of the nation-state.

It is very clear that the ideological core of the MHP is the ultra-nationalism that exalts the existence and greatness of the nation. As the founder of the MHP, Alparslan Türkeş states that pro-MHP people believe that history is in fact a

---

[3] *Ülkü Ocağı* is the youth organization of the MHP. Sometimes the plural form of *Ülkü Ocağı* is used in the following: *Ülkü Ocakları*.

Turkish Ultra-nationalism in Germany

struggle of nations (quoted in Ülkü, 1995, p. 18). However, the term fascism indicates more specific features than the term ultra-nationalism. Unlike ultra-nationalism, fascism is not only an ideology but also a movement. The most important distinguishing feature of fascism is that it requires a mass movement. In the following section, I shall deal with the orientation of its followers, its exaltation of the nation and the state, its mobilisation of the masses, and its leader cult with a view to exposing the fascist as well as neo-fascistic nature of the ülkücü movement.

The MHP and its Followers

With the exception of Italian fascism, no fascist movement or regime has defined itself as such. Neither Germany's Nazism nor Turkey's *ülkücülük* acknowledge their ideological and structural similarities with fascism. However, by comparing the Turkish case with the Italian case as an example of classic fascism, and applying Antonio Gramsci's (1994) analysis of fascism, we may be better able to explain the politics of the MHP. First, as in the case of Italian fascism, we can identify the rural basis of the MHP grass roots. Central and Eastern parts of Turkey, where traditional economic, social and cultural conditions still prevail, are the most important centres of MHP support. Secondly, the ideology of the MHP reflects and reformulates the fears, prejudices and the demands of the traditional petty bourgeoisie, which lost its secure and stable economic position as a result of the dramatic side-effects of the penetration of capitalism into traditional areas.

Prior to 1980, several writers attempted to explain the class character of Turkish fascism. According to these analyses, the fascist movement in Turkey was strengthened in the context of the Sunnis' reaction to the Alevi migration to Sunni-based towns.[4] This reaction is considered to be a response, especially in central Anatolia, to the relative improvement in the Alevis' economic and social situation. In the 1980s and 1990s, Kurdish (compulsory or voluntary) migration to the Mediterranean and the Aegean regions led to similar responses. The tradesmen, artisans, small-scale retailers or other members of the petty bourgeoisie of these regions also responded with reactionary nationalism. Today, moreover, the negative effects of the globalisation process, such as an increase in economic differentiation, marginalisation and unemployment, foster discontent in the lower and marginalised classes and feed the MHP ideology.

In the early Republican period, the activities of ultra-nationalist currents (not movements) were limited to founding cultural organisations that would shape or influence the official ideology (Bora, 1994, p. 52). Unlike fascist movements, these

---

[4] As an example, see Ömer Laçiner, Mayıs 1978, 'Malatya Olayı-Turkiye'deki Faşist Hareketin Yapısı ve Gelişimi' Birikim, and the special issues on 'Maraş'tan Sonra', Birikim December 1978/ January 1979. For a critique of these analyses, see Erdost, M. (1980). According to Erdost, there is no class relation between Alevis and Sunnis, rather the class relations cut cross both Alevi and Sunni people in Central Anatolia (1980, p. 75).

114   *Transnational Social Spaces*

currents tried to create an image of being beyond political discussion. Their ideologies depended not only on corporatist nationalism like Kemalism, but also on a Turkist and racist understanding of national character. Because of their elitism, their political projects did not meet the expectations of the majority of the Turkish population; instead, they depended mainly on campaigns or conspiracies at the state level (Bora, 1994, p. 43).

With the rise of communism as a political movement in Turkey during the 1970s, fascism emerged as a counter-movement for protecting the totality of the nation and the state. Türkeş, in his memoirs, explains the role of the rise of Marxism in the foundation of the *ülkücü* movement:

> Following 1968, an extremely active Marxist and separatist youth movement began. In an evaluation meeting of the party, we said that only a more attractive ideology could overcome this separatist movement. Then we discussed which ideology we could use. We decided that Turkish nationalism could be the counter-ideology and that we should rally around this ideology (quoted in Turgut, pp. 400-401).

Recent empirical research conducted by Mustafa Çalık in the less developed areas of Turkey suggests that the rise of the fascist movement was mainly related to the rise of a 'communist threat', which was then equated with atheism and immorality (Çalık, 1995, p. 155). In this survey, a large majority (81.5 percent) of the *ülkücüs* claimed that the fear of communism had strongly influenced their decision to join the *ülkücü* movement. The extreme reactionary character of the followers of the MHP implies that they came from the traditional areas of Turkey which had been undergoing dramatic changes. Furthermore, most of the participants stated that the masculine discourse of the party and the manly image of Türkeş positively affected their opinion about the party (Çalık, 1995, p. 156).

The petty bourgeois, the unemployed, the young and the male social base is not a feature that is specific to MHP; other fascist parties and movements have similar supporters. Many scholars mention this feature of fascistic movements as crucial in their specific analyses. For example, in his essay on the French *Front National*, Christopher Flood states that 'polling more strongly men than women, the FN gets its most substantial support from owners of small business, self-employed artisans and other traders, clerical workers, manual workers and unemployed' (1998, p. 25). Although there is a difference to the FN, Wolin states that the social basis of fascism is composed of those he refers to as the potential 'losers of the modernisation process' (1998, p. 59). The followers of fascist parties tend to support patriarchal and traditional values. As a result of its masculine-based ideology, like other fascist movements[5] the social base of the MHP is mainly

---

[5] In the German neo-fascist case, Kagedan states that the 'German *Bundesverfassungsschutz* (Office for the Protection of the Constitution) statistics published in 1994 characterize the militant right extremist category as consisting overwhelmingly of males (96 percent male vs. 4 percent female)' (Kagedan, 1997, p. 117).

Turkish Ultra-nationalism in Germany 115

composed of males. In a survey on the 1999 elections, it is claimed that 75 percent of all voters of the MHP were male and almost half of the first-time voters voted for the MHP (Erdem, 1999).

Myths of the Nation and the State

One of the most significant characteristic features of fascism is its extreme usage of myths, symbols and rituals. In Turkish fascism, there are also some popular mythical symbols such as *Bozkurt* (Grey Wolf), *Ergenekon, Asena, Kızıl Elma* (Red Apple), and *Nizam-ı Alem* (The Order of the Universe). Most of these myths go back to the 'invented' experiences of Turks in Central Asia, which is assumed to be the original home of the Turkish 'race'. In the words of a first-generation ultra-nationalist, Zeki Velidi Togan, one can see that the Grey Wolves espouse a ultra-nationalist ideology:

> The Grey Wolf is the totem of the Turkish nation. A totem is a social symbol. The Grey Wolf totem was understood differently in various Turkish societies. In the *Göktürk* society, the ancestor is the female wolf, whereas it is the male wolf for *Uygurs*. For the Oğuz society, the male wolf is a national leader who leads society in the great wars (1996, pp. 32-9).

The leaders of MHP and pro-MHP writers have always suggested that the Grey Wolf is the national symbol of the Turks. According to Türkeş, 'being an enemy of the Grey Wolf also means being an enemy of the Turkish nation. If being against the Grey Wolf is being against the Turkish nation, then it must openly be declared and everyone has to state his position' (1995b, p. 40). In his 'Handbook of the *Ülkücülük*', Enver Yaşarbaş claims that Turks have been strongly influenced by the way of life of the grey wolves (1996, pp. 105-8). In his view, Turks adopted not only the military tactics of grey wolves, but also their family relations. In his words, 'Turks have strongly been influenced by the family structure of this animal. For example, the grey wolfe lives together with his child until its death. So do Turks. On the other hand, Christians who eat pig meat and are influenced by the features of this animal expel their children when they are eighteen' (1996, p. 107).

In ultra-nationalist mythology, while *Asena* is the female wolf that is the mother of *Göktürks*, a Turkish clan (Togan, 1996, p. 35), *Ergenekon* is the heaven that is striven for by the Central Asian Turks (Çay, 1998, p. 77). Like these myths, the myth *Red Apple* derives from the experiences of Central Asian Turks.

> An old Central Asian Turkish clan was defeated by an enemy clan. The commander of the enemy clan was living in a silk tent that had a golden red apple on the top. Turks plotted to capture that tent and determined this aim as the ideal of the clan. After this ideal had been achieved, Turks pursued other ideals. [...] So, the ideal of the red apple is a target which Turks want to achieve (Yaşarbaş, 1996, p. 108).

116   *Transnational Social Spaces*

For many MHP nationalists, gaining political power is the Red Apple of Turkish people. Following the party's electoral success in 1999, a pro-MHP columnist declared that '*Ergenekon* is the place of salvation and the Red Apple tent of the Turks. In the elections of April 18th, Grey Wolves reached Ergenekon again' (Önkibar, 1999). While the above-mentioned myths originated from Central Asian Turks, the Nizam-ı Alem derives from religious ideas. In the view of ultra-nationalists, 'following the domination of the Holy Koran and the implementation of its principles throughout the world, happiness will be spread all over the world. The idea of Nizam-ı Alem must be the ideal of all *ülkücüs'* (Yaşarbaş, 1996, p. 112). As we can infer from these examples, all these ideals and myths depend on imperial feelings and racist visions.

In fascist discourse, the state and the nation are assumed to be a totality, combining all the elements of the society in one whole. Furthermore, fascist movements or parties view themselves as the real representatives of the nation. As a consequence of this view, the devotion of the nationalists to the greatness and protection of the nation is seen as a natural duty. Such a vision is also adopted by the MHP. In his defence at the MHP trial following the 1980 coup, Mehmet Doğan, the vice president of the party, declared that 'a property owner seeks peace and quiet, integrity and fraternity within the boundaries of his property. Since we regard ourselves as the real owner of this property of the Turkish nation, we are against all sorts of terror and separatism. This is our natural mission' (1993, p. 26) However, following the coup of September 12, 1980, the situation of the 'real owner of this property of the Turkish nation' was not so favourable. Like other fascist movements, *ülkücülük* mainly legitimised the unfortunate situation of its militants through the discourse of the man in the street, on which I shall focus in the following section.

Mobilising Masses through the Discourse of the 'Man in the Street'

Without mass support, racism remains a version of ultra-nationalism. However, one of the typical features of fascism is its strong appeal and the mobilisation of the masses. Fascist movements invoke images of a native, just and honest authority instead of the existing authority, which they accuse of being immoral, hypocritical and alien to the society. Using this image of a just authority, it provokes and organises the 'blind hatred' of the lower, subordinated masses, and in this way attracts the 'man in the street'. However, fascism always puts limits and at the same time reins this 'man in the street' in, and never allows the complete demonstration of the energy of its supporters (Bora, 1995a, p. 78). This 'man in the street' is praised for his deficient, weak and oppressed position but is not encouraged into practising any form of political activity that might change this situation.

This term 'man in the street' is used by Wilhelm Reich in a psychoanalysis of the fascistic personality (1980). According to him, fascism attracts the 'man in the street' by stressing his weaknesses. It does not challenge or discuss the conditions that give rise to this weakness; instead it normalises and naturalises the man in the street's position. The ordinary man remains small and weak. Furthermore, his individuality is absorbed into the state or nation, which is pictured as a huge and sacred organism. In this sense, on the one hand, he becomes part of a great community, while on the other, he becomes even smaller than before vis-à-vis the state and the nation. Particularly following the people's disappointment over the state's oppression of the idealist militants after the military take-over on September 12, 1980, there emerged a fruitful discourse on the Grey Wolves as 'little men' who were arrested and punished by the state they revered. They were seen by the Grey Wolves as the real sons of the Turkish state and nation; but, as the image went, the father slapped the son when the son was trying to kiss his hands.[6]

Especially in the 1980s, many idealists directly attacked the existing Turkish state. In these years, many novels and memoirs expressing the harsh treatment and torture by the military regime were published. Remzi Çayır, an *ülkücü* militant, states that the harsh treatment of the *ülkücü* community by the Turkish state began even before the 1980 coup.

> We are tortured, crushed while we want to serve. There is no state. People are continuously dying. Our community, whose parents are Muslims, has been used as a tool (Çayır, 1987, p. 132).[7]

This disappointment and friction with the state however, did not lead the *ülkücü* community to a radical questioning of state authority. The exaltation of the man in the street by equating him with the state was the dominant solution to the paradoxical relation between the *ülkücüs'* and the state. In Çayır's novel, when the *ülkücüs* in prison are talking, one of them declares:

> The state and we are not distinct. We know that the state is the identical to our existence. Nation is state; state is nation. One cannot exist without the other. The founder of the state is the nation. And we are the nation (1987, p. 286).

The words of Beşir Ayvazoğlu, an ultra-nationalist writer, are a good example of the exaltation of the oppressed man in the street after the 'unjust behaviour' of the regime and state towards them on September 12, 1980. He idealises and mystifies disappointed idealists in such a way:

---

[6] For more information about the disappointment and contradictory feelings of idealist writers after the 1980 coup d'etat, see Bora, 1994, pp. 101-46).

[7] There are other novels and memoirs that narrate how the *ülkücüs* were misjudged by the military regime (Çayır, 1987b; Mete, 1990; Durak, 1987).

118   *Transnational Social Spaces*

> They were all pure, young men. They were not just lovers of the country but rather melancholic lovers of their country. If you could persuade them that they are the enemies of the Turks and Turkishness, they would defy even the mountains. At last, they were beaten by the State for which they had fought. It was natural, the state could both love and beat; both its kindness and unjust treatment were right. They (the Grey Wolves) were crushed, they were oppressed, and they were despised. Despite these facts, if the state were to appoint them to a duty, they would forget everything and devote themselves to that duty again [...]. (1998, p. 182).

Clearly, Ayvazoğlu exalts the oppressed *ülkücüs* because of their weak position and their blind devotion to the state. While the *ülkücü* masses are seen as an active part of politics, it is implied that the energy of the man in the steet little men must be reined in for the sake of the state. As the words of Ayvazoğlu imply, if the state and the dominant bloc could persuade the *ülkücüs* that it were necessary for the fate of the state and the nation, they would even deny themselves. In this sense, an idea of the homogeneous interests of the state and the nation lead *ülkücüs* to identify themselves with the state and the dominant ideologies.

Leadership Cult

Fascist parties lack organicity between the upper cadres and their power base. In other words, there exists a gap or a wedge between the cultivated fascism of the leadership and the pure reactionary radicalism of the base (Bora, 1994, p. 46). Whilst fascist parties seek to activate the blind hatred and reactionary feelings of the lower classes, they have to restrain the activities of these members since they need to have relate organically with the upper classes, too. One of the most distinguishing features of fascist parties is their strict, hierarchical organisational structure. In Turkish public opinion or imagination, the MHP also has a tough, strong image. Moreover, in various speeches made by its leader and other members of the MHP, we can find an exaltation of, and even an obsession with, military discipline. The trinity of leader, organisation and doctrine is a famous formula of the party. In Türkeş's words:

> A political party, first of all, is a large organisation. We call it the leader-organisation-doctrine. We must acquire discipline and maturity, as required by the formula (1995c, p. 196).

In the analysis of Can and Bora, the real nature of the leader-organisation-doctrine corresponds to the trinity of '*devlet-ocak-dergah*'.[8]

---

[8] '*Devlet-Ocak-Dergah*' is also the name of their book about the *ülkücü* movement. *Devlet*: the State, the Supreme Being or the leader; *Ocak*: local headquarters of the idealist youth where they organize; *Dergah*: building or place where a dervish group meets and receives the doctrine.

Turkish Ultra-nationalism in Germany 119

It may be argued that no fascist party is immune to the problem of inorganicity because of the contradictory interests of the leadership and the rank and file.[9] In their proto-fascist periods, German and Italian fascism also faced the problem of dealing with a heterogeneous power base. In both historical cases, during the stabilisation process of their fascist regimes, there were bloody confrontations.[10] Leadership cult is one solution, even the necessary solution, for the congenital inorganicity of fascist parties. In the 'Handbook of the *Ülkücü*', Enver Yaşarbaş describes the *ülkücü* leader:

> Whatever the number of the members in his control, a leader must be in contact with a relatively small group personally, intensively and regularly. He should trust only this small group in order to realise his intentions (Yaşarbaş, 1996, p. 76).

In fact, hierarchical relations between the leader and the rest exist in all fascist parties, not just in the MHP.[11] At its 1969 congress, the party accepted a new regulation, which was to enlarge the authority of Türkeş over the organisation and institutionalise a strict hierarchical structure within the party. MHP members and *ülkücüs* define Türkeş as a charismatic leader. In their view, 'in the *ülkücü* movement, the devotion and faithfulness to Başbuğ Alparslan Türkeş, who is our natural leader, derives from his militaristic background and nationalist spirit and consciousness' (Yaşarbaş, 1996, p. 85). Türkeş also likens relations within the party to a military structure and sees himself as the commander of the *ülkücüs*. He claims that he is the only founder and paragon of idealism. As with other fascist parties, the MHP mainly relies on repression, military discipline and fear. As a result, leaving fascist parties is much more difficult than leaving other parties. The words (or the order) of Türkeş exemplify and reveal how and why it is a problem to leave the party:

> Shoot anyone who turns his back on the cause. Shoot me if I turn my back on the cause (quoted in Parlar, 1996, p. 297).

In fascist parties, the leaders have their special titles. For instance, Türkeş was identified as '*Başbuğ*' (leader); the new leader of the party, Devlet Bahçeli, is now called '*İlteber Devlet*' (Chief of the state) (MHP, 1999, p. 16). Furthermore, the inorganicity between the party basis and the leadership still exists. The

---

[9] As Nicos Poulantzas puts it, poor peasants and rural and new petty bourgeoisie were victims of fascist regimes (1980, p. 266).

[10] Poulantzas states that fascism eliminates its power bases in the stabilization period by using force (1980, pp. 66-7).

[11] Neocleous points out the commonality between the leadership cult of a fascist party and religious understanding. When he analyses the Italian case, he states that 'the leadership cult [...] assumes the air of religious devotion - the fascist leader being analogous to the Pope in the Catholic Church - and expulsion from public life the equivalent of excommunication' (1987, p. 15).

120 *Transnational Social Spaces*

members of the party believe that decisions about the future of the party totally depend on Bahçeli. The words of a pro-MHP writer about the future orientations of the party after the elections of April 18, 1998 prove this fact:

> What will the MHP do after this success? Only the new leader of the MHP and *ülkücü* movement, Dr. Devlet BAHÇELİ,[12] and no one else, can decide about this (Kaplan, 1999, p. 60).

Turkish Ultra-Nationalism outside the Nation-State: The Construction of the Ülkücü Transnational Space

In the late 1960s and especially in the 1970s, the population of Turkish people in Germany increased sharply. While the earlier Turkish newcomers were primarily workers, after this first influx the increase in the Turkish immigrants was largely due to family integration. After Germany terminated its guestworker programme in 1973, despite those who returned to Turkey, the population of Turks in Germany increased, mainly owing to family integration and births. When Turkish immigrants decided to live in Germany longer than they (and the German authorities) had initially anticipated, it became clear that the Turks' immigration to Germany was not only an economic but also a social phenomenon.

The dramatic change in the number and the composition of Turkish immigrants has created a new social phenomenon in German society, with specific features. First, Turks make up the largest group of immigrants in Germany. Another factor that distinguishes the Turkish case from that of other immigrants concerns the relation between immigrants and their homeland. Prior to its dissolution, the Yugoslavian government worked closely with Yugoslav organisations in Germany. Therefore, as Jürgen Fijalkowski states, 'the Yugoslavs operated a rather uniform but highly effective self-help system through the so-called Yugoslav Clubs, of which there were about 350 in the early 1980s' (1994, p. 27). Although Italians were less rigid and more diverse than Yugoslavs, they also had rather unified organisations. Most Italian societies were represented by one of four organisations: AGLI (the Catholic Association of Italian Workers), FILEF (a supporter organisation of the Italian Communist Party), FAIEG (the Christian Union of Parent and Family Associations) and CTIM (an organisation that co-operates with the Italian neo-fascist party) (Fijalkowski, 1994, p. 127). In the early 1980s, the number of Italian societies in Germany was around 200, including sports clubs (Thraenhardt, 1989, p. 10).

On the other hand, the Turkish state was not as interested in the social conditions of Turkish immigrants in Germany. One important factor in the structural discrimination employed by the German state was the unequal nature of the contracts between Turkey and Germany. The Turkish side was weaker and not

---

[12] The capital letters exist in the original text.

concerned with imposing certain rights, such as family integration, for its citizens (Okyayüz, 1999, p. 37). In various speeches and writings of Turkish immigrants, one can find a good deal of reproachful criticism of the Turkish state. As an example, Tatar writes that 'it is impossible to say that our governments up to now have been interested in our problems. They have considered us only as providers of foreign currency' (Tatar, 1994, p. 14). Another ultra-nationalist writer blames not only Germans but also the Turkish state for the 'assimilation' of third-generation Turks in Germany:

> Germans, who protect their own culture in every place they have emigrated to and who are proud of this situation, aim at weakening the Turkish ties of the third generation by employing their existing cultural policies. Moreover, our own state has been passive against these policies and could not intervene in the developments concerning this issue (Aytemiz, 1992, p. 23).

Starting in the mid 1960s, one can distinguish three kinds of Turkish right-wing organisations in Germany. The first kind of organisation were the ultra-nationalist Turkish organisations such as *Türkische Kulturvereine* (Turkish Cultural Clubs), *Türkische Gemeinschaften* (Turkish Communities), *Türkische Zentren* (Turkish Centres), and *Nationalsozialistische Arbeitervereinigungen* (National Socialist Worker Associations) (Özcan, 1992, p. 176). In the 1970s, *MHP-Ausländerorganisationen* (MHP-Foreign organisations) and the *Föderation Türkisch-Demokratischer Idealisten-Vereine in Europa* (Federation of European Democratic Idealist Associations) were founded in Germany. The second sort of right-wing Turkish organisations are Orthodox-Islamist organisations such as *Kultur-und-Solidaritäts-Vereine* (Culture and Solidarity Associations), *Islamische Zentren* (Islamic Centres), *Vereinigung der Dienste islamischer Gemeinden* (The Union of the Services of Islamic Communities) and *Verein des Koran-Kurses* (Association of Koran Courses). The *Milli Görüş* movement contacted and controlled most of the Islamist movements in Germany. Apart from the *Süleymanlı* and *Nurculuk* movements, almost all of the Islamist associations have been under the control of this movement. A third kind of right-wing Turkish organisation were the conservative-liberal organisations. Since 1977, the *Freiheitliche deutsche-türkische Freundschaftsgesellschaft* (Free German and Turkish Friendship Society) has become the most important representative of conservative and liberal Turks.

Generally, when the influence of the MHP widens in Turkey, the influence of the *ülkücü* movement in Germany increases proportionately. Following the 1980 military coup in Turkey, the party was shut down. Similarly, the *ülkücü* movement in Germany was relatively inactive during the 1980s. However, the number of *ülkücü* organisations in Germany rose sharply in the 1990s, when the MHP in Turkey also underwent a revival. These matching developments in both countries suggest the importance of correlated dynamics, which helped stimulate their renewed popularity.

122   *Transnational Social Spaces*

In this section, I shall focus on the intensity and extensity of the transnational relations between *ülkücü* organisations in Turkey and in Germany. The extensity of transnational relations refers to their location and physical sphere of influence, the actors included and the fields covered. However, for a broader comprehension, one should also take into account the intensity of transnational relations, that is, the density of ties and speed of transactions (Faist, 2000, p. 5). In order to cover both dimensions, I will scrutinize to what degree there are informational, organisational and personal exchanges between Turkey and Germany. Although it is to be expected that the *ülkücüs* in Germany have been materially conditioned by the German nation-state sphere, these transnational exchanges between Turkish and German *ülkücüs* shape the nature of *ülkücüs* in Germany and sometimes may challenge the party policies of the *ülkücüs* in Germany. Focusing on these transnational exchanges may be helpful in understanding some underlying factors that affect *ülkücülük* in Germany.

Ideas

As a political ideology, *Ülkücülük* has a set of views on society and politics. Although these views are not always immune to contradiction, one may characterise them as ultra-nationalist, authoritarian and fascist. And it seems that these ideas flow from Turkey to Germany. First of all, in *Ülkü Ocakları* one can read ultra-nationalist newspapers coming from Turkey. Some conservative, ultra-nationalist newspapers like *Türkiye* and *Tercüman*, however, have special editions for Europe. In these newspapers, one can find many news items about the activities of *Ülkü Ocakları* in Germany. Secondly, in *Ülkü Ocakları* people watch Turkish channels, including those with ultra-nationalist tendencies. *Ülkü Ocakları* that I have visited also have cafés, in which young people can eat or drink or play billiards and other games. Here one can also watch television. During my visits, Turkish channels were always running. Especially during the football matches of Turkish teams, the young come together and watch TV. Many old *ülkücüs* and officers that I interviewed made reference to the weak Turkish of the young members as one of the biggest problems. Therefore they try to prevent, sometimes even to forbid, the German language at the *Ülkü Ocakları*. The *ülkücüs* never watch German channels in these *Ocaks*. Although such an affinity to the Turkish-language mass media is not limited to *ülkücüs*,[13] such an exclusive use seems to be a peculiar of theirs.

Another instrument for the transmission of ideas is books printed in Turkey. In both of the *Ocaks* there are often bookshelves, and one can in fact also buy the books. Most of these books come from Turkey and almost none of them are about

---

[13] In recent years, Turkish language mass media spread so vastly that the Berlin Commissioner for Immigrant Affairs 'spoke of the dangers of the "3 Ts": eased access to Turkish language television, cheaper costs in telecommunication and long-distance travel' (Faist, 2000, p. 14).

the problems of Turkish people in Germany. The majority of books include the views or speeches of Türkeş or other *ülkücü* leaders on Turkish society from an ultra-nationalist point of view. Another substantial section of the library consists of religious books that explain the religious rules or recount the lives of religious figures. There are also many books that focus on the great *heroes* of Turkish history and on mythical stories about Turks.

Throughout the history of *ülkücüs* in Germany, we can witness an intensive transmission of ideas from Turkey. Throughout the transformations that took place in Turkey, the prevailing discourse of the 'man in the street' and ultra-nationalism has been maintained within Germany. *Ülkücü* organisations in Germany also organise educational programmes. In these programmes, although there are specific lectures about the situation of Turkish people in Germany, most of them have more or less the same content as their counterparts in Turkey. Furthermore, most of the lecturers come from Turkey. For example, in a three-day intensive workshop in Wuppertal, the main subjects of the lectures were Turkish history, Islam, the organisation of the party, and the problems of Turkish youngsters in Germany.[14] The Vice-President of the party and some deputies and teachers from Turkey participated in this workshop. In 2000, an education centre in France opened for all the *ülkücüs* in Europe. This school is just another version of the party school in Ankara (Tekin, 2000, p. 94).

> The main target of these seminars is to explain national and spiritual issues to young people who live in Europe.

1. The Grey Wolf as the national symbol of the Turkish nation.
2. The nine Lights (Part 1) of Alparslan Türkeş' Nationalism, Idealism, Morality, Village-orientation, Solidarism.
3. East Turkistan (Slave Turkish State).
4. The nine Lights (Part 2) Scientific orientation, Freedom and Personalisation, Development and Populism, Industry and or Technological orientation.
5. Çanakkale Victory.
6. 4th April, Black Day (death of the leader).
7. 3rd May 1944, Turkists Day.
8. 29th May 1453, The Conquering of İstanbul.
9. The Geo-Political Importance of Turkey.
10. Freedom to East Turkistan.
11. Victory Month: August.
12. The campaign against the *Ülkücü* Movement in the military coup of September 12th 1980.
13. Our soul Kerkük (Although this city was in the National Pact, today it is outside of the Turkish boundary).
14. In memorial of Kemal Atatürk.

---

[14] http://www.ergenekon.de/faaliyet.htm.

124   *Transnational Social Spaces*

  15. Religious Conversation discourse.[15]

As is evident, all of the items are related to issues totally remote from the problems of Turkish youth in Germany. Most of the themes concern symbols, myths or glories of Turkish history, which provide the background for an ultra-nationalist identity for young *ülkücü* in Germany.

Organisational Sources

Between 1975 and 1977, the MHP was able to establish its foreign organisations. Then in the summer of 1977 the MHP had to disband its foreign organisations owing to a decision by the Turkish Constitutional Court that prohibited Turkish political parties from organising activities abroad. This shows that events taking place within the Turkish state by all means affect the nature of *ülkücü* transnational space. Shortly after the decision of the Turkish constitutional court, the party constituted other kinds of organisations in Europe, like *Türk Ocağı* (Turkish Hearths), *Ülkücü Derneği* (Idealist Clubs), *Büyük Ülkü Derneği* (Greater Ideal Club). On the 17th and 18th of June 1978, the MHP established the Federation of Democratic Turkish Idealist Associations in Europe (ADÜTDF).

Many believe that the real importance of *ülkücü* organisations for the party comes from its financial contributions to the 'movement'. According to Pekmezci and Büyükyıldız, Turgut Özal[16] attempted to influence *Ülkü Ocakları* in Germany because of its financial power (1999, p. 19). Although Özal tried to capture these *Ülkü Ocakları* by gaining an important place in the organisations, he did not succeed. It is extremely difficult to establish how much money the German *ülkücüs* actually transfer to Turkey. Nevertheless, it is quite clear that such remittances are not very regular. The amount of the financial remittances depends mainly on the commitment of the members in Germany, which varies according to the political situation in Turkey and in Germany.

In recent times, even the *ülkücüs* themselves have complained about their image as a financial guarantor of their Turkish counterpart. The *ülkücüs* I interviewed stressed that there has been a large drop in the amoung of funding transferred from Germany to Turkey. The first explanation for this is the situation of the MHP in Turkey. After its unexpected success in 1999, the MHP became part of the coalition government. During this period, there were large financial contributions from *ülkücüs* in Germany to the party. Due to its relatively passive performance in the government, however, it lost many members not only in Turkey but also in Germany. Especially after the big disappointment in the recent elections

---

[15] See http://www.ulkuOcağı-augsburg.de/SEMINERLER.htm for the below mentioned list.

[16] Turgut Özal was the 8th president of Turkey and Prime Minister between 1983 and 1990. His Motherland Party (ANAP) was composed of four political tendencies including ultra-nationalist Turkism, conservative Islamism, liberalism and social democracy.

in 2002, the party is now no longer represented in parliament, which has also contributed to a decline in the interest of the *ülkücü* organisations in Germany.

There is however, another reason why there is a decrease in financial payments from Germany to Turkey. This is the dramatic change in the sociological situation of Turkish people in Germany. The young people, having grown up in Germany, have little knowledge of the real political and social situation in Turkey. Although they still conceive of themselves as Turks, their imagination and expectation of Turkey is different from that of the people living in Turkey. Also the older people, who grew up in Turkey but live in Germany, have chosen Germany as the focal point of their life. Since the late 1980s, Turkish organisations in Germany have been campaigning for the right to German citizenship. *Ülkücü* organisations have also emphasised that Turkish people in Germany must concentrate on their problems in Germany, and not on Turkish politics. The Turkish organisations in Germany are aware that Turkish people in Germany are becoming less and less interested in Turkish politics.

In 1986, the *ülkücü* organisation in Germany split off from the mother organisation in Turkey because of an argument between the leader in Turkey and the chairman of the German organisation. After this split, Musa Serdar Çelebi, who was the head of the organisation in Germany, founded a new organisation called the European-Turkish Islam Union (ATİB). According to the General Secretary of the ATİB, Mahmut Aşkar,

> this split was a result of the members' experiences in Germany: [...] We had our own difficulties and aims here in Germany. The organisation that is located in Germany had to be active here. [...] All of our all endeavours are aimed at the problems of our people who live here. We do not have any other concerns.[17]

A further split in the organisation of the MHP in Germany took place in 1994. But this time the cause was the break-up of the party in Turkey. A small part of the MHP split off under the leadership of Muhsin Yazıcıoğlu and set up a new party called Grand Unity Party (BBP). After this division in Turkey, a few of the organisations in Germany also splintered off and set up a new organisation called Nizam-ı Alem Ocakları. BBP and its organisation in Germany, Nizam-ı Alem, are more emphatically Islamic than the MHP. Unlike the ATİB case, this split originated in Turkey and did not arise out of a change in the situation of Turkish people in Germany. On the other hand, it would also be wrong to believe that the *ülkücü* organisations that are not affiliated to the ATİB have totally Turkey-orientated policies. Although they have organic relations with political parties in Turkey, the officers are aware of the new expectations and orientations of Turkish people in Germany. One functionary of Nizam-ı Alem stated:

---

[17] From my interview with him on June 27, 2003.

126 *Transnational Social Spaces*

> Now, our aim is to save the Turkish youth in Germany. We have no other aim. We are not in a position to help Turkey. We can not even solve our own problems [...]. The transfer of funds to Turkey is over. The Turks did not see the realities in the 1990s, but in the 2000s. If those resources had been spent in Germany, we would now be in a much better situation.[18]

Almost all *Ülkü Ocakları* in Germany have mosques, and these mosques are quite substantial elements of their organisational resources. For the *ülkücüs*, functioning both as a mosque association and a political organisation has two advantages: first, such a policy is more appropriate to German legal procedures. It is more practical and legitimate to present themselves as a religious group rather than a political organisation holding Turkish nationalist views. Secondly, the appeal to religious Turks is an advantage. Some old people explain that they visit an *ülkücü* mosque although they are not *ülkücü*. The location of the *ülkücü* mosque might be more convenient than that of other mosques. However, the situation of the mosques is not immune to the internal debate of the *ülkücüs*. Some officers and members of ATİB, Nizam-ı Alem und the *Türk Federasyon* say that in order to attract young people, they need to transcend the 'mosque mentality' and create places for games or cafés for the young people.

Sending Envoys

Beginning as early as the 1970s, the MHP foreign representatives were active in Holland, Denmark, Belgium, France, Switzerland, Austria and Germany. From the beginning, Germany has always been the centre of the European organisation of the party. Türkeş visited Germany in 1970 and participated in the General Conferences of the party there (Türkeş, 1998, p. 222). In late December 1975, the MHP European General Assembly (*Europarat*) was established by the party. At the opening plenary it was clearly emphasised that

> The European MHP organisation functions under the leadership of the party and its chairmen and its scope of work should be organised and controlled by them (quoted in Aslan and Bozay, 1975, p. 177).

There is another dimension of sending representatives from Turkey to Germany. Especially after the 1980 coup, although most of the Turkish refugees were left-wing, there were also some *ülkücüs* who escaped from the military regime in Turkey. After 1980, *Ülkü Ocaklari* in Germany was a shelter for many *ülkücü* militants.[19] Ozan Arif, the most celebrated folkloric poet (*ozan*) of *ülkücüs*,

---

[18] From my interview with him on July 6, 2003.

[19] An *ülkücü* militant describes his experience like this: ‚When I came to Europe, I had lots of problems. First, I went to Germany. I had no job, no German language, and no idea about the life in Germany. My friends who lived in Germany tried to help me financially and

was also a refugee and wrote many poems about the situation of such people. Some of his poems represent the clichéd *gurbet* discourse: *Acı Gurbet* [Sore out of Homeland] (1995, pp. 245-6), *Almanya Adresim* [Germany, My Address] (1995, pp. 249-51), *Almanya Yarası* [The Wound of Germany] (1995, p. 256), *Gurbette Ölürsem* [When I Die away from my Homeland] (1995, pp. 274-5). The *Ülkü Ocağı* in Bad Oeynhausen[20] edited a book called *12 Eylül ve Ülkücüler* [12th September and *Ülkücüs*] containing recollections of the *ülkücü* militants, who were tortured by the military regime after the coup (Bahadır, n.d.).

Besides this extraordinary situation after the military take-over, there have been other influxes of people from Turkey because of their political, religious or educational activities. In particular, certain important political positions within the ultra-nationalist movement were assigned to persons from Turkey. Like other Turkish organisations with mosques, the *ülkücü* organisations have invited *imams* from Turkey. Teachers (especially of Turkish language and history) are also invited by the *ülkücü* organisations of various towns. The guests often stay in Germany for a long time and sometimes decide to settle there.

Another occasion for sending representatives is when guests are invited from Turkey for specific activities only. Among other activities, each of the *ülkücü* organisations in Germany (Türk Federation, Nizam-ı Alem and ATİB) holds an annual general meeting. In 2003, the *Türk Federasyon* organised its 24th annual conference with more than 20,000 participants. As in earlier years, there were also many guests from Turkey, including the leader of the party, Devlet Bahçeli. The party leader of the BBP, Muhsin Yazıcıoğlu, and other important politicians of that party attended the annual general meeting of Nizam-ı Alem. At this conference, with almost 2,000 participants, different politicians from Turkey made speeches about political developments in Turkey from an ultra-nationalist point of view. Yazıcıoğlu's speech took more than two hours. At the ATİB's annual general meeting, attended by more than 2,000, there was no party leader from Turkey, because the ATİB is not affiliated to a party in Turkey. The officers of the ATİB emphasised this point again and again. On the other hand, the founder of the ATİB, Musa Serdar Çelebi, was a special guest and his aura likened that of a political leader. Furthermore, Çelebi is now the vice-president of the BBP in Turkey. Another vice-president of the BBP, Eyüp Aşık, was a guest both at the conference of Nizam-ı Alem and of the ATİB. In this sense, the ATİB is indirectly related to the BBP. On the other hand, the ATİB tries to invite politicians from different parties, mainly conservative and liberal. They even invited a social democratic politician from Turkey, who did not attend, however. Another difference is the appearance of some local German politicians from different political parties,

---

spiritually. But this was not enough. Especially after the military coup, with the increasing number of *ülkücüs* who escaped from Turkey, the situation was getting worse. I was trying to live with the help and to sleep on the carpet of the *Ülkü Ocakları*' (in Kırcı, 2002, p. 132).

[20] This *Ülkü Ocağı* is named after Mustafa Pehlivanoğlu, who was hanged by the military regime *after* 1980.

128   *Transnational Social Spaces*

including the *SPD, CDU* and *Die Grünen* at the ATİB conferences. At all the annual general meetings of these three *ülkücü* organisations, besides politicians, one can see many other guests such as musicians, artists, and local singers from Turkey.

Not only at annual conferences, but also at other events, it is usual to see guests from Turkey. At a Ramadan gathering that I visited, there were two rows of guests seated at the front. The most important guests sat in the first row; these were functionaries of *Ülkü Ocakları* in Germany and from Turkey. Sponsors, who financially support the meetings, sat in the second row. These are generally the owners of small businesses in Germany. At this traditional Ramadan gathering, there was also a deputy president and some other guests from Turkey. In his speech, the deputy explained that he had travelled for weeks in Europe in order to strengthen relations between the European movement and that of Turkey. He mainly talked about the problems of the people in Turkey. The participation of top-ranking Turkish MHP politicians is quite common at such gatherings. The other participants were composed of ordinary families, and altogether the gathering looked more like a wedding-party than a political meeting.

Revealing Characteristics of Ülkücülük in Germany

Followers of the MHP

Like most Turkish people in Germany, *ülkücüs* are composed of the lower section of the working class in Germany. Some writers label Turkish immigrants as an underclass (Horrocks and Kolansky, 1996, p. xxiv). Although the term underclass has some insightful points that explain their situation, the fact that Turkish immigrants still play quite an important role in the economic life of Germany implies the limitation of this concept. If they work for the production of material life, then the term underclass ignores their role in the economy by implying that they are outside of the existing system. In this sense, it is better to consider Turkish immigrants as members of the lower working class in Germany. Their distinguishing features are their direct relation to and dependence on the state, and their limited political and civil rights.

Their limited legal, political and civil rights in a liberal democratic country is legitimised by institutional racism. Although much of their situation contradicts the rules of liberal democratic discourse, their belonging to another nation or ethnicity provides a justification for this contradictory situation. In other words, their lack of rights is legitimised by taking them as an exceptional case that cannot be evaluated with the normal liberal laws. Because this exceptional situation within German legal, political and economic life is legitimised by their belonging to another ethnicity, ideologies that rely on the concept of ethnicity become more attractive than others for immigrants in the host country. Therefore, among immigrants, reactionary and nationalist ideologies have considerable scope in which they can take effect.

Ultra-nationalism offers a simple answer for young people who feel discriminated or repressed in everyday life because of their ethnicity. One of the young *ülkücü* men explains why he supports the Grey Wolves:

> They give me a feeling that I can be proud of being Turkish. Turkish people need this feeling more than ever (quoted in Heitmeyer, 1997, p. 21).

Especially after incendiary attacks against Turks in Solingen and Mölln in the early 1990s, the perception of *ülkücülük* changed in the eyes of many young Turkish people. These attacks by the German extreme right against Turks strengthened the Turkish extreme right, as its responses to these attacks appeared to be natural and proper to some youths. One *ülkücü* officer explains the attraction of their organisations to Turkish youth after this event:

> Until the Solingen fire attack, Turkish youths did not pay much attention to *ülkücülük* or to nationalism. I do not know how they felt after this event, maybe they felt like the victims of an attacker, maybe they bore a psychological burden [...]. I know some people who had no interest in Islam or in being Turkish. Beforehand, I was always trying to explain our cause to them and to invite them to join our organisation. Youths who had never come to our Ocaks came to me after the Solingen event. Then they had great respect for me as the head of *ülkücüs*, they asked me about the organisation, about the Grey Wolves, and about Turkish nationalism. [...].[21]

Some *Ülkücü* youths explained to me how influential the Solingen fire attack was in shaping their identity. One young *ülkücü* describes the Solingen and Mölln events as a trauma and a shock for him:

> I began to hate Germans. After this event, I really hated Germans. I did all kinds of things to show that I am different from them. I hung out a Turkish flag, I spoke only Turkish. I am a Turk, and I speak Turkish.[22]

A dominant feature of the ultra-nationalist ideology is its male-based or masculine structure. The role of women among *ülkücüs* in Germany does not seem very different to that in Turkey. All of the committee leaders of the organisations are male in the *Ocaks* and one can only come into contact with men there. It is unthinkable for a woman to sit, drink or play a game in the cafe of the *Ocak* like a man. A young *ülkücü* officer explained that his endeavour to integrate girls in the *Ocaks* was unsuccessful because of the moral concerns of older *ülkücü* officers. In

---

[21] My interview with him on May 22, 2003.

[22] My interview with him on June 6, 2003.

130 *Transnational Social Spaces*

another case, a theatre workshop was cancelled because girls were performing with boys.

However, some *ülkü Ocakları* have women's branches. On one *ülkücü* web site, an *ülkücü* women's branch is presented as follows:

> *Ülkü-han* is the name of an *Ülkücü* women's branch. They organise fairs, boat trips, and sewing courses. Furthermore, they help organise entertainment and quizzes for our children. *Ülkü-Han* seeks to maintain our customs and traditions in this very country where neighbourly visits, tea hours and eating together do not exist.[23]

As is evident, although women are sometimes a part of the organisations, they have no political role. As in Turkey, the main role of women for *ülkücüs* is that of raising children and cultivating customs and traditions. Furthermore, in Germany, as in Turkey, males support *ülkücü* ideology more than women. In a survey taken of Turkish youth, it was found that while 35.4 percent of men supported *ülkücülük*, just 19.8 percent of women believed that the Grey Wolves represent them. (Heitmeyer, 1997, p. 139) If we compare these figures with those of another reactionary ideology, we can see the difference: the most influential Islamic organisation, Milli Görüş (National View), has the support of 22.9 percent of men and 19.7 percent of women (Heitmeyer, 1997, p. 141). On the other hand, a director of a branch of the *Türk Federasyon* says that:

> Suddenly, we could not pay our rent. [...] It was difficult to obtain donations. We established a women's branch, and immediately everything began to run smoothly again (Tekin, 2000, p. 90).

These words may be seen as a motivation for increasing the role of women in the *ülkücüs* organisations.

Young people support ultra-nationalist ideologies to a greater degree than older people. This also seems to hold true for *ülkücüs* in Germany. Both the MHP and Türk Federasyon attach special importance to attracting and organising Turkish youths in Germany. For example, Şefkat Çetin, the Vice-President of the party, declares that:

> The most useful generation for our country is the third one. We constituted the necessary infra-structure for organising this generation. In each association, youth branches have been created (quoted in Tekin, 2000, p. 98).

One of the most salient features of *ülkücü* youth is their refusal to mix with German youth to a greater extent than any other youth section of Turkish organisations in Germany. For example, Heitmeyer's survey indicates that while

---

[23] http://www.ergenekon.de/ulkuhan.htm.

Turkish Ultra-nationalism in Germany   131

39.2 percent of Grey Wolves spend their spare time with Turkish people only, 24.1 percent of Islamists spend their spare time with Turks only (1997, p. 165).

According to Paul Geiersbach's observation of an *ülkücü* social event, ⅔ of the participants were aged between 14 and 25 (1990, p, 183). There were also a number of female participants. My observation at different *ülkücüs* meetings was similar. Although young males were dominant at the meetings, there was also a degree of female participation.[24] On the other hand, *ülkücü* women do not visit the *Ocaks*. This can be seen as evidence that women may participate in the activities at a social level, but not at a political level.

Myth of Nation and State

As in Turkey, several icons that are attributed to Turkish mythology are still widely used by *ülkücüs* in Germany. As an indicator of this tendency, wearing a grey wolf, the crescent and the Turkish flag are common among Turkish nationalists.[25] Furthermore, a brief examination of the names of *ülkücü* websites in Germany reveals their reverence for pan-Turkist, ultra-nationalist and mythological figures such as the Grey Wolf, Ötüken, and Ergenakon. Such mythical elements from Turkish history give the *ülkücü* youth a basis for their ultra-nationalist identity that emphasises their distinction from German people. Although such an emphasis on the myths of their country of origin does not always mean indifference to the political life of the host country, it makes it difficult to struggle for equal rights in Germany. Many *ülkücü* organisations consider themselves as a natural lobby for Turkey. The observations of the *ülkücü* journalist, Arslan Tekin, underscore this point:

> The MHP has an extremely dynamic and conscious power that follows the permanence of the state. The biggest lobby in Europe is *ülkücüs*. They are very well organised and they (have) succeeded in gathering thousands or ten thousands of members. The *Türk Federasyon* does what the Turkish state cannot do. Turkish associations function as a natural lobby (2000, p. 88).

This tendency to act as a lobby is also related to a change in the policies of the Turkish state. Recently, the Turkish state has begun to consider Turkish people in Germany as a lobby group (Kaya, 2000, p. 60). However, we should not think that the *ülkücü* movement always acts in the service of the Turkish state. Several events have shown that the leadership of the party is not prepared to remain simply an instrument of the state. For instance, when the Turkish ambassador in Paris

---

[24] On the other hand, in the meetings of the ATİB, the number of young people was less in proportion to the Türk Federation and Nizam-ı Alem. A prominent officer of the ATİB admits that their biggest problem is the lack of interest among young people.
[25] Compare Kaya, 2000, p. 142.

132 *Transnational Social Spaces*

proposed a demonstration to commemorate the Armenian genocide in 1915, the MHP refused this proposal. Şefkat Çetin, Vice-President of the party, declared:

> We refused this proposal. No one can manipulate us. We will not be a service element (quoted in Tekin, 2000, p. 101).

A prominent officer of the *Türk Federasyon* who I interviewed labelled the behaviour of the Turkish state a 'remote control mentality'.

As I mentioned earlier, in 1986 the *ülkücü* organisation in Germany was split into two organisations. The chairman of the organisation at that time, Musa Serdar Çelebi, established a new organisation called the Europe Turkish Islamic Unity (ATİB). As one can gather from the name of this new organisation, it has more religious overtones than does the mainstream *ülkücü* organisation in Germany. In fact, such an Islamisation process of the *ülkücüs* in Germany was directly related to the developments in Turkey. Such a process was also experienced in Turkey. Following the 1980 coup, the party was banned by the military regime and most of the high-level leaders of the party were imprisoned. The harsh treatment of the *ülkücü* movement by the Turkish state was a real shock for the rank and file of the MHP. This is in fact understandable when one takes into account the unconditional respect and love of the *ülkücüs* towards the Turkish state. Following this 'shock', many of the *ülkücüs* tended to adopt more Islamic, critical views instead of statist and nationalist views. During the prohibition of the party in Turkey in the 1980s, the activities of the Grey Wolves were also very quiet and subdued.

During the 1980s, relations between *ülkücüs* and the Turkish state were quite difficult. At that time, open contact between Turkish officers and *ülkücüs* was not easy. The policy of the Turkish state against *ülkücüs* was hostile and aloof. In his observation of an *ülkücü* social event in the 1980s, Geiersbach notes that a high-ranking Turkish officer sent his greetings but did not disclose his name (1990, p. 184). However, during the 1990s, relations between the Turkish state and the *ülkücüs* were more cordial. The participation of Turkish officers in such organisations became normal in the 1990s. The main reason was the rise of the Kurdish movement in Turkey. In contrast to Turkey, Kurdish people could openly maintain their identity and politics in Germany. They have been at much greater liberty than in Turkey. Under such conditions there emerged more space for the role and function of *ülkücüs* in Europe as Turkish nationalist groups working against Kurdish nationalism. In some German cities and towns, *ülkücüs* even control certain streets (Aslan and Bozay, 1997, p. 185).

Discourse of the Man in the Street to Mobilise the Masses

While *ülkücü* organisations can sometimes organise huge demonstrations in Germany, these are not for their own rights but for the political interests of the Turkish state. The natural lobby mentality is symptom of an important feature of

Turkish Ultra-nationalism in Germany   133

ultra-nationalism: mobilising the masses through the discourse of the man in the street. The leader of the MHP, Bahçeli, declared for example that

> Ankara should see this power. Turks in Europe are very important for Turkey from the economical, political and cultural point of view (quoted in Tekin, 2000, p. 96).

Such a one-sided perception neglects the substantial issues of Turkish immigrants living in Germany. Officers of the MHP in Turkey mainly emphasise the interests of the Turkish State. From the *ülkücü* point of view, this is a contradiction, since the interests of the Turkish state and those of *ülkücüs* are one and the same. When the Turkish state becomes stronger, they believe that they will also become stronger.

Since the early 1970s, Turkish ultra-nationalists in Germany have become more active in their struggle against Turkish socialist groups and movements. This kind of anti-communist politics of the Turkish ülkücüs was also pursued by the *ülkücüs* in Turkey. A brochure published by the Berlin *Türk Ocağı* declares the following:

> Do not fight against each other but against foreigners. [...] You have no home except where your flag is flying. Since this home is your everything, you have to love it. Protecting home with foreign doctrines which imitate other nations is not a dream but treason [...]. Everything you do, your entire struggle should be for Turkishness and for Anatolia [...]. (quoted in Feyizoğlu, 2000, p. 550).

European *ülkücüs* and *Ülkü Ocakları* are especially important for the MHP leadership in Turkey. They are, in a sense, a reserve of organisational resources, in terms of both finance and manpower. Of course, one of the most important political aspects of the *ülkücüs* in terms of manpower for the MHP is their right to vote in Turkey. Like other political parties, the party tries to mobilise its rank and file in times of elections in Turkey, as most of the *ülkücüs* are citizens of Turkey in Germany. An extreme form of the significance of *ülkücüs* in terms of manpower was the co-operation of some young *ülkücü* with the secret service of Turkey. Haluk Kırcı, an *ülkücü* militant, who worked with the Turkish secret service against Kurdish nationalists and Turkish left-wing activists, recounts their co-operation with some young *ülkücüs* from Germany. In his memoirs, he writes that his superior officer found several young people from *ülkücü* organisations in Europe within a space of two weeks. His superior articulated the readiness of the young nationalists in Germany for violent action against opponents:

> I was often abroad. I have met so many agitated and patriotic young people there who would immediately come and fight in the mountains if I invited them (Kırcı, 2002, p. 22).

134   *Transnational Social Spaces*

According to an *ülkücü* journalist, Arslan Tekin, there were two differences between the situation of *ülkücüs* in Germany and their fellow-members in Turkey: First, they were in *gurbet* (away from home) and second, there were many *ülkücüs* who had to flee following the 1980 coup (2000, p. 85). From this perspective, Germany is not a territory where they chose to live but a necessary place of exile. They are in *gurbet*, they are excluded, exploited and marginalized and this is their fate. Since it is widely believed that exclusion and marginalisation is quite normal in *gurbet* conditions for *ülkücüs*, their answer to these conditions is not to struggle for equal rights but instead to initiate a self-ethnicisation process. However, this *gurbet* psychology is shared by all *ülkücüs*. Young members of the organisation in particular have a tendency, and also the opportunity, to see Germany and Turkey differently than their parents. Although they emphasise their Turkish identity, many of them are well aware that Germany is their new home territory. A young *ülkücü* tries to overcome this paradox between home and living location as follows:

> Although Germany is not my home, it is of course my living location. [...] I have no plans to move back to Turkey. What makes Germany what it is for me is the existence of Turkish people here. This situation leads to a new phenomenon: 'European Turkishness'. It is very important for me. That also means there is a great difference between the Turkishness in Turkey and in Germany. [...] It is nothing special to be a Turk in Turkey. [...] But here in Germany it is something special to be a Turk.[26]

Leadership Cult and Strict Hierarchy

The leadership of the MHP has always been sensitive about the European *ülkücü* organisations. In the MHP, there are only two organisations that are directly under the control of the party leader. The first is the *Ülkü Ocakları*, the informal youth organisation of the party, and the second are the European *ülkücü* organisations. The leadership cadres of German-Turkish *ülkücü* organisations are composed of appointees of the MHP. For the most part, these people are sent by the party directly from Turkey. As in Turkey, *ülkücü* organisations in Germany have a very strict, hierarchical structure. All *ülkücü* associations in Europe are organised under the umbrella of a federation in the respective country in which they were founded. Furthermore, there are plans to combine all of these in one confederation.

Alparslan Türkeş, the founder of the MHP, is a cult figure for *ülkücü* people both in Turkey and Germany. A large number of them hang the portrait of Türkeş in their offices, and even, like in Augsburg,[27] give his name to their *ülkücü* hearths. In many ordinary news articles, one can see the exaltation of the leader of the MHP:

---

[26] My interview with him on June 22, 2003.

[27] http://www.ulkuOcağı-augsburg.de.

Young *ülkücü* promise to preserve and glorify everything that comes from the legacy of leader Alparslan Türkeş. They say that their aim is to make young Turkish people dependent on their culture, religion and history and to maintain Turkish identity in Europe.[28]

Ülkücüs in Germany behave like part of the grass roots of the MHP in Turkey. Therefore, their attitude about changes or new developments in the party is no less important than that of *ülkücüs* in Turkey. For example, just after his election as president of the party, Bahçeli visited Europe in order to gain support. He and the higher functionaries of the party joined the 20th Conference of the *Türk Federasyon*.

As in Turkey the internal structure of *ülkücü* organisations in Germany are authoritarian and militaristic. The *ülkücü* writer Tekin praises the organisational features of *Türk Federasyon* using militaristic terminology:

> *Ülkücüs* are the most dynamic section of Turkish elements in Europe. No other institution can compete with them in terms of authority, logistics and organisation (2000, p. 87).

However, the officers of the organisations and older *ülkücü* militants are not happy with the relatively liberal behaviour of the young members of the organisations. They believe that they have forgotten Turkish customs, practices and habits because of the German educational system. One chairman of an *ülkücü* association in a German city explains the new situation nostalgically and regretfully:

> Unfortunately, we have no more military discipline. In former times the members stood up when the chairman came into the room. Nowadays, we cannot teach our young members such rules, because they grow up too liberally here. In former days we called back at gunpoint the people who attempted to leave the organisation. Now, we are trying to find different ways of attracting the young people just one day a week to the organisation.[29]

Conclusion

The parallelism of dominant discourse, elements and strategy of *ülkücüs* in Germany and in Turkey is a sign of the strong organisational and ideological unity between the movements in the two countries. Although the *ülkücü* ideology in Turkey (the original one) cannot totally determine the German form, *ülkücüs* in Germany depend on their fellows in Turkey more than any other ideology since

---

[28] http://www.turkfederasyon.com/bulten/Ocak2001/html/teskilat.html.
[29] My interview with him on July 8, 2003.

136 *Transnational Social Spaces*

this ideology requires a strict and rigid organisational structure. The administrative cadres of *ülkücü* organisations in Germany are directly assigned by the MHP leadership and European *ülkücü* organisations depend directly on the party's leader.

Ideology is not only a set of beliefs, ideas or notions. It is also embedded in the production, reproduction and legitimation of social relations in a given society. From this point of view, the *ülkücü* Turkishness in Germany and in Turkey have, of course, quite distinct tendencies and natures. As time passes, there seems to be a divergence between the discourse of German *ülkücüs* and the discourse of Turkish *ülkücüs*. However, this divergence does not imply a serious rupture between the German *ülkücülük* from the Turkish one. Certainly, there is no balanced relationship between the European and the Turkish side. It is clear that the European movement is dependent on the MHP leadership in Turkey.

As a matter of fact, the strict dependence of *ülkücü* organisations in Germany on the leadership of the MHP has led many *ülkücü* German Turks to deal primarily with Turkey-centred questions. For an ultra-nationalist ideology, the existence of a specific nation-state is an indispensable and distinguishing aspect. For other ideologies such as Islamism, liberalism and socialism, in contrast, living in another nation-state is not an ontological obstacle to supporting their ideology. For the ultra-nationalist ideology, living in another nation-state has more decisive effects than other ideologies. This strict relation between them differentiates German-Turkish *ülkücüs* from other German Turks. Since its ideological formation is Turkey-centred, reactionary and authoritarian, *ülkücü* ideology has made a very limited contribution to the equal rights campaign of immigrants in Germany.

On the other hand, like other German Turks, German-Turkish *ülkücüs* are quite resolved to live on a long-term basis or even permanently in Germany. Although politically they concentrate on building a Turkish lobby in Germany or in Europe in order to defend the interests of Turkey, sociologically, they are becoming more and more a part of the material, cultural and social life in German society. In that sense, they are becoming increasingly alienated from the agenda of their counterparts in Turkey. Most of them are aware of their peculiar problems and opportunities in the German social formation and therefore they try to find new ways of overcoming the tension between their imagined home and their real living location by finding identities such as European Turkishness, or by emphasising the distinctiveness of being a Turk away from home.

References

Ağaoğulları, Mehmet Ali. (1987), 'The Ultranationalist Right', in Irwin Cemil Schick and E. Ahmet Tonak (eds.), *Turkey in Transition: New Perspectives*, Oxford University Press, New York.

Aslan, Fikret and Bozay, Kemal (1997), Grauer Wolf Heult Wieder, Unrast, Münster.

Turkish Ultra-nationalism in Germany 137

Atsız, Nihal (1999-05-14), 'Soğukkanlı, Vakur ve Vazifeşinas', in Dilek Zaptçıoğlu, 'Asenanın Kızları-3', in *Yeni Yüzyıl.*

Aytemiz, A., (1992), *Batı Avrupa Türkleri: Almanya'da 30. Yıl*, Avrupa Türk-İslam Birliği Yayınları, Frankfurt am Main.

Ayvazoğlu, Beşir (March-April 1998), 'Ah! O eski ülkücüler', in *Türkiye Günlüğü.*

Bahadır, Muhammed (n.d.), *12 Eylül ve Ülkücüler*, Şehit Mustafa Pehlivanlıoğlu Türk Kültür Ülkü Ocağı, Bad Oeynhausen.

von Beyme, Klaus (ed.) (1988), 'Right wing Extremism in Post-War Europe', in *Right Wing Extremism in Post-War Europe*, K.B. Frank Cass, London.

Bora, Tanıl (1994), *Devlet, Ocak, Dergah*, İletişim yayınları, İstanbul.

Bora, Tanıl (1995), '"Sıradan Faşizm": Yurttan Sesler', in *Birikim.*

Bora, Tanıl (May 1999), 'Zifiri Karanlık Seçimleri', in *Birikim.*

Çalık, Mustafa (1995), *MHP Hareketi*, Cedit Neşriyat, İstanbul.

Çay, Abdülhaluk (1988), *Türk Ergenekon Bayramı: Nevruz*, Türk Kültürünü Araştırma Yayınları, Ankara.

Çayır, Remzi (1987), *Onlar Diridirler*, Ocak yayınları, Ankara.

Darendelioğlu, İlhan (1968), *Türkiye'de Milliyetçilik Hareketleri*, Toker Yayınları, İstanbul.

Doğan, Mehmet (1993), *Savunma*, Ocak yayınları, Ankara.

Donat, Yavuz (1997-04-08), 'Başbuğ'dan Sonra', *Milliyet.*

Durak, Yılma (1987), *Mamak Mektupları*, Ocak Yayınları, Ankara.

Dural, Baran (1992), *Milliyetçiliğe Farklı Bir Bakış ve Turan İdealinin Doğuşu*, Kamer yayınları, İstanbul.

Erdem, Tarhan (1999-04-20), 'Seçim Sonuçları', in *Radikal.*

Faist, Thomas (2000), 'The Border-Crossing Expansion of Spaces: Common Questions, Concepts and Topics', in Institute for Intercultural and International Studies (INIIS) (ed.), *German-Turkish Summer Institute Working Papers No. 1/2000*, University of Bremen, Bremen.

Feyizoğlu, Turan (2000), *Fırtınalı Yıllarda Ülkücü Hareket*, Ozan Yayınları, İstanbul.

Fijalkowski, Jürgen (1994), 'Conditions of Ethnic-Mobilisation: The German Case', in John Rex and Betrice Dury (eds.), *Ethnic Mobilisation in a Multi-Cultural Europe*, Aldershot, Avebury.

Flood, Christopher (1998), 'Organising Fear and Indignation', in Richard Golsan (ed.), *Fascism Return: Scandal, Revision, and Ideology since 1980*, University of Nebraska Press, Lincoln and London.

Geiersbach, Paul (1990), *Gott auch in der Fremde Dienen: Ein Türkenghetto in Deutschland*, Mink Verlag, Berlin, Vol. 2.

Golsan, Richard (ed.) (1998), 'Introduction', in *Return of Fascism: Scandal, Revision, and Ideology since 1980*, University of Nebraska Press, Lincoln and London.

Gramsci, Antonio (1994), 'The Two Fascisms', in *Pre-Prison Writings*, Cambridge University Press, Cambridge.

Gür, Metin (1993), *Türkisch-islamische Vereinigungen in der Bundesrepublik Deutschland*, Brandes & Apsel, Frankfurt am Main.

Heitmeyer, Wilhelm, Müller, Joachim and Schröder, Helmut (1997), *Verlockender Fundamentalismus. Türkische Jugendliche in Deutschland*, Suhrkamp Verlag, Frankfurt am Main.

Horrocks, Eva and Kolansky, David (1996), *Turkish Culture in German Society*, Berghahn Books, Oxford and New York.

Kagedan, Ian (ed.) (1997), 'Contemporary Right Wing Extremism in Germany. In Aurel Braun and Stephen Scheinberg Search of Definition', *The Extreme Right: Freedom and Security at Risk*, Westview Press, Oxford.

138   *Transnational Social Spaces*

Kaplan, M., (July 1999), '18 Nisan 99 Seçim Sonuçları Üzerine Bir Tahlil Denemesi', in *Ülkü Ocakları Dergisi*.

Kaya, Ayhan (2000), *Berlin'deki Küçük İstanbul: Diyasporada Kimliğin Oluşumu*, Büke yayınları, İstanbul.

Kaya, Ayhan (Fall 1999), 'Türk Diyasporasında Etnik Stratejiler ve "Çok-KÜLT-ürlülük" ideolojisi', in *Toplum ve Bilim*.

Kılıçarslan, Ayten (1992), *Batı Avrupa Türkleri: Almanya'da 30. Yıl*, Avrupa Türk-İslam Birliği Yayınları, Frankfurt am Main.

Kırcı, Haluk (2002), *Zor Zamanda Kurt Duruşu*, Burak Yayınları, İstanbul.

Küçük, Abdurrahman (1999), 'İslam ve Türk Milliyetçiliği', in *MHP Siyaset Okulu- Eğitim Serisi 3*, Tutibay yayınları, Ankara.

Laçiner, Ömer (ed.) (1978/1979), 'Maraş'tan Sonra', in *Birikim*, Vol. December 1978/ January 1979, special issues.

Laçiner, Ömer (May 1978), 'Malatya Olayı-Türkiye'deki Faşist Hareketin Yapısı ve Gelişimi', in *Birikim*.

Landau, Jacob (1974), *Radical Politics in Modern Turkey*, E.J. Brill, Leiden.

Landau, Jacob (1981), *Pan-Turkism in Turkey*, Hurst publication, London.

Mete, Ömer Lütfi (1990), *Çığlığın Ardı Çığlık*, Yeni Düşünce Yayınları, Ankara.

Miles, Robert (1987), *Capitalism and Unfree Labour: Anomaly or Necessity?*, Tavistock, London and New York.

Neocleous, Mark (1997), *Fascism*, Open University Press, Birmingham.

Nuhoğlu Soysal, Yasemin (1994), *Limits of Citizenship; Migrants and Post-national Membership in Europe*, The University of Chicago Press, Chicago and London.

Okyayuz, Mehmet (1999), *Federal Almanya'nın Yabancılar Politikası*, Doruk yayınları, Ankara.

Ozan Arif (1995), *Bir Devrin Destanı*, Hamle yayınları, İstanbul.

Önkibar, Sebahattin (1999-04-20), „Politika Günlüğü", *Türkiye*.

Özcan, Ertekin (1992), *Türkische Immigrantenorganisationen Bundesrepublik Deutschland*, Hitit Verlag, Berlin.

Parlar, Suat (1996), *Osmanlıdan Günümüze Gizli Devlet*, Spartaküs yayınları, İstanbul.

Pekmezci, Necdet and Büyükyıldız, Nurşen (1999), *Ülkücüler: Öteki Devletin Şehitleri*, Kaynak yayınları, İstanbul.

Poulantzas, Nicos (1980), *Faşizm ve Diktatörlük*, Birikim yayınları, İstanbul.

Radtke, Franz Olaf (1993) Multikulturalismus-Ein Gegengift gegen Ausländerfeindlichkeit und Rassismus? In (Ed.) Manfred Hessler, Zwischen Nationalstaat und Multikultureller Gesellschaft, Berlin: Hitit.

Reich, Wilhelm (1970), *The Mass Psychology of Fascism*, Simon & Schuster, New York.

Soytemiz, İsmail (1989), 'Türkiye'de Sivil Faşist Hareketin Askeri Stratejisi', in Murat Belge (ed.), *Sosyalizm ve Toplumsal Mücadeleler Ansiklopedesi*, İletişim yayınları, İstanbul, pp. 2338-9.

Tatar, E., (1994), 'Göçmenlik Sürecimiz', in Işın Greiner (ed.) *Bizim Almanya: 'Yabancılar Sorunu' Üzerine Merhaba Gazetesinden Derleme*, Merhaba yayınları, Ulm.

Tekin, Arslan (2000), *Devlet Bahçeli ve Milliyetçi Hareket Partisi*, Tütibay yayınları, Ankara.

Thraenhardt, D. (1989), 'Patterns of Organization among Different Ethnic Minorities', in *New German Critique*, Ithaca, Vol. 46.

Togan, Zeki Velidi (1995), 'Bozkurt Efsanesi', in Cemal Anadol and Alparslan Türkeş, *MHP ve Bozkurtlar*, Kamer yayınları, İstanbul.

Türkeş, Alparslan (ed.) (1995a), 'Nazizm, Faşizm Uydurması', in *Yeni Ufuklara Doğru*, Kamer yayınları, İstanbul.

Turkish Ultra-nationalism in Germany 139

Türkeş, Alparslan (1995b), 'Bozkurt Düşmanı Olmak Türk Düşmanı Olmaktır', in Cemal Anadol and Alparslan Türkeş, *MHP ve Bozkurtlar*, Kamer yayınları, İstanbul.

Türkeş, Alparslan (1995c), 'Teşkilatli Çalışmamızın Esasları', in Cemal Anadol and Alparslan Türkeş, *MHP ve Bozkurtlar*, Kamer Yayınları, İstanbul.

Türkeş, Alparslan (1996), 'Açılış Konulması', in *MHP Parti İçi Eğitim Faaliyetleri 1.*, MHP Genel Merkezi, Ankara.

Türkeş, Alparslan (1998), *Her Türlü Emperyalizme Karşı*, Kamer Yayınları, İstanbul.

Ülkü, İrfan (1995), *12 Eylülde Ülkücüler*, Kamer Yayınları, İstanbul.

Ülkü Ocağı, http://www.ulkuOcağı-augsburg.de/SEMINERLER.htm, *Augsburg*.

Wolin, Richard (1998), 'Designer Fascism', in Richard J. Golsan (ed.), *Fascism Return: Scandal, Revision, and Ideology since 1980*, University of Nebraska Press, Lincoln and London.

Yaşarbaş, Enver (1996), *Ülkücünün El Kitabı*, Kamer yayınları, İstanbul.

PART II

ENTREPRENEURSHIP AND MANAGEMENT

Chapter 6

Transnational and Local Entrepreneurship

Cem Dişbudak

Introduction

International migration affects many countries, be they sending or receiving countries. As a rule, the developed countries are the labour receiving countries (or the countries of destination, or host countries), and the developing or underdeveloped countries are labour sending countries (or the source, or home countries). When international migration takes the form of mass migration, then it obviously has significant effects on both sending and receiving countries. The impact on the sending and receiving countries differs considerably. The most important effect of international labour migration on the receiving countries is that it covers their labour shortages, and in this sense these countries have clearly benefited from international migration (Gitmez, 1981; Salt, 1983). However, the impact of international migration on the sending countries remains quite controversial, and different schools of thought reach opposite conclusions. Since most of the early researchers concentrated upon the determinants of international migration, namely the impacts of these movements on the receiving countries and the impacts of remittances on sending countries (Lucas, 1981; Keely, 1989; Appleyard, 1989; Borjas, 1989), they could not consider the later effects of international migration on the sending countries.

At present, rapid developments in the technology of transportation and telecommunications have directed international migration studies towards the entrepreneurial activities of migrants returning to their home countries (Ghosh, 1996; Kalantaridis, 1997; Portes, 1997; Kyle, 1999; Gorter, 2000; Amassari, 2001). Studies on return migration reveal that the labour exporting countries may gain more from international migration than expected (Ghosh, 1997; Papademetriou, 1998). However, this gain does not arise automatically; usually certain conditions such as a favourable economic situation, a business-friendly environment, suitable labour market conditions, and supportive government policies are required.

One of the most remarkable waves of labour migration took place after the Second World War from various countries to the Western Europe. From the 1960s onwards, one of the countries faced with mass emigration was Turkey. Inevitably,

144   *Transnational Social Spaces*

this mass migration affected the Turkish economy, and attention at the time focussed on the remittances usually sent home by migrant workers. While the positive effect of these remittances on the balance of payments cannot be denied, there were many other effects of migration and researchers concluded that in general these effects were negative. Interest in international migration declined, however, and its long-term effects on the Turkish economy could not be investigated in detail. The most important effect of international migration in the long run is the business activities of the return migrants. Here, these entrepreneurs are called 'transnational entrepreneurs', thus distinguishing them from indigenous entrepreneurs. The activities of the transnational entrepreneurs inevitably affect the whole economy, but the most important effect can be felt more immediately in the city where these entrepreneurs set up their businesses.

This chapter concentrates mainly on the activities of transnational entrepreneurs in Çorum. This city is one of the fastest growing cities of Turkey; the city has shown unprecedented growth rates in its recent history. The increase in exports from Çorum is especially striking over the past three decades. A significant part of this economic growth is related to the activities of transnational entrepreneurs in the city. The main purpose of this chapter is to construct a general framework within which the relationship between international migration, entrepreneurship and regional economic development can be examined and understood.

Transnational entrepreneurship is inevitably related to other concepts such as globalisation, transnational social spaces, networks, and social capital. All these issues are discussed with special reference to Faist (this volume). He identifies three dimensions in these relations: extensity and intensity of exchange, the organisation of exchange, the impact and consequences of the transboundary expansion of social spaces on varied aspects, such as politics, everyday social life and entrepreneurship.

This chapter is organised as follows: the next section gives a broad outline of Çorum and discusses the recent economic development of the city. In the third section, the Turkish migration experience and its effect on the economy is discussed. The fourth section presents entrepreneurship theory, transnational entrepreneurship, and other countries' experiences. Section five introduces the activities of transnational entrepreneurs in Çorum. The final section summarises the findings.

The City of Çorum

Çorum has long been known as one of the most famous historic sites of Turkey, but the city lately also became renowned for its high economic growth rates. The city shows unprecedented growth rates between 1980 and 1995. In this period, the economic growth rate for Turkey is 71.16 percent while that of Çorum is 124.67 percent. Furthermore, the difference between the growth rates of Çorum and her neighbouring cities is much higher[1] (Eraydın, 1997). These growth rates qualify Çorum as an extremely interesting case that necessitates further scrutiny.

Çorum is in the Black Sea region, neighbouring the provinces of Amasya, Samsun, Sinop, Kastamonu, Çankırı, Kırıkkale and Yozgat. The city connects the Black Sea region with East Anatolia and the capital of Turkey, Ankara. The city covers an area of 12,820 km^2, which corresponds to approximately 1.6 percent of the country. It has 13 districts, these are Alaca, Bayat, Boğazkale, Dodurga, İskilip, Kargı, Laçin, Mecitözü, Oğuzlar, Ortaköy, Osmancık, Sungurlu, and Uludağ; among these, the districts of Sungurlu, Alaca and İskilip appear to be significant in terms of their economy and population. The population of the city is approximately 600,000.

Çorum was the earliest settlement in Anatolia. The capital of the Hittites, Hattusas, is in Çorum. Because of its heritage, the city has many sites of touristic interest. However, the city was not able to take advantage of these places of touristic interest for a long time because the city's public relations were poor. Although there have been some improvements, the potential of the city is still not fully developed.

Economy

Çorum did not begin to gain economic strength until the 1980s; historically, it has always been an agricultural region. The accumulation of capital in the city therefore depended on this sector. Although some significant industrial activities have developed in the city, the agricultural sector is still significant at almost 70 percent of the city's economic output. The share of industry is 10 percent, and the rest is services (Tuğlu, 1998). However, if the recent economic activities continue, this picture will have changed radically within a few years. In order to better understand recent economic developments, it is necessary to examine the history of the industrial developments in the city over the past seventy years.

There were a few flourmills in the city in the 1930s. The industrial sector did not exist in the city until 1950s. The city showed some improvements in the 1950s. In 1957, the state-owned cement factory was established and later a sugar factory was founded by the state. The remarkable success of the state-owned factories encouraged local people, and in the 1970s huge private investments were made in other areas such as the brick and tile industry. At present, this industry has the capacity to meet 25 to 30 percent of the country's demand. Until the 1980s, this sector was the leading sector in the city and it was alone in creating industrial employment. In the late 1950s, some new industrial enterprises were established. The actual turning point of the industrial sector was 1980; after this date there were

---

[1] The neighboring cities of Çorum are Çankırı, Amasya, and Yozgat. The growth rates of these cities for the period 1980-1995 are 14.2 percent, 41.79 percent and 52.36 percent respectively.

146 *Transnational Social Spaces*

high rates of economic growth in the city. It is for this reason that the city has recently become known as one of the 'Anatolian tigers'.

From 1975 to 1998 Çorum's industrial production proportionate to the production figures for the whole of Turkey increased steadily, from 0.11 percent in 1975 to 0.12 percent in 1980, 0.14 percent in 1987, 0.2 percent in 1995 and 0.3 percent in 1998. Furthermore, industrial employment in Çorum increased from 0.16 percent of national industrial employment in 1975 to 0.46 percent in 1997 (*Bölgesel Gelişme*, 2000; Büyükkılıç, Arpacıoğlu and Artar, 1990). It can be said that the region has been transformed from a completely agricultural structure to a semi-industrialised one.

This change might be explained by many factors, including state investments. In the earlier stage of development of a less developed province, it is very important to have considerable government support to build an industrial and agricultural base. This support may include direct industrial investment, infrastructural investment, and subsidies. As a second step, the government may provide incentives, but this should not distort our understanding of the development process at work. It should be remembered that economic development is a dynamic process, and endogenous factors are no less important than exogenous ones. Although there are other less developed provinces that obtained more incentives than Çorum, they did not grow as fast (see Table 6.1). During the period 1983-1997 the annual per capita average investment related to government incentives for Çorum is 29.5 million TL in constant 1997 prices, while the respective average figure for Turkey is 63.8 million TL (*Bölgesel Gelişme*, 2000). It is therefore worthwhile to look at the different factors explaining the development of Çorum.

Entrepreneurship is one of the reasons behind this fast development, if not the most important factor, since economic development is a dynamic process and that entrepreneurs are its main actors. Before discussing the role of the entrepreneurs in the economic development, in the next section, international return migration and the impact of this process on the Turkish economy are reviewed.

International Migration and the Turkish Experience

Turkey experienced a period of major social change during the 1950s, characterised by migration from rural areas to urban areas. The increased labour demand of the Western countries coincided with this movement, and the internal migration pattern turned instead to these countries. People went to Western countries without hesitation. Many believed they could soon save enough money to return to Turkey rich. Some dreamed of saving enough money so as not to have to work after returning. Others went abroad to save enough money to set up their own

Transnational and Local Entrepreneurship 147

business in their home country.[2] Almost one million people left the country with such dreams during the 1960s and 1970s. At first, most thought that migration was a temporary phenomenon and that after a period of time they would return to Turkey. While some of them returned after spending some time abroad, many settled there permanently. Today, there are over 3 million Turkish people in the Western countries and over 2.5 million of these are in Germany (Migration Newsletter, 2001).

The export of workers pleased the Turkish government because it meant the workers would send remittances home, and it eased unemployment pressures. Various governments signed bilateral agreements with the host countries in the first year of migration, but later the governments lost control over the Turkish migration process. Overall, the Turkish State has been unconcerned and generally ignorant about the migration process in the past.

The whole process was controlled by the countries requiring labour (Gitmez, 1981). They founded offices in the main cities of Turkey and imported workers according to their needs.[3] The Turkish governments seemed unconcerned, possibly because they underestimated the importance of losing so many labourers. They set their sights on the remittances and the unemployment pressures, failing to see the other possible effects of international migration.

The Impacts of the Immigration on the Turkish Economy

It is obvious that sending over a million workers abroad in the space of a decade will deeply affect an economy. There are both positive and negative effects of this event on the Turkish economy. Without denying the importance of the remittances, the majority of researchers concluded that the mass emigration did not bring the benefits to the Turkish economy that had been expected (Gitmez, 1981; Abadan-Unat, 1976). The remittances covered Turkey's trade deficit for some years and relieved the pressure that hard currency was bringing to bear on the economy. However, economists still have reasons for emphasising the negative effects of the remittances. The importance of the remittances decreased over time, but in some years the total amount of remittances is still high (see Table 6.2).

For the most part remittances have been used in unproductive ways, for instance, for consumption and construction activities; both of which create an inflationary pressure on the economy. The second effect is an increased tendency to import, which causes a problem for the balance of payments. Finally, the increased dependency on remittances reduces the capacity and willingness to improve export performance. Another impact is the dependency on remittances; a

---

[2] There are many Turkish immigrant entrepreneurs in Germany and in other Western European countries. They are not covered them in this paper because it is impossible to examine this related subject in a single paper. Pecoud (2000) can be seen for the entrepreneurial activities of the Turkish immigrant entrepreneurs in Germany.

[3] For the story of workers' recruitment, see Gitmez (1981) and Abadan-Unat (1976).

148 *Transnational Social Spaces*

regular and substantial amount of remittances may reduce the incentive to earn foreign currency.

These effects were observed in the Turkish economy to differing degrees (Gitmez, 1981; Gökdere, 1978). It is not possible to deny the positive effects of remittances but if these remittances could be used in more productive areas, their impact would be more beneficial to the Turkish economy. An example of the productive use of remittances is the setting up successful businesses by migrant workers. There are several examples of these types of efforts, such as workers' co-operatives and village development co-operatives; the number of these co-operatives reached 225 in the late 1970s (Apak, 1993). However, most of them failed for a variety of reasons and did not fulfil the purposes attributed to them.

Apak (1993) identifies several reasons for the failure of the workers' co-operatives. According to him, management problems, the wrong choice of sites, and marketing problems are possible reasons. Two important reasons have to be added to the list. The first is the overall macroeconomic conditions in Turkey and the second is the structure of the world economy. De Castro (1994) argues that a country can benefit from migrant workers if these workers set up their own enterprises.

The following section discusses the effect of entrepreneurship in general and transnational entrepreneurship in particular on economic development.

Entrepreneurship, Transnational Entrepreneurs and Economic Development

Entrepreneurship

Entrepreneurship is widely accepted as the most important factor in economic growth and development (Schumpeter, 1934; Baumol, 1968; Baumol, 1990; Kirzner, 1973). The importance of entrepreneurial activities became more apparent after the crisis of the Fordist production system, and awareness of their importance gained strength with the increasing role of *small and medium-sized enterprises* (SMEs). Hence, the governments of all countries started to pay special attention to the SMEs and their founders.

Entrepreneurs are supposed to organise production and to foster economic growth, thus they are the main agents of change. Joseph A. Schumpeter elucidated the role of entrepreneurs and entrepreneurship in a more detailed fashion, and placed entrepreneurs at the centre of his economic theory as the pivotal factor of economic development. In his well-known books, *The Theory of Economic Development* (1989) and *Capitalism, Socialism, and Democracy* (1957), he devoted tens of pages to explaining the roles of entrepreneur and entrepreneurship in economic development, and is thus the first economist who systematically constructed a consistent theory of entrepreneurship. He claimed that without entrepreneurial activity there would be no changes in an economy. Schumpeter called this simplified version of economy the 'circular flow of economy' which

Transnational and Local Entrepreneurship 149

resembles the neo-classical stationary state of economy. However, there is an important difference between the two views; in a Schumpeterian system, an economy starts off from the circular flow of economy, while in the neo-classical system, an economy remains static in the final analysis. For Schumpeter, the main importance of the entrepreneur comes from his ability to innovate, but this is not the only function of an entrepreneur. He defines the enterprise and entrepreneur as follows:

> The carrying out of new combinations we call enterprise; the individuals whose function is to carry them out we call entrepreneurs (Schumpeter, 1989, p. 74).

By carrying out new combinations, he not only means the innovative design of new products but also enumerates the other functions of entrepreneurs, and with these functions they can change and cause economic development. According to Schumpeter, the functions of entrepreneurs include the following:

1. the introduction of new goods, or goods of a new quality,
2. the introduction of new methods of production,
3. the opening of new markets,
4. the tapping of new sources such as raw materials, and finally
5. the reorganisation or restructuring of any industry (Schumpeter, 1989).

A close inspection of these functions shows us that only two of them are related to production, the remaining three functions are related to other activities. The opening of new markets and the tapping of new sources of raw materials can easily be related to the activities of the return migrants in their home countries, since their entrepreneurial activities seldom comprise the first two functions of entrepreneurs.

Casson (1998) also stresses this point. According to him, many economic activities such as creating new markets and exporting to new markets are initiated by transnational entrepreneurs. However, substantial obstacles to trade can arise when an entrepreneur acts as a mediator between two countries. The most important obstacles to trade are the problem with meeting the right people, the money, the price, and contractual compliance. These problems are solved by the entrepreneurial networks created by the transnational entrepreneurs.

The Role of the Network

In a capitalist economy, entrepreneurs are supposed to work individually: this brings competition and effectiveness. Today, however, many economists argue that entrepreneurs work better in a competitive network than as a collection of competitive individuals (Casson, 1998). A network may be defined here as a basis of trust between the two parties or the third parties, which are directly or indirectly

150 *Transnational Social Spaces*

involved in these relations. The formation of the network necessitates a high degree of trust, and thus parties are usually very cautious in this process.

The change of the economic structure of the world economy has enhanced the role of networks. Over the past three decades, as the number of SMEs world-wide has increased, relationships among these firms has been widely questioned by economists. Studies show that one of the most important factors behind the success of SMEs is the formation of networks (Butler and Hansen, 1991). However, these investigations are mainly limited to local business networks. In a global world, the formation of networks across national borders becomes increasingly important as spatial distances become less and less important.

Entrepreneurs in different countries are usually reluctant to trade with people they do not know, because small global players are sometimes not dependable. For this reason, entrepreneurs from the developed countries hesitate to do business with the entrepreneurs in developing countries. The transnational entrepreneurs solve this problem by forming networks.

Entrepreneurial networks solve many problems that an individual entrepreneur may face in business life. These problems might be transaction costs, cheating, and other social and ethical problems. The members of a network do not encounter these kinds of problems because they know and trust each other. The importance of the network increases when transactions are made between two different countries.

Transnational Entrepreneurs and Economic Development

As already mentioned above, entrepreneurs are the main driving force behind economic development; an increase in the number of entrepreneurs in a region automatically gives rise to economic growth and development. However, people often do not engage in entrepreneurial activities for many reasons. There might not be any business opportunities, there might be some opportunities but not enough capital to start up a business, or entrepreneurs simply may not know whom to work with. Governments all over the world try to overcome some of these problems by providing support schemes as well as information, but it is difficult to say whether these measures always work. The significance of transnational entrepreneurs is clearly that without having any substantial government support they become entrepreneurs in their region, producing positive externalities.

Transnational entrepreneurs have important attributes such as enough capital, skill, knowing a foreign country with friends, business and family contacts, and courage. All these qualifications make them valuable. Return migrants may modernise or enlarge a farm or start a small business, or they can help their acquaintances by applying the skills they obtained in the foreign country (Rogers, 1983). With their networks, they may change a region economically. Casson (1998) claims that the chance of migrants, in many cases, engaging in entrepreneurial activities may be higher than non-migrants because entrepreneurial ideas are usually generated on the basis of travel experiences. This seems plausible,

Transnational and Local Entrepreneurship · 151

since migrants have a better chance to see business opportunities in different countries. There are many examples of this fact in history and in today's business world.

Kalantaridis (1997) reports on the development of an important garment industry in the Greek region of Polikastro-Peonia and how the transnational entrepreneurs returning from Germany, in co-operation with their relatives at home, played an important role in this process. The transnational entrepreneurs were mostly engaged in the garment industry and they provided important assistance to the local entrepreneurs by liaising with foreign partners and markets. In addition to the firms they established, they created an important bridge between Greece and Germany.

There are examples of transnational spaces created by transnational entrepreneurs in other parts of the world. Portes (1997) indicates the activities of Dominican transnational entrepreneurs in the Dominican Republic after returning from the USA; Kyle (1999) studied the transnational entrepreneurs of Otavalo in Ecuador. All these examples relate to the recent increased trend towards globalisation. This trend has inevitably affected Turkish people in Western Europe, and many migrant workers have returned to their homeland and founded their own businesses.

Çorum is one such city where these entrepreneurs returned and established their businesses. Previous efforts in the city, combined with the activities of the transnational entrepreneurs triggered a major economic boom. This is especially clear when the volume of exports is taken into account. The next section discusses the activities of the transnational entrepreneurs and their contribution to the city and transnational spaces between Germany and Turkey.

Transnational Entrepreneurships in Çorum

This section explores the extent to which transnational entrepreneurs have affected the economy of the city, their activities before migrating and whilst in Germany, the role of savings made in Germany in founding their firms, the scale of their employment creation, and the type of work they engage in. The interviews prove how the migration process can create new entrepreneurs by enabling them to learn new skills and accumulate capital.

The transnational entrepreneurs interviewed for this study were identified through a kind of snowball system; after contacting one of them, it was easy to track down others. A semi-structured questionnaire was prepared, however, since the interviews were made face-to-face, open-ended questions were used. The interviewees were mostly co-operative, but hesitant in answering some questions, especially those concerning their income, volume of exports and tax payments. The information given was confirmed by enquiring with the local institutions and some local entrepreneurs. Hence, some of the figures presented here are at best estimates based on the information obtained from them.

152 *Transnational Social Spaces*

The Çorum case shows that sometimes a small number of entrepreneurs may have a substantial effect on the economy. There are 10 firms owned by transnational entrepreneurs in the city.[4] All of them were contacted and interviewed, and these interviews revealed that while their numbers are few, their effect on the city is considerable, as will be explained below. There is no claim that they are the exclusive impetus for the recent developments in the city, but they have played an important role in terms of increasing the export volume for the city, in particular to Germany.

All the transnational entrepreneurs interviewed are originally from Çorum, and all of them have close relatives in the city. They all stayed in Germany for a long time but they made frequent visits to Çorum and their relatives. These visits and their close ties with relatives enabled them to keep up-to-date with what was going on in the city and in Turkey. They therefore did not experience many difficulties in establishing their businesses after returning. This is a great advantage for them because besides being familiar with the city, they had enough money (capital) to set up a business, and they had contacts with relatives in Germany to sell what they produced. Their innovative ability becomes apparent here; they see Germany and the other Western Europe countries as new markets and Çorum as the new supply source. Innovative skill is the main feature of entrepreneurial activity in Schumpeterian terms.

Entrepreneurial activities encompassed the following industries; two firms were in the textile and clothing sectors, two firms in the food and beverages sector, five firms manufactured metal products, machinery and equipment. Moreover, the last firm, which is the largest, engages in several different sectors such as food and beverages, building and basic metal industries. This is a community-based enterprise, established as a workers' co-operative. This co-operative owns several firms but here it is treated as a single firm. Most of the entrepreneurs launched their businesses in the mid-1990s, except for one who founded his business in the mid-1980s. This is important because it is consistent with the view that entrepreneurship can flourish if an enabling environment exists. Moreover, the need for skilled workers can only arise if the economic situation is sustainable. The fast development in Çorum after the 1980s attracted people who had left Çorum for educational purposes. Thus, in many branches there was no lack of skilled labour in the region; and transnational entrepreneurs had no trouble finding skilled labour. With the exception of one firm, all the businesses export 10-90 percent of their products, and their main export target is naturally Germany, which is the single most important destination. Other countries include Israel, the Turkic Republics, and France, but the export figures to the latter countries are relatively low.

---

[4] There are other return migrants in the city engaging in their own businesses on a micro-scale. Their economic impacts are negligible since they either work alone or employ a few family members. Therefore, the transnational entrepreneurs who employ more than ten workers in their firms are included.

The majority of the entrepreneurs worked in Germany for long periods, and in two cases the owners of the firms still live in Germany in order to remain in close contact with their customers. The long work experience in Germany is not surprising since saving enough money for setting up a business requires time. When the firm is big, as in the case of the two firms, shareholding is inevitable: one firm is shared by five individuals and the other was established as a workers' co-operative.

The entrepreneurs interviewed did not have any formal business training except for one who attended a language school. He is an engineer and highly educated, and a very innovative person. The other entrepreneurs only had work experience and learned everything through their work experience in Germany. All of them describe themselves as unskilled before going to Germany, and they claim that they learned everything in Germany. This is an example of the well-known 'learning-by-doing' hypothesis.

Among the transnational entrepreneurs, just one of them initially went abroad as a student; all the others went to Germany as immigrant workers, and their education finished at primary level. This is quite surprising, since many studies proved that there is a high correlation between education and entrepreneurship, and this ought to be expected for return migrants as well. McCormick and Wahba (1999), for example, argue that there is a high correlation between entrepreneurship and education among Egyptian return migrants. The Çorum case is not consistent with these findings. However, most of them work with their relatives, and at least one of their relatives is a university graduate. It may be that they somehow compensate their lack of educational through their partnership with more educated relatives. Some of their success can be explained by their social capital.

One entrepreneur, the engineer, did not import the machines in his factory from Germany; all of them were produced domestically. However, he claims that he had technical assistance from his German contacts when setting up his business. The other firms imported 50-100 percent of their machines from Germany. In the case of the two firms whose owners still live in Germany, all of their machines were imported complete from Germany. One firm produces for a large enterprise in Germany while the other produces only for the domestic market. The remaining businesses produce for both domestic and foreign markets.

Those entrepreneurs producing food and beverages initially targeted the Turkish population living in Germany, but later changed this marketing strategy and targeted both Germans and Turks. Although, they sell the same product they use different brand names for different groups. This brand name differentiation contributed significantly to the increase in their sales.

The contribution of these firms to the region is important because they meanwhile employ more than four hundred people, introduced some relatively advanced technology to the region, and most importantly, they encouraged local entrepreneurs to venture into export business. All these factors are very important for a city that is newly developing. The number of jobs created may seem to be

154 *Transnational Social Spaces*

rather low, but it is a significant number considering that total employment in the manufacturing sector in Çorum is about 6,000 people. Therefore, the number of jobs created by these firms is quite significant.

The number of businesses comprises almost 10 percent of all businesses in the city if traditional firms that produce agricultural products are not counted. Moreover, most of these firms use relatively advanced technology compared to other local firms, so it can be said that these firms improve the standard of technology in the region.

The firms of the transnational entrepreneurs are export-oriented. Although their exact export volume is not known, the estimate is that it is around 15 percent to 20 percent of total exports from the city.[5] This exporting tendency stems from their familiarity with foreign countries, especially with Germany, and this familiarity provides them with a very solid network. However, our findings indicate that except for one firm, none of them have formal networking facilities; all the network activities are based exclusively on informal relations, such as friends and relatives.

Typology of the Entrepreneurs

It is argued here that entrepreneurs are the driving force of economic development, as exemplified in the economic development of Çorum. These entrepreneurs closely correspond to the Schumpeterian model. In the literature, the focus on Schumpeterian entrepreneurs is the introduction of new products. However, there are other functions of Schumpeterian entrepreneurs, such as opening up new markets and establishing new supply sources.

In the Çorum case, transnational entrepreneurs mainly fulfil the above two functions described by Schumpeter. Although local entrepreneurs had heard of Germany, they traditionally preferred to export mainly agricultural products to this market. Germany is therefore a new market for industrial products from the region. Transnational entrepreneurs have returned to Çorum and started their businesses in this region instead of in Germany. Therefore, this can be equated with finding a new market and new sources of supply.

Another point is that transnational entrepreneurs in Çorum usually prefer to engage in activities that are unknown to the region. Four of the firms manufacture completely new products, and have created enough demand for their new products. Furthermore, other firms have imitated two of the transnational firms since their activities have proven to be quite profitable.

These transnational entrepreneurs differ from Schumpeterian entrepreneurs in an important way. While Schumpeterian entrepreneurs are highly individualised, in our case 4 out of 10 businesses were established by more than one individual.

---

[5] Most of the entrepreneurs were hesitant in giving exact figures concerning their business activities, and instead provided approximate indicators. As a rule, when considering their activity, they understate their financial situation.

Transnational and Local Entrepreneurship 155

This is mainly out of financial considerations. The savings of a single person are not usually enough to set up a business, especially when one considers the lack of credit institutions in Turkey. Therefore, it is natural for people to set up a business together.

The Ties, Areas of Impacts, and Transnational Social Spaces

The relations of the transnational entrepreneurs are economic but even in business relations a high degree of mutual trust is vital. As part of a business network, the transnational entrepreneurs proved their reliability. Most of the business relations of the transnational entrepreneurs date back at least two decades, so that members of these networks know each other very well. Sometimes transactions take place without the need for official contracts because of this high level of trust. This is rarely seen in the business world, especially when transactions are made between two countries.

Transnational entrepreneurs maintain strong ties with their contacts in Germany due to business relations. Business partners frequently communicate by telephone, e-mail, and fax for regular business arrangements. Moreover, entrepreneurs often travel to Germany for face-to-face meetings. In some cases, entrepreneurs spend half of the year in Germany where they have a home. Therefore, besides the extensity, the relations are very intensive. They do not miss any fair or event that is directly related to their businesses.

These ties depend mostly on relations between the individual entrepreneurs and are to a large extent based on kinship and friendship in Germany, while relations in Turkey are based on kinship. However, it seems that religious ties are important in the case of the workers' co-operative. The manager interviewed was hesitant to confirm these religious ties but the local people claim that it is the case.

The extensity and intensity of these relations inevitably affect several areas; it is clear that involved parties are directly affected in economic terms, but there are other agents who are also affected by these relations. The most important impact of these relations can be seen on the indigenous entrepreneurs operating in Çorum. Several entrepreneurs started to export their products with help from one or more of the transnational entrepreneurs. In some cases, the local entrepreneurs imported their machines with the help of the transnational entrepreneurs. This is an important example of the enlargement of the transnational spaces created by immigrant workers.

As Faist (chapter 1, this volume) noted, transnational social spaces should be thought of as

> relatively stable, enduring and dense sets of ties reaching beyond and across the borders of sovereign states.

Therefore, it is natural to conclude that a new transnational social space has developed in Çorum.

156 *Transnational Social Spaces*

Globalisation and Transnational Entrepreneurs

In recent years, economic relations between countries have increased dramatically. There are many reasons for this development; the presence of multinational companies, the reduction in the costs of communication and transportation; still another important reason is the activities of small global players. The economic activities of these small global players increase over time. Portes (1997) calls these activities 'globalisation from below'; for him the most important part of this process is performed by transnational entrepreneurs. On the one hand, globalisation processes stimulate migration, but especially economic migration and transnational entrepreneurship. On the other hand, these developments further deepen the process in question.

The activities of the transnational entrepreneurs reinforce the globalisation process, but globalisation at the same time creates new small global players by forcing the governments of the world to liberalise commercial relations. No single government can prevent or stop this process. One of the economic implications of globalisation is the reduction of barriers to international trade. Hence, countries are forced to adopt export-oriented policies; this creates in turn, new opportunities for transnational entrepreneurs.

Martin (1991) argues that if Turkey were to implement an export-oriented policy, then return migrants would be even more successful. There is a lost of evidence for this view. As stated above, the workers' co-operatives might not have failed if the country had implemented export-oriented policies. This process is irreversible. As part of this process, the number of transnational entrepreneurs will increase all over the world as well as in Turkey, including Çorum.

Conclusions

Çorum is a city in which transnational entrepreneurs returning from Germany have established their own firms and created income and employment opportunities. Their contribution to the city cannot be denied; the numbers of firms and workers are proof of their contribution. Furthermore, since most of their products are produced for export, these activities have resulted in substantial increases in the amount of exports from the city.

Other positive effects result from the interaction between transnational entrepreneurs and other local entrepreneurs in the city. Their success in the export trade has encouraged others in the city to follow suit, and has thus indirectly affected the production structure. The exchange of information between transnational entrepreneurs and local entrepreneurs has also changed the ways new technologies are acquired. Local entrepreneurs now try to contact German firms with the help of the transnational entrepreneurs; this direct contact reduces the cost of capital goods and inputs they use in their production.

Transnational and Local Entrepreneurship 157

These economic activities of transnational entrepreneurs should be taken into account within the context of transnational social spaces. As these transnational spaces enlarge, economic and social relations are likely to improve. Immigration and return migrants, however, cannot solve all the economic problems of a country or a region. Furthermore, a country or a region can only benefit from return migration if the necessary infrastructure and institutions exist. The Çorum case shows that already existing economic activity may serve to attract entrepreneurs. Once there, however, the transnational entrepreneurs certainly have important effects on the economic and social life of the city.

158   *Transnational Social Spaces*

Appendix

**Table 6.1 1983-1997 Period: Total Government Subsidised Investment
in the Less Developed Provinces (1997 Constant Prices million TL)**

Cities	Total (Government Subsidised Investment)	Annual Average (per Capita Government Subsidised Investment)	INDEX (per Capita Government Subsidised Investment)
Afyon	95,416,501	8.6	13.5
Bilecik	403,290,109	153.2	240.0
Çorum	269,056,247	29.5	46.2
Denizli	932,076,485	82.8	129.7
Eskişehir	641,534,546	66.7	104.5
Gaziantep	2,190,311,262	144.5	226.4
Kahramanmaraş	1,895,713,808	141.3	221.4
Karaman *	80,138,435	37.2	58.4
Kayseri	722,211,848	51.0	79.7
Konya	564,722,793	21.5	33.7
Malatya	871,194,469	82.7	129.6
Uşak	161,626,470	37.1	58.1
Turkey	54,062,031,491	63.8	100.0

* Karaman became a province in 1988, therefore the data only exists after this year.

Source: Regional Development; Eighth Five-year Development Plan

Transnational and Local Entrepreneurship 159

Table 6.2 1964-1998 Workers' Remittances and Trade Balance

Years	Remittances	Trade Balance
1964	9	-126
1965	70	-108
1966	115	-228
1967	93	-162
1968	107	-268
1969	141	-264
1970	273	-360
1971	471	-494
1972	740	-678
1973	1,183	-769
1974	1,426	-2,246
1975	1,312	-3,101
1976	982	-2,912
1977	982	-3,753
1978	983	-2,081
1979	1,694	-2,554
1980	2,071	-4,603
1981	2,490	-3,864
1982	2,140	-2,628
1983	1,513	-2,990
1984	1,807	-2,942

Years	Remittances	Trade Balance
1985	1,714	-2,975
1986	1,634	-3,081
1987	2,021	-3,229
1988	1,776	-1,777
1989	3,040	-4,219
1990	3,246	-9,555
1991	2,819	-7,340
1992	3,008	-8,190
1993	2,919	-14,160
1994	2,627	-4,216
1995	3,327	-13,212
1996	3,542	-9,989
1997	3,400	-12,200
1998	3,500	-13,100

Source: State Planning Organisation: Economic and Social Indicators, 1950-1998

Transnational and Local Entrepreneurship   161

References

Abadan-Unat, N. vd (1975), *Göç ve Gelişme*, Ajans-Türk Matbaacılık, Ankara.
Apak, S. (1993), *Yurt Dışındaki İşçi Potansiyeli ve Türkiye Ekonomisi*, Cem yayınevi, İstanbul.
Appleyard, T. R. (1989), 'Migration and Development: Myths and Reality', in *International Migration Review*, Vol. 23(3), pp. 486-99.
Baumol, W. J. (1968), 'Entrepreneurship in Economic Theory', in *American Economic Review*, Vol. 58, pp. 64-71.
Baumol, W. J. (1990), 'Entrepreneurship: Productive, Unproductive, and Destructive', in *Journal of Political Economy*, Vol. 98(5), pp. 893-921.
Butler, J.E. and Hansen, G.S. (1991), 'Network evolution, entrepreneurial success and regional development', in *Entrepreneurship and Regional Development*, Vol. 3, pp. 1-16.
Bölgesel Gelişme (Regional Development) (2000), DPT yayınları, Ankara.
Casson, M. (1998), 'Entrepreneurial Networks: A Theoretical Perspective', in C. E. Nunez Sevilla (ed.), *Entrepreneurial Networks and Business Culture*, Universidad de Sevilla, Sevilla.
De Castro, V. H. (1994), 'Financial Strategies for Collecting and Employing the Savings of Portuguese Emigrants and Regional Development Policies', in *Migration and Development içinde*, OECD publications, Paris.
Eraydın, A. (1997), 'From a Locality in the Center of A Less Developed Region to a Node of Growth: The Experience of Çorum', in *yayınlanmamış makale*.
Ghosh (1996), *Migration and Development: Some Selected Issues*, http://oim.web.cl/15/arting.htm.
Gitmez, A. (1980), *Göçmen İşçilerin Dönüşü*. ODTÜ İktisadi İdari Bilimler Fakültesi Yayını, Ankara.
Gorter, C. (2000), 'Migrant Entreprenurs in East Indonesia', in *Tinbergen Institute Discussion Paper*, Vol. TI 2000-082/3.
Gökdere, A.Y. (1978), *Yabancı Ülkelere İşgücü Akımı ve Türk Ekonomisi Üzerrindeki Etkileri*, İş bankası Yayını, İstanbul.
Henderson, J. and Castells, M. (1987), *Global Restructuring and Territorial Development*, Sage Publications, Bristol.
Kirzner, I. M. (1973), *Competition and Entrepreneurship*, University of Chicago press, Chicago.
Kyle, D. (1999), 'The Ottavalo Trade Diaspora: Social Capital and Transnational Entrpreneurship', in *Ethnic and Racial Studies*, Vol. 22(2), pp. 422-47.
Martin, P.L. (1991), *The Unfinished Story: Turkish Labor Migration To Western Europe*, International Labor Office, Geneva.
McCormick, B. and Wahba, J. (2001), 'Return Migration and Entrepreneurship in Egypt', *University of Southhampton Working Paper Series*, University of Southhampton, Southhampton.
Migration Newsletter (2001), Ministry of Labor and social Security, General Directorate of External Relations and Services for Workers Abroad, Ankara, Vol. 1(3).
Özcan, G.B. (1995), *Small Firms and Local Economic Development*, Ashgate Publishing Limited, Aldershot.
Papademetriou, G. D. (1998), *Reflections on the Relationship between Migration and Development*, http://rcms.org/investigation/reflections.htm.

Pecoud, A. (2000), 'Cosmopolitanism and Business: Entrepreneurship and Idendity among German-Turks in Berlin', in *Princeton University Working Paper Series*, Princeton University Press, Princeton, Vol. WPTC-2K-05.

Portes, A. (1997), 'Globalization from Below: The Rise of Transnational Communities', in *Princeton University Working Paper Series*, Princeton University Press, Princeton, Vol. WPTC-98-01.

Portes, A., Guarnizo, Luis and Haller, William (2001), 'Transnational Entrepreneurs: The Emergence and Determinants of an Alternative form of Immigrant', in *Economic Adaptation Working Paper*, Princeton University Press, Princeton.

Rogers, R. (1983), 'Incentives to Return: Patterns of Polcies and Migrants' Responses', in Mary Kritz, Charles Keely and Silvano M. Thomasi (eds.), *Global Trends in Migration Theory and Research on International Population*, The Center for Migration Studies, New York, pp. 338-64.

Salt, J. (1983), 'International Labor Migration in Western Europe: A Geographical Review', in Mary Kritz, Charles Keely and Silvano M. Thomasi (eds.), *Global Trends in Migration Theory and Research on International Population*, The Center for Migration Studies, New York, pp. 133-57.

Schumpeter, J. A. (1957), *Capitalism, Socialism, and Democracy*, Harper, New York.

Schumpeter, J. A. (1989), *The Theory of Economic Development*, Harvard University Press, Cambridge (Mass.).

Thomas-Hope, E. (1999), 'Return Migration to Jamica and its Development Potential', in *International Migration*, Vol. 37(1), pp. 183-205.

Tuğlu, P. (1998), *Yerel Ekonomik Gelişme Raporu*, TKB Matbaası, Ankara.

Chapter 7

Intercultural Encounters:
German and Turkish Managers
in Joint Ventures

Marita Lintfert

Introduction

The continuing expansion of business mergers to joint ventures or even global players heightens the awareness for the need of efficient communication and co-operation on global markets. Nowadays, an expert clientele in the international business world is confronted with key terms such as communicative competence and intercultural competence, which are regarded as essential tools to optimise the interaction among colleagues with similar, dissimilar or totally different backgrounds. In the context of existing trans-state spaces between Turkey and Germany, the following paper outlines the perceptions and experiences of German and Turkish managers interacting in German-Turkish enterprises, subsidiaries or joint ventures in İstanbul and Ankara. The aim of this paper is to convey different points of view towards interaction in the context of business life held by Turkish and German managers working in licensed German companies on Turkish territory. Focusing on their experience articulated in narrative descriptions, the aim of this approach is to bring to light the views of Turkish and German female and male managers with regard to their perceived working experience and patterns of the quality of interaction, as well as with regard to the infrastructure, specific phenomena, patterns and ties in the context of doing business.

The empirical questions with respect to the quality of interaction between Turkish and German manager-colleagues are as follows: How do German and Turkish female and male managers in multicultural working relations conceive and identify their partners? How do Turkish managers perceive German colleagues in their host country? Are there internalised assumptions, presuppositions or prejudices in relation to the other person and, if they exist, how do Turkish managers deal with conceived prejudices towards their partners and vice versa? In addition, under what circumstances do German managers become more comfortable, more sensitive and more aware of the complexity of interaction in business with regard to dissimilar communicative patterns, unfamiliar social

164   *Transnational Social Spaces*

contexts or different cultural elements regarding their Turkish partners? Do these play a minor or rather a major role during managers' interaction at work?

The above-mentioned questions were put to an audience of eighteen managers and consultants who are working in German-Turkish enterprises, subsidiaries or German licensed companies in İstanbul or Ankara. Their points of view are regarded as personal-business-diary-material, or – as mentioned above – as narrative descriptions. Thus, the main emphasis in this paper is on the views of expatriates and indigenous staff with respect to their perceptions, experiences and actions in business life that pertain to successful or less successful interaction in local business proceedings. What will be introduced in the following are conceived relationships with German and Turkish colleagues in elite positions. There may or may not exist different norms, cultural elements, religious beliefs, and traditions. If there are elements which might interfere with smooth business proceedings, it should be assessed how far they are interrelated with linguistic, social and cultural differences.

Although the categories of gender, hierarchy and power are undoubtedly omnipresent for German and Turkish female and male managers even during their working lives, it is not the author's intention to discuss these categories before the empirical section has been dealt with. By transcribing selected excerpts from the interviews, the potential relevance of communicative, non-verbal socially or culturally bounded patterns display the manager's experience with regard to attributions, negotiations, presumptions, prejudices or prepossessions. The results of the interviews reveal their central opinions and their points of view on Turkish-German work settings and conditions.

Methodology

The methodological principles of Critical Discourse Analysis (CDA) underlie the empirical chapter in this paper. CDA claims to reveal diverse critical dimensions of the interrelation between language and culture, and explains how language and other symbolic systems work in the construction of ideologies (Erickson, 1982; Fairlough, 1989; van Dijk, 1993 and 1998). CDA is an approach in discourse analysis which aims to focus on language and discourse in cultural and social-economical contexts. It is a method which maps out the interaction between language and social structures and explains how social structures are constituted. According to van Dijk, CDA research merely describes political issues and tries to illuminate the way discourse structures confirm, legitimize, negotiate, reconstruct or challenge relations of interdependency, power or dominance in society. Van Dijk's discourse theory works as a means of studying the reproduction and functioning of ideologies, which he understands as very general and abstract mental representations. In his view, ideologies are the 'basis of social representations shared by members of a group' (van Dijk, 1998, p. 8). He defines socially shared mental representations as 'organised clusters of socially shared beliefs (knowledge, opinions, attitudes etc.) as located in social memory' (1998, p. 46). Organised clusters of socially shared beliefs should be regarded as beliefs embedded in knowledge, opinions or attitudes and shared by group members via social practices. Discourse is an instrument and medium through which one perceives and receives the world.

Turning to the business world of Turkish-German managers, one should take into consideration that communicative abilities in terms of conventions, traditions or particularities are not restricted to cultural and communicative features. Interaction between persons in elite positions and their relationships are based on hierarchical structures such as status, power and gender which determine the interface of business interaction in general. It goes without saying that German and Turkish colleagues who are involved in everyday communication and co-operation are also involved in economic, social and political hierarchies. Thus, it is an omnipresent phenomenon that groups in national, bilateral or international contexts have their characteristic hierarchical patterns. What is questionable or debatable are the points of view of the managers' perception and successively their description and articulation. Where are there manifest or latent patterns with regard to linguistic, cultural and social bonds and ties between German and Turkish business partners?

However, the selected excerpts show phenomena in shared beliefs, social ties, mutual conditions and obligations and, moreover, a de facto corporate identity in enterprises. If social ties can be defined as continuing actions of involved participants who refer to shared values and norms, it may be questionable whether deep symbolic ties exist between, for instance, a German marketing manager who works only with Turkish colleagues in a German licensed firm in İstanbul. And how deep is the interrelation of social capital in Turkish-German settings, i.e. mutual expectations, conditions and obligations of involved partners on Turkish territory? The premises of exchanging social capital can be seen in a system which is based on several mutual conditions, i.e. the guarantee of reciprocity, the ability to trust each other and the continuity of successful mutual transaction between the actors involved (cf. Faist, chapter 1, this volume). Last but not least, how representative is the model of transnational social spaces with its function of bridging social capital as a facilitating linkage for Turkish and German colleagues in leading positions? How do managers facilitate and continue interaction in Turkish-German business relations on Turkish territory within the framework of professional expectations and social inclinations such as reciprocity, solidarity, and loyalty? Symbolic ties represent imagined chains of shared beliefs, meanings, expectations, and representations. In the context of Turkish-German business relations, the relevance of symbolic ties – with a view to optimising and facilitating interaction – should be taken into consideration.

The empirical data of this paper consists of eighteen tape-recorded face-to-face interviews which lasted approximately nine hours in total. The participating female and male managers and consultants were aged roughly between 30 and 55 years. The interviews were carried out in English or German in January 2001. The

166 *Transnational Social Spaces*

names of the enterprises, subsidiaries or joint ventures will be kept anonymous. The names of the informants are indicated only by an alphabetical letter or the possessive pronoun. The protection of anonymity was assured to informants before the questionnaire was handed out. The process of finding interview partners was initiated by sending a one-page fax with information about the research interests and conditions to enterprises in İstanbul and Ankara and by attaching data about my lectureship at the Marmara University (İstanbul) in the Departments for German Economics and Informational Systems from 1996 to 2000 (see Table 7.1 for the list of informants and Table 7.2 for the questionnaire). The criteria for selecting relevant German and Turkish interview partners in leading positions were:

- a sound knowledge of spoken English and / or German,
- experience in elite positions or as a manager in a German company or subsidiary in Turkey for several years,
- an ongoing exchange and communication with colleagues with a Turkish and / or German background,
- a willingness to answer the questions as realistically as possible.

Table 7.1 Essential Data of the Informants

Title / Position / Residence in Turkey	Nationality / Sex / Age	Place / Language of the Interview
A Consultant for German Subsidiaries since 1996	German-Turk Female ~30	İstanbul German
B Senior Re-presentative since 1990	German Male ~40	İstanbul German
C General Manager brought up and Educated in the USA	Turk Male ~45	Ankara English
D Assistant to the General Manager Since 1995	American Female ~35	İstanbul English

Title / Position / Residence in Turkey	Nationality / Sex / Age	Place / Language of the Interview
E General Manager Since 1998	German-Turk n/a 36	İstanbul German
F General Manager Since 1998	Swiss n/a ~55	İstanbul German
G Managing Director Since 1996	German n/a ~45	İstanbul German
H Managing Director Since 1995	German n/a ~40	İstanbul German
I Managing Director	Turk n/a ~50	İstanbul German
J Assistant to Managing Director G Born in Germany, working in İstanbul Since 1996	Turk Female ~30	İstanbul German
K Head of Department of an Enterprise Since 1999	German Male ~35	İstanbul German
L Head of Department of a Company Since 1995	Austrian-Turk, Male 36	İstanbul German
M Product Manager Born in Turkey	Turk Male ~30	İstanbul English

Title / Position / Residence in Turkey	Nationality / Sex / Age	Place / Language of the Interview
N Consultant Since 1983	German Female ~50	İstanbul German
O General Manager Since 1996	German Yugoslavian family background Male, 30	İstanbul German
P General Manager Born in Turkey	Turk Female ~ 45	Ankara English
Q Product Manager Born in Turkey, studied in Germany	Turk Male ~45	Ankara German

Table 7.2 Questionnaire

1. When do you believe in success or failure, when do you recognise success or failure in concrete communicative encounters between Turkish and German colleagues? Where are the strong, and where the weak points while communicating? When, in your view, do Turkish-German encounters fail?
2. Under what circumstances might relations improve between Turkish and German colleagues? In other words: What are the preconditions for an agreeable work setting with a pleasant working atmosphere between them?
3. What do you have in mind when you think about the reality, the dynamics and the dimension of cultural values, social representations, and religious traditions between Turkish and German colleagues at work? What is your impression? What is your experience?
4. What effects and developments do you observe and perceive in German-Turkish transnational spaces? The term transnational spaces is used to describe the implicit and explicit interrelation and interconnections that exist between Turkish and German organisations, initiatives, enterprises, and the social, political and cultural arrangements and resources which flow back and forth.

German and Turkish Managers in Joint Ventures

Empirical Chapter

Question 1 and 2 (in the following referred to as (1) and (2))

Person *M* (1) and (2)

> I believe that German companies are far behind American companies in globalisation process. First of all, eh, our German colleagues do not speak very well English. If you want to work global, your colleagues should speak fluently English. And our colleagues are far back to this. So there is a space for improvement. Eh, we communicate in English, and we are having hard times in real communication. That's the first problem. So, the medium of communication is not very sound. Eh, secondly, the worst thing is, German people still have not learned to think locally, you know. They still think, that things are like in Germany – everywhere in the world. This is another point where they are behind the American companies and globalisation because eh, conditions are much different here than it is in the Western European countries. So that should be regarded. Therefore, sometimes we have difficulties with expressing the situations here. For instance, they think their business orderly, like it is in Germany. Another example, there, only money counts: price, that is the big difference in the Western European countries. – So, we have to express sometimes the difficulties which we are trying to reduce as much as possible, but it is improving, because they like the business in Turkey. [...] So, all in all, it includes technical knowledge, market knowledge and the way how people think, the real thinking for Turkish people, for instance, is extremely different than that of German people. They should come here and communicate with them and than see it more open. That will help. But they have many responsibilities, time consuming, duties anyway – I believe, more frequencies would solve this, and I don't say they are overconfident, but the harmful thing is introspection in mind. So if you focus on your local market then you will be successful in your local market. If you say, my local market is enough for me, okay, than no problem. But if they want to work globally, you have to change.

M's answer regarding communication is on the one hand focused on linguistic problems, i.e. translating or transferring contents into the common foreign language, which is English. On the other hand, *M* mentions several times the inability of his German colleagues, who work in Hamburg, to think in global dimensions. He expresses the need for German colleagues to get to know local systems and characterises his partners as not open enough for local settings, conditions, and circumstances. In his view, global business is productive when partners acknowledge local circumstances and conditions when interacting and co-operating in order to optimise conditions on both sides. In his argument, he indicates the status quo of his colleagues, i.e. a relatively high degree of ignorance with respect to local systems.

170 *Transnational Social Spaces*

Person *J* (1)

Kommunikation am Arbeitsplatz, also, ich kann ja nur vom Verhältnis Vorgesetzter – Mitarbeiter sprechen – ähm, ich glaube, hier ist schon direkt der Kernpunkt, wie die Kommunikation abläuft, und daran kann man schon relativ viel ableiten. Ähm, da treffen natürlich zwei verschiedene Kommunikationsformen aufeinander, und das hängt von vielen Faktoren ab: von der Ausbildung, von der eigenen Person, von der Machtposition usw., und äh, da sind zwei, eigentlich zwei unterschiedliche Denkweisen, die aufeinander treffen. Ich glaube, in der Türkei besteht ein eindeutiges Machtsystem, äh, ich habe jetzt von einem Bekannten gehört, ein Türke, also, er hat zusammengefasst: Also, wer die Macht hat, hat Recht. Äh, spiegelt sich auch hier, bei uns wieder. Ist zwar nicht mein Ansatz, aber ich kann ihn nachvollziehen und verstehen. Äh, mein Hintergrund ist eigentlich ein anderer. Äh, ich komme aus dem Marketing-Bereich, und im Marketing-Bereich ist es eher so, dass man versucht, sehr viel zu diskutieren und gemeinsam eine Lösung zu finden. Jeder hat das gleiche Recht. Jeder hat die gleiche Stimme, und, dann versucht man die beste Lösung zu finden. Den Ansatz versuche ich auch hier zu praktizieren, aber, um auf Stärken und Schwächen zu kommen, man sieht eindeutig, das ist schwierig. Es ist schwierig, so ein System des Teamgedankens umzusetzen, weil die eigentlich gewohnt sind: Wir haben ein Problem, und der Chef trifft die Entscheidung und dann machen wir das so. Es ist schwierig umzusetzen [...] Die Entscheidungsfindung ist normalerweise relativ einfach, wenn der Chef sagt: Wir machen dies, dann machen wir das. Äh, Schwäche ist natürlich die Diskussion. Da müssen die Leute sich dran gewöhnen, dass sie mitdiskutieren und auch eine Entscheidung mittragen, also, Verantwortung übernehmen, äh, wie gesagt, ist, glaube ich, nicht die Stärke. Die möchten das schon nach oben delegieren und die letztendliche Entscheidung dem Vorgesetzten überlassen. Das heißt auch – man kann direkt zur zweiten Frage kommen. Ich glaube, das funktioniert nur, wenn – ich meine, ja gut, das funktioniert überall so, nicht nur in der Türkei, wenn beide Seiten verstehen, was die andere will und warum die andere das so macht, und das sie das nachvollziehen können. Das heißt für mich, äh, ich muss nachvollziehen können, oder muss eben wissen: okay, die wollen eine klare Entscheidung haben, dann ist es für sie in Ordnung. Auf der anderen Seite müssen sie auch verstehen, warum ich gerne diskutieren möchte, warum ich, eh, ich sag es mal im konkreten Beispiel, warum ich bei einer Problemstellung frage: Wie sieht das der Vertriebsleiter, wie sieht das der Finanzleiter und wie sieht das die Marketingleiterin in dem Fall? Und äh, wenn wir dann alle zu einer Entscheidung kommen und die tragen können, ist das in Ordnung. Nur das Verständnis muss da sein, und das dauert schon etwas, bis man das mal klargemacht hat, seine eigene Position klargemacht hat, und es braucht eine gewisse Zeit, bis die Gruppe auch versteht, was man genau will und warum man das so machen möchte, weil das Ergebnis, nach meiner Meinung ein Besseres ist.

German and Turkish Managers in Joint Ventures   171

Person *J* (2)

> Kommunikation in der Türkei, untereinander – ist, glaube ich, äh, auf einer anderen Ebene, viel emotionaler, aber dadurch auch viel enger. Ich glaube die Leute sind viel enger, wenn sie Kontakt haben, viel enger zusammen als Deutsche. Äh, sehr emotional, was ich auch hier täglich erlebe. Ich kann emotionale Reaktionen manchmal nicht ganz nachvollziehen, warum die direkt so ausschlagen, die Reaktionen. In Deutschland, gut, würde man auch reagieren, aber – eher auf einer sachlichen Ebene. Also, das merkt man schon, also so ne – die Sachlichkeit, und, und, und hier diese emotionale Ebene, das ist für mich ein großer Unterschied.

The German manager *J* avoids any distinction between his colleagues and himself. He works with possessive terms like 'my group', 'my colleagues', 'we', 'they' and 'the people' and is eager to get to know how and why colleagues behave and think as they do. *J* points out certain systems, values, and habitual conventions combined with political implications at work. *J* names teamwork as a principle he is used to and tries to activate the ideas, thoughts and resources of Turkish colleagues find a common denominator. This process, if successful, influences values and may additionally be an experiment in socially and culturally bounded assumptions and patterns. *J* indicates his own and local elements of corporate culture and wants to weigh up all potential possibilities to get on with business as a German Marketing manager in İstanbul, which means finding a compromise between educational and academic concepts and distinct habitual attitudes towards authority and hierarchy.

As manager *J* articulated the strong hierarchical continuum in Turkish business relations and pointed out that he considered teamwork essential, it should be added that the internal circle of strong hierarchical structures among Turkish colleagues is encompassed by an external circle predominated by the principles of work ethics or the habitual attitudes of German partners. In terms of power relations it is this external circle which dominates and has an impact on working conditions, communication and co-operation at work. Several interviews, especially with Turkish managers and also with both consultants, address the aspect of power and inherent hierarchical structures among Turkish and German colleagues at work on Turkish territory. It seems there are at least two circles: the internal one which outlines local dispositions towards hierarchical systems, and the external one which overshadows the complex system of socio-economic and socio-political occurrences and the positions of both partners with respect to the dimension of equality and power at work on Turkish territory.

In the following excerpts, instances and negotiations of affirmative reactions are apparent. Human, social and political aspects particularly with respect to co-operation are described as well-balanced, especially regarding the constitution of social identities, social relations and perspectives towards values at work. They refer to a collection of types of systems or values such as education, politics or

172 *Transnational Social Spaces*

media, which the informants regard as occurrences of social practice. They define them as properties of working life and try to manage working relations and business interaction in combination with local social practice, i.e. approaches towards communication, co-ordination and co-operation.

Person *G* (1)

> Gutes Funktionieren am Arbeitsplatz, da würde ich keinen Unterschied machen, genau das, was ein gutes Arbeitsklima zwischen Deutschen und Deutschen ausmacht: Fairness, Offenheit, mal ein Auge zudrücken, äh, 'give and take' [...]. Und, ich glaube, dass das Arbeitsklima in der Türkei freundlicher ist, als ich das in Deutschland erlebt habe.

Person *H* (1)

> Also, die Stärke – in der Kommunikation zu Türken – und mir als Deutschem, ich gehe subjektiv von mir aus. Vielleicht machen andere Deutsche ganz andere Erfahrungen. Die Stärke, oder die Vereinfachung, liegt darin, dass ich eine Kommunikation, glaube ich, leicht beginnen kann, man kann sie leicht in Gang bringen, und kann Kontakte, auch einfache, knüpfen. Das ist eine Stärke, insbesondere für unser Geschäft – im Messebereich, was im weitesten Sinne zu den Medien gehört. Das erleichtert die Sache. Ja, die Stärke ist auch ein, ein, ein Freund – ein, ein, in erster Linie, am Anfang, ein freundliches Wesen der Menschen, hier. Ich würde mal sagen, die Stärke liegt insbesondere in der Phase: Kontaktanbahnung, äh, dort. Ja, die Schwäche in der Kommunikation – ergibt sich oft – um es mal so zu sagen, innerbetrieblich, ja, innerbetrieblich.

Person *L* (1)

> [...] global gibt es insofern keine Probleme, als die deutschen Kollegen eigentlich mit System arbeiten. Wenn es mal, vielleicht Probleme gibt, gibt es von unserer Seite zeitweise Probleme, weil man jetzt, äh, nicht die, diese, das strukturelle Arbeiten gewöhnt ist. Da kann es von der Mentalität her, weil man ein bisschen lockerer alles nimmt, des öfteren hier ein Problem, – wie man ja so weiß – wenn, dann geht es von unserer Seite aus. Von den deutschen Kollegen her, von der Arbeitsweise her, von der Kommunikation her – wenn man sagt: Ich rufe am Mittwoch an, um zehn Uhr!, wird man auch am Mittwoch (lacht) um zehn Uhr angerufen. (lacht lauter) Äh, im Geschäftsleben hängt alles von der Minute ab, von der Sekunde ab, manchmal. – Ja, und das sind jetzt die Stärken der deutschen Partner, und manchmal unsere Schwächen. Manchmal ist es auch unsere Stärke, weil wir – weil die Kollegen, die hier sind oder in der Türkei, viel flexibler sind in mancher Sicht. Das sie nicht so ganz eingeengt sind in manchen Sachen, so sehe ich das. – Wenn – also die Kommunikation, äh, die ist eigentlich nie ein Problem bei uns. Die Kommunikationssprache bei uns ist Englisch, manche Kollegen, die hier arbeiten, die machen es auch auf Deutsch, weil sie in Deutschland mal gelebt

German and Turkish Managers in Joint Ventures   173

> haben. Also, wir haben beide Sprachen: Deutsch und Englisch. Und deswegen
> fällt es uns nicht schwer, also, die Kommunikation herzustellen.

Person *L* (2)

> Ich bin der Überzeugung, dass sowieso eine super Verbindung herrscht. Die
> Kollegen, die hier in der Gruppe arbeiten, mit denen wir hier zusammen arbeiten,
> die nicht mit Deutschland oder Österreich oder Europa, äh, dort gelebt haben, die
> sagen das Gleiche, weil, von der anderen Seite kommt wirklich diese Zuneigung –
> auch, von den Deutschen Kollegen, da gibt es wirklich keine Probleme. – Ich
> meine, für eine Kommunikation ist für Türken immer die Einstellung wichtig. Ich
> meine, wenn wir jetzt die Einstellung der hier arbeitenden Kollegen nehmen, und
> die Kollegen, die in Deutschland arbeiten, da ist eine positive Einstellung da.
> Durch diese positive Einstellung ist die Kommunikation einfach viel leichter. Es
> sind keine Vorurteile gegenseitig – vorhanden. Keiner fühlt sich irgendwie besser
> als der Andere, jetzt im Gespräch oder so. Jeder fühlt sich wie ein gleicher
> Partner. – Es wird aber auch sehr viel dafür getan, weil ja, (Firmenname) an sich
> ein interkulturelles, also – im Headquarters arbeiten was-weiß-ich wie viele zig
> Nationen, und da ist schon die Atmosphäre gegeben und somit – man arbeitet ja
> mit Asien, man arbeitet mit Amerika, man arbeitet mit allen Kontinenten,
> eigentlich. – Also, diese Arroganz, die man normalerweise über Deutsche sagt,
> die spüren wir hier überhaupt nicht. Manchmal sagt man dazu, äh, so hört man es
> überall, das die Überheblichkeit da wäre, ja, jetzt, äh, des Minder – jetzt kulturell
> und wirtschaftlich steht man ja besser da und – aber das spürt man hier eigentlich
> nicht. Ich meine, wir haben ein gleiches Verhältnis. Ich meine, man lernt sich
> kennen. Das ist das Wichtigste bei (Firmenname). Wie wir hier das Office
> aufgemacht haben – jeder Angestellte, der war hier im Headquarters, hat seinen
> Counter-Partner mal kennen gelernt. Das hat sicher auch dazu beigetragen, weil,
> es gibt viele Firmen, wo man den Counter-Partner, mit dem man den ganzen Tag
> spricht (lächelt), oder über Monate kommuniziert, gar nicht kennen gelernt. Dann
> hat man so eine Vorstellung über den Counter-Partner: Und, schaut der vielleicht
> so aus oder so. (lacht) Wenn man sich einmal kennen gelernt hat, schaut das alles
> schon besser aus, mit der Kommunikation. Also, Zusammenarbeit jetzt, hier bei
> uns, funktioniert super.

What is implicitly mentioned in the excerpts cited in the passages above is
the attitude and the attempt to concentrate on working conditions and on the
partner and to focus on the willingness to find a common ground while working
together. In the following excerpt, informant *P* points out the premises for an
appropriate and adequate working atmosphere: awareness, neutrality, background
information, experience and the acknowledgement that prejudices are part of being
human. People have to perceive and categorise environmental conditions and filter
the perceived world in subcategories – this is human and cognitively necessary.
With the appropriate awareness it is not necessarily harmful to have prejudices and

174   *Transnational Social Spaces*

pictures in one's mind. They are ubiquitous. The question is, how, when and whether people have the disposition to interact with people from other communities and cultures under specific circumstances. At multi-national conferences, the common attitude in novel situations is a decisive and sensitive aspect, i.e. it is vital to focus on present contexts and not on pre-existing associations. The aspect of hierarchy and power is evident in *P*'s statement. Hierarchical structures and competition are predominant in national and transnational business relations. Nonetheless, in the German-Turkish context the relation is more delicate. As *P* points out, various constellations of hierarchy and power-positions, the systems of (re)production of inequality are evident: the prestige of Germans is high or higher than that of the Turkish partner. Thus, if the German partner may order and command or know a situation better as a matter of fact, then the Turkish colleague is seemingly in the weaker position – at least as far as the matter at hand is concerned. This can be read as an ubiquitous system of relations and as a discourse of hierarchy and power which is nationally or ethnically defined and which can be seen through various filters of perception:

Person *P* (1) and (2)

> Ich schätze sie sehr ambivalent ein. Ich kann auch sagen warum, weil es, wie ich es oft gesehen habe, gerade in einem so genannten urdeutschen office-environment, d.h. also wo, wo Leute schon lange zusammen arbeiten, wo also schon bestimmte Freundschaften bestehen, das immer sehr anfällig ist, so eine Meinung und so ein Verhältnis. Das heißt, es hängt auch viel von der Optik ab. Äh, ich soll ja ganz ehrlich sein. Sieht ein Türke so aus, wie wir uns in Deutschland den klassischen Türken vorstellen, dann ist oft die Kommunikation schlecht oder blockiert oder da ist eine Barriere. Es hängt eben oft von solchen Dingen ab. Ich merke das eben auch ganz oft, wenn bestimmte Dienstleistende ankommen, nehme wir mal an Kurierpost, wenn da also ein richtig sichtbarer Türke oder Südländer, es muss ja nicht nur ein Türke sein, es geht ja im Grunde genommen auch um die ganzen Südländer: Iraner, Araber, Marokkaner, etc., wenn so jemand reinkommt, dann ist die Haltung bei demjenigen, der die Post aufgibt, als wenn jemand wie 0815 reinkommt, den man gar nicht registriert. [...] Das heißt ambivalent, ich sehe es als ambivalent in dem Sinne, dass, äh – man kann es positiv und negativ sehen. Positiv heißt: Die werden registriert. Mehr als vielleicht so ein blonder 0815-Typ, der da einfach nur reinkommt und das Zeug abholt und wieder weg ist. Und auf der anderen Seite kann das natürlich auch ins Negative gleich umschlagen, dass die zwar registriert werden, aber da wird gesagt, das ist ein Türke, der spricht nicht so gut Deutsch, der kann das nicht so gut ausfüllen, diesen Schein, auf den kann man sich nicht verlassen. Also, es ist, es ist, die ganze Palette ist da. Es – Kommunikation unterliegt starken Schwankungen. Eben einmal geprägt durch das Äußere, durch die Sprache und dann vielleicht auch durch die Meinung desjenigen, der, der den Türken sieht. Umgekehrt: Wenn ich jetzt als Türke am Schreibtisch sitze, dann unterliegt das

auch Schwankungen, weil im Grunde genommen da auch wieder die Wahrnehmung anders ist, d.h. wenn der äh, wenn der Türke, äh, meinetwegen einem Deutschen einen Auftrag erteilt, dann hängt es auch wieder davon ab, wie er es macht: Macht er es sprachlich ganz richtig? Sagt er – die Betonung – wir erleben es ja auch oft – ich habe es gerade vorgestern Abend erlebt, in Frankfurt, im Bus: unglaublich netter türkischer Busfahrer, trifft aber den Ton in der deutschen Sprache überhaupt nicht, weil er es einfach nicht kann. Äh, das muss man ihm ja nicht zum Vorwurf machen. Aber er trifft den Ton nicht, er hat einen sehr befehlenden Ton: Komm rein, rein, im Bus! Obwohl er es unglaublich nett meint. Aber das kommt bei Leuten halt falsch an. Bei mir kam es richtig an, weil ich mehr weiß, und wir fingen auch gleich an, dann auf Türkisch zu reden. Aber, das heißt, noch einmal zusammenfassend: Es unterliegt starken Schwankungen. Wo liegen Stärken? Wo liegen Schwächen? Stärken? Da beziehe ich mich im Grunde genommen auf das, was ich gesagt habe. Die Wahrnehmung ist halt anders oder genauer: man nimmt, also, die Leute nehmen sich mehr wahr, das ist eine Stärke. Äh, die Schwäche ist, dass unter Umständen gleich Vorurteile im Raum stehen, und die eben im Laufe des Gespräches, der Kommunikation nicht sofort abgebaut werden kann. [...] Die Kommunikation am Arbeitsplatz hängt von der Kompromissbereitschaft ab, weil man sich ja – im Grunde genommen ist ein Büro wie eine WG. Das ist ein Privatraum, den man sich mit Anderen teilen muss, d.h. Kompromissbereitschaft, Toleranz, Loyalität dem Anderen gegenüber, was man selbst macht und was andere machen. Also, da würde ich das nicht so offensichtlich auf dieses Türken-Deutschen-Verhältnis beziehen. Ich versuche immer, neutral zu sehen, also, die Farbe loszuwerden, die Farbe eines Türken, die Farbe eines Franzosen, die Farbe eines Deutschen. Das passiert halt sehr oft, tagtäglich im Alltag: Wenn jemand etwas sagt, dann denkst du gleich: Aha, warum sagt er das? Woher kommt das? Warum sagt er das, was er sagt? Ich versuche im Grunde genommen, die Person neutral zu sehen, nicht als Türken, nichts als Deutschen. Das ist ja auch das klassische Arbeitsverhältnis, Chef und Arbeiter. Wenn es ein türkischer Chef ist und ein deutscher Arbeiter, der ihm untergeordnet ist, und der türkische Chef gibt seine Anweisungen, dann muss man sich mal in den Arbeiter reindenken: Was sagt er? Sagt er: Okay, ich akzeptiere das! Oder: Ich lehne das ab, weil ich denke, das ist falsch oder richtig! Oder: Ich lehne es ab, weil es von einem Türken kommt. Von einem Türken lasse ich mir nichts sagen! – Ich treffe diese Aussage zigmal am Tag. Nicht mit Türken sondern mit Franzosen. Ich habe vier Jahre lang schlechte Erfahrungen mit Franzosen gemacht, und mein Standardspruch ist: Von einem Franzosen lasse ich mir nichts sagen, oder von einem Franzosen lasse ich mich nicht mehr beleidigen. Also, im Grunde genommen sollte ich sagen: Von diesem Menschen lasse ich mich nicht mehr beleidigen. Von diesem Menschen lasse ich mir nichts sagen, weil ich denke, dass er nicht gebildet genug ist oder blöd ist oder was auch immer der Grund ist, aber nicht weil er Türke oder Deutscher ist. Also, einfach Neutralität in diesem Punkt.

176 *Transnational Social Spaces*

Consultant *N*, who has worked in Turkey since 1983, refers to various occurrences and representations through which Turkish and German colleagues interact. Mental stereotypes of both groups are illustrated by culturally and socially oriented representations. In her view, interaction and co-operation in Turkish and German business relations in elite positions may not be a question of emphasising differences. It may be a question of realising moments of discontent and the question of how to cope with various forms of in-group and out-group phenomena:

Person *N* (2)

> Also, die Kommunikation zwischen Deutschen und Türken am Arbeitsplatz funktioniert am Besten, wenn man als Deutscher über die türkische Mentalität die Kommunikation mit den Türken führt, das heißt, wenn man das Deutsche, was man hat, zurücknimmt, nicht aufgibt, zurücknimmt, und praktisch auf der Basis, mit der Art der türkischen Mentalität mit den türkischen Mitarbeitern, mit dem türkischen Personal kommuniziert. Das heißt: Wir Deutsche sind immer sehr direkt. Das ist eine Schwäche von uns. Das liegt nicht in der türkischen Mentalität. Wir kritisieren in Gegenwart von dritten Personen. Das ist auch eine Schwäche von uns. Das darf auch nicht sein. Nicht nach der türkischen Mentalität. Wir können ab und zu die Stimme erheben. Äh, das ist auch eine Schwäche, das darf man also auch nicht machen. Man muss eigentlich dem türkischen Mitarbeiter – dass, was man gerne von ihm erwartet, so herüberbringen, dass er meint, dass es letztendlich von ihm selbst kommt, und dass er voll dahintersteht und es logisch nachvollziehen und akzeptieren kann, für sich. Man darf ihn nicht in irgendwelche Gewissenskonflikte bringen. Vor allen Dingen nicht mit anderen Mitarbeitern, mit seinen Kollegen, dann blockt er sofort ab.

Question 3

What do you have in mind when you think about the reality, the dynamics and the dimension of cultural values, social representations, religious traditions between Turkish and German colleagues at work? What is your impression? What is your experience?

Person *H*

> Fangen wir mal mit dem letztem Faktor an, zu den religiösen Werten: Da sehe ich keine größeren Probleme, zumindest hier mit meinen Erfahrungen in der Westtürkei, das – die religiösen Werte werden gegenseitig respektiert. Also, wenn wir ein Weihnachtsfest haben, also, und umgekehrt auch. Dann glaube ich auch, dass durch diese laizistische Struktur, na ja, durch die gewisse Umgestaltung, die vorgenommen wurde, keine große Probleme entstehen oder eine große Rolle spielt. Aber in kulturellen Unterschieden, je nach dem, was man kulturell – wie man es definiert. Ich glaube, das ist eine Angelegenheit, wo man das Augenmerk

German and Turkish Managers in Joint Ventures 177

drauf richten sollte. Ich denke, dass gerade in der Türkei das Schwierige für uns ist, dass sie halt zwischen den Welten sich befinden, die Türken. Das sie einmal eine europäische Dimension in sich haben, die Türken, mit der wir dann auch problemlos, äh, kommunizieren können, aber auf der anderen Seite auch eine halt orientalische Dimension haben – in einem gleichen Kopf sitzt manchmal beides drin, und natürlich, die Menschen sind so unterschiedlich gewichtet. Das ist eigentlich für mich ein größeres Problem, äh, damit zurechtzukommen, äh, weil, das führt persönlich, dann oft zu Missverständnissen, Enttäuschungen, weil – also wenn man mit Leuten zu tun hat, also, die Anbahnung ist europäisch, ja, und das, was man machen kann, was man gestalten kann, so, und dann, in einer weiteren Phase kommt – denken wir, es geht so weiter, und dann kommt aber die orientalische Komponente durch, das also Besprochenes nicht unbedingt zu gelten hat – mehr – oder irgendwelche anderen Dinge, womit man nicht, äh, zurechtkommt. Es ist vielleicht sogar, wenn man jetzt mit einem [...] ach, Araber oder so, darauf muss ich aufpassen und so und so. Aber hier, da das so schwankend ist, ist das sehr kompliziert. Das glaube ich, das lässt sich auch gar nicht so leicht lösen.

At first it seems that *H* articulates questions which he has in mind in order to locate the personality and identity of Turkish business partners. From his point of view, his own, or European, or western-biased principles at work seem to indicate transparent and straightforward work ethics. He conveys the impression that his own working conditions have a solid foundation, and criticises the unstable working conditions of his counterparts. His answer exemplifies the intermediate character of the oft-mentioned discourse around the kaleidoscopic facets of reality arising out of Turkey's almost eighty-year history as a nation-state, her unique geopolitical position and her secular constitution. Turkey seems to represent a neither-nor-position: neither occidental nor oriental, neither European nor Asian, and neither Islamic nor familiar. In *H*'s argumentation, he works with the 'us-and-them scheme'. He toys with his own seemingly better self-representation and signals implications of the other-presentation with biased mental models of their social representation, i.e. the difficulty of (re)locating the social practices, behaviour and attitudes of Turkish colleagues in business life. The text implicitly embodies one symptomatic example of a typical, though not exclusive, image of the partner: being business-orientated and clever, but – as *H* cannot locate the position of the partner – not trustworthy. His perception of the in-between-position may arise out of feelings of helplessness and anxiety. It is impossible, he claims, to decode his partner's profile and performance. If the Turkish partner were an Arab, it might be easier to decode social, cultural or linguistic patterns. This statement implies a discourse of mental stereotypes as well. What is intriguing about *H*'s statement is his position and location – as a German manager in an elite position, where he has had to cope with reality for years.

Transnational Social Spaces

Person *A*

> Also, (seufzt) die Redeweise ist sehr unterschiedlich, also, die Türken sind einfach – meinen einfach, viel höflicher reden zu müssen, sagen vieles nicht so direkt, und wenn dann der deutsche Mitarbeiter Kritiken eher direkter, offener äußert, dann fühlen sie sich schneller verletzt. Also, die Höflichkeit, – äh – und der Gedanke, man muss die Fehler des Anderen gar nicht aufzeigen, sind Werte für den Türken, die dann, sozusagen, nahe Zusammenarbeit erschweren. Es ist auch ein anderes Gefälligkeitsverständnis zwischen den zwei Kulturen gegeben. Also, die Türken sehen im Rahmen ihrer Gastfreundschaft es immer so, dass sie auch ausländischen Mitarbeitern gegenüber vielleicht gefälliger sein müssen, als das Verständnis auf der anderen Seite ist. Ich meine, wir hatten damals bei (Firmenname), um ein Beispiel zu nennen, hatten wir immer den Fall, dass, wenn Mitarbeiter aus Deutschland gekommen sind, egal welcher äh, welches Führungsniveau oder [...] wir in der Firma hatten, haben (seufzt) unsere Mitarbeiter eigentlich in der Türkei sich um die gekümmert, sind mit ihnen abends weggegangen etc., und haben sie ausgeführt, beziehungsweise haben sich darum gekümmert, dass sie auch gut versorgt sind. Umgekehrt war das nicht der Fall. Wenn also Mitarbeiter nach Deutschland gefahren sind, äh, haben die Mitarbeiter das dort eher so angesehen: Man muss sich eben von 8:00 bis 17:00 Uhr um sie kümmern, aber danach, äh, werden sie schon selber ihren Weg finden. Und das ist dann zum Beispiel wieder – das beleidigt dann zum Teil wieder die türkischen Mitarbeiter.

Person *B*

> Der Grundunterschied für mich ist sicherlich in der Erziehung begründet, und da spielen natürlich auch religiöse Werte eine Rolle, obwohl ich eine richtige Religiosität, sowohl im Alltag als auch am Arbeitsplatz, zumindest in unserem Büro, nicht feststellen kann. Trotzdem sind Verhaltensweisen und Muster daraus abgeleitet [...] und, ich, für meinen Teil, habe sicherlich in mancherlei Beziehung auch relativ lange gebraucht, um zu verstehen, dass es da prinzipielle Unterschiede gibt. [...] Welche Reaktionen zum Teil auf Äußerungen fallen?, etwas, – man muss sehr vorsichtig sein, was man in Bezug auf das Türkischsein, oder das, was man darunter versteht, wenn man das falsch rüberbringt, eben, dann werden die Leute doch echt persönlich angesprochen, sie empfinden, ähm, ihre eigene Existenz, – oder wenn man sagt 'das Volk' oder 'die Menschen in der Türkei', pauschal, wenn man die anspricht, wenn da etwas nicht sehr taktvoll geäußert wird, dann kann das durchaus zu Missverständnissen auf der anderen Seite führen. Ähm, dieses persönliche Empfinden, dieses persönliche Sich-angegriffen-Fühlen, dieses Sehr-emotional-Reagieren, das ist sehr stark ausgeprägt. Und das, – dafür braucht jemand, der hier arbeitet als Ausländer eine gewisse Zeit, um das richtig umzusetzen, um das richtig zu verarbeiten und entsprechend vorsichtig damit umzugehen. Ähm, das ist aber alles kein – keine unbeherrschbare Geschichte. Es ist sicherlich so, dass, wenn man sich mit der

German and Turkish Managers in Joint Ventures   179

> Kultur ein wenig auseinandersetzt, auch sicherlich sich darauf gut einstellen kann.
> Die Leute sind nicht unberechenbar. Ganz im Gegenteil. Ich glaube, wenn man
> das kulturelle System hier einigermaßen überblickt, dann sind die türkischen
> Mitarbeiter in ihren Verhaltensweisen auch sehr planbar, und auch manipulierbar,
> man kann geradezu mit ihnen spielen, was sie auch können. Türken sind sehr gute
> Spieler – im Gegensatz zu den Deutschen. [...] Und mit der Emotionalität, wenn
> man jemanden provozieren möchte, in positiver wie negativer Art, dann kann man
> das sehr gut machen, viel eher, als man das in Deutschland machen könnte.

It is apparent that emotions, overwhelming gestures, and simply uncontrollable personal features seem to constrain and disturb business relationships in the eyes of several German informants. However, *A* maintains that the Turkish side is too polite, too careful with regard to its own demands and intentions, not strict enough in articulating personal points of view in business. While *B* discusses the profiles of German and Turkish colleagues – features like emotionality and spontaneous actions on the Turkish side and the dependability and rationality of the German profile – *A* notices the lack of forcefulness or possibly self-assertiveness among Turkish colleagues. The characterisation of a generalisation (being emotional) to some extent becomes an explanation, if not an excuse for the partner's profile. *C, D, E, G, H, K, N* and *O* mentioned the aspect of emotionality or uncontrolled reaction among Turkish colleagues. What makes the discourse of the virtually emotional character of Turkish colleagues interesting is the question why both German and Turkish managers avoided a discourse about politeness interrelated with power. Only *A* and *N* addressed questions like the politeness of Turkish colleagues and their somehow altruistic state of mind towards business partners. Furthermore, one may ask why German colleagues have a problem with emotionality. Being rational, strict and scientific are categorised as positive representations, whereas negative images such as being emotional are described as a problem.

Question 4

What effects and developments do you observe and perceive in German-Turkish transnational spaces? The term transnational spaces is used to describe the implicit and explicit interrelation and interconnections that exist between Turkish and German organisations, initiatives, enterprises, and the social, political and cultural arrangements and resources which flow back and forth.

Person *I*

> [...] Es gibt hier viele Deutsche, äh, Geschäftsmänner, Geschäftsführer oder sagen
> wir Logistik-Manager, äh, die haben ihre Gemeinde, die sind mehr zusammen.
> Was wir in Deutschland über Türken denken, gilt auch für die Deutschen hier.
> Und wenn die hier leben, sollten sie meinetwegen die lokale Kultur auch

180 *Transnational Social Spaces*

verstehen, äh. zu verstehen versuchen, ein bisschen Türkisch denken. Wenn ich mal, sagen wir, (Firmenname)-Manager, den Logistik-Manager besuche, sehe ich noch immer einen deutschen Mann vor mir, der Deutsch denkt, der Deutsch agiert, der Deutsch entscheidet. Nicht jemand, der ein bisschen versucht, den türkischen Kontext zu verstehen. also, wie sich der Türke benimmt. Also, wenn ich mal ein bisschen ausführlicher spreche, der, der, äh, fühlt sich unwohl. Also, äh, was habe ich am Anfang gesagt? Generell kann ich sagen: Die Deutschen reden direkt. Die Türken reden um. In einem Gespräch, in dem ich nicht ganz direkt meine Meinung mitteile, sollte der Andere schon meine Mentalität irgendwie, äh, irgendwie, äh, er muss es nicht wissen, aber – derjenige der herkommt. um zu arbeiten, hätte schon früher mal die türkische Mentalität – irgendwie schon untersuchen sollen. Denn, ein Deutscher, der hier arbeitet, kommt. um hier Erfolg zu haben. in seiner Branche. Also, wenn jemand zu mir kommt. möchte ich gerne einen Tee bestellen. Ganz einfach. Wenn ich aber einen Deutschen besuche, und er mir überhaupt nichts, äh, anbietet, äh, das ist nicht Türkisch. – Also die Deutschen. die ich hier kennen lerne, die haben hier einfach so ein Problem. Die kommen mit deren totalen deutschen Mentalität her, die sind nicht bereit, sich irgendwie zu bewegen, geschäftlich. Aber in deren privaten Leben benehmen sie sich mehr Türkisch, denn, dass gefällt denen – wie wir uns, äh wie wir essen. wie wir tanzen wie wir singen, das gefällt denen, das ist mediterran. äh, man kann das genießen. Aber geschäftlich, die sind Deutsch. Ich denke. dass ich als ein Türke, äh, mit meiner Mentalität, mit meiner Kultur, mit meiner Lebenserfahrung am besten ans Ziel kommen kann, äh, hier, also ich meine. in der Türkei, äh, nicht mit einer deutschen Mentalität. Äh, ansonsten würden alle deutschen Arbeitsstellen hier voll mit Deutschen sein, die, die, die bringen nur bestimmtes Personal. sagen wir, äh, den Geschäftsführer – das hat nur einen Sinn. wenn er sich darauf einlässt. Man kann anders nicht leben.

Person *H*

Also. ich meine, dass es – schon einen sehr, – dass es sich um eine langfristig dynamische Angelegenheit, dass also schon, die Verflechtungen, also auch zunehmen. allein schon durch die vielen Verbindungen der Türken, die in Deutschland Leben. Dass das schon mal eine, äh, Brücke ist. Die Rückkehrer, die hierher kommen. die bei uns mitarbeiten, und – es positive, also, Effekte hat, hier und auch umgekehrt, auch Deutschland. Deutschland hat sich auch etwas verändert durch die Beziehungen durch die Anwesenheit der Ausländer, und hier, die, die – wenn jetzt Deutsche hier arbeiten, im Land, mit Beispielen, das es so ganz. ganz. ganz langsam. das auch die Gesellschaft mitbeeinflusst oder die Arbeitswelt mitbeeinflusst, nicht nur Deutsche auch andere. Ja, sonst, äh, glaube ich. das außerhalb dieser Räume. äh, wo Türken und Deutsche zugleich tätig sind, meine ich. dass da noch sehr, sehr, sehr große Unterschiede bestehen. Also, ich will sagen. dass die Distanz der Deutschen zu den Türken noch sehr, sehr groß ist, wenn ich nach Deutschland komme. (Zwischenfrage nach der Distanz) Ja,

Misstrauen, Misstrauen und Distanz. Der Türke hat ja einen, äh, ich weiß nicht woher das kommt, er hat ein negatives Bild sich irgendwann mal aufgebaut. Sie kennen ja den Begriff: Ich bin getürkt worden. Das muss ja irgendwoher kommen. Und was es hier also auch noch oft gibt, was aber zum Teil auch unberechtigt ist, und, und da in der Richtung muss man viel, muss man viel arbeiten. Ich sehe es auch in der Arbeitswelt, nach wie vor, da sind noch große Unterschiede mit Partnern zu arbeiten. [...] Aber auf der anderen Seite, vielleicht kommt aus Deutschland vielleicht immer noch, eine gewisse – diese Arroganz, die in Deutschland herrscht, zum Beispiel in Hannover, immer wenn es darum geht, türkische Firmen zu platzieren, heißt es: Na, was ist mit dem? Also, ungerechtfertigte Arroganz besteht und der Mangel der Offenheit von deutscher Seite. – Was Solidarität und Loyalität am Arbeitsplatz betrifft, Hilfsbereitschaft, ja, im Gegenteil, da muss ich sagen, da sind die Türken – eigentlich oft einsatzbereiter als Deutsche – einsatzbereiter, verantwortungsbewusster, was ich hier gesehen und erlebt habe. Ja, was Deutsche sagen: Bis hierhin und nicht weiter. Und Loyalität, damit habe ich überhaupt keine Probleme, ja, nun ist es auch so, das solche Leute keine Chance haben, die sind sofort raus, oder wenn sie hinter dem Rücken reden. Das überstehen die nicht.

Person *N*

Äh, tja, im transnationalen Raum, die Brücken zum Beispiel, ähm,, da ich immer nur praktisch in Unternehmen tätig bin, habe ich mit diesen Dingen sehr wenig zu tun. Ähm, was mir nur in der Anfangszeit aufgefallen ist, vor zwanzig Jahren, da kamen also diese – nach – also diese, diese in Deutschland Geborenen, also klein nach Deutschland gegangen und dann nach, äh, so mit 16, 17 wieder zurückgekommen, die sprachen zwar alle Deutsch, teilweise gut, teilweise nicht gut, aber die waren ziemlich entwurzelt. Was ich heute feststelle ist, wenn die, wenn die Türken zurückkommen, die auch einen deutschen Pass haben, die fühlen sich eigentlich multikultureller als früher. Äh, früher hatten die so ihre Wurzeln verloren. Die waren keine Türken mehr, wurden auch so gar nicht betrachtet und angeguckt, und waren auch keine Deutschen. Was ich festgestellt habe, jetzt im Moment, bei der Generation, die jetzt in Deutschland lebt und auch wieder zurückkommt mit ihren Eltern, äh, oder auch alleine, die fühlen sich irgendwo als Bürger von zwei Staaten, die fühlen sich sowohl als Deutsche als auch als Türken. Das war früher nicht so. Vor 15, 18 Jahren war das nicht so. Da waren die entwurzelt. Heute sind die nicht mehr entwurzelt. Heute sind die, die Bürger von zwei Staaten, und die versuchen von Beiden, das Beste zu nehmen und davon zu profitieren. Also, sie verleugnen auch nicht mehr ihre Eigenarten, die sie haben, wie es früher so gewesen ist, sondern die stehen heute dazu und sagen: Ich bin so. Aber ich kann auch ein bisschen anders. Wenn ich meine deutsche Seite zum Beispiel herauskehre, kann ich auch anders. – Ich habe viele Türken, die Türken sind mit einem deutschen Pass, wo der Kopf aber Deutsch ist, die hier riesige Probleme haben, wenn der Kopf zu Deutsch ist. Das darf nicht sein. Die werden nicht anerkannt. Ich habe ungern in Firmen Türken, die aus Deutschland kommen, auch einen deutschen Pass haben, die mir hingesetzt werden und wo gesagt wird: Also, der ist toll. Das ist also jetzt der (Name). Der hat in Deutschland studiert. Der kommt aus Deutschland. Der ist also jetzt unser Ingenieur hier. Das geht in 80 Prozent der Fälle schief, weil die türkischen Mitarbeiter den Mann nicht anerkennen, weil der deutsche Manieren hat. Der arbeitet nicht bis nachts, der hat ein Zeitproblem, weil er das aus Deutschland nicht kennt. Der hat ein Autoritätsproblem, weil die Türken ihn erst einmal nicht akzeptieren, und er sich erst einmal durch Leistung Anerkennung verschaffen muss. Das kennen die nicht. Die sagen: Ich habe studiert. Ich brauche dem Typen doch nicht zu beweisen wie gut ich bin. Aber leider ist das so. Und, äh, der hat also das Problem, dass er natürlich gewisse Dinge hat, auf die die türkischen Mitarbeiter sehr viel Wert legen, was für ihn aber nicht mehr wichtig ist, so die gewissen Koordinationsprobleme, diese Kleinigkeiten. Und, äh, wenn ich das als Ausländer habe, wird mir das verziehen, weil ich ja Ausländer bin. Aber dem Türken wird das nicht verziehen, der hat das zu wissen. Da sagt man: Der ist über, über, über, äh, abgehoben. Äh, arrogant, äh, und das sind so die Attribute, deshalb hat dieser Mann extreme Probleme. Also 80 Prozent dieser Experimente scheitern. Deshalb heute geht es also darum, wie der Mann sich selbst rüberbringt. Wenn die also sagen: Der ist arrogant. Guck dir den mal an, wie der uns behandelt hier und so. Was will der denn da? Äh, das sagt man aber erst dann, wenn der Mann selbst signalisiert, das er sich selbst nicht rüberbringen kann. Er muss sich selbst – die Leute haben die Probleme, dass sie zum Beispiel in Deutschland studiert haben, und sie sind jetzt wer. Aber in der Türkei sind sie nichts. Zum Beispiel, man fängt buff mit irgend einer Bemerkung an und haut den Leuten die um den Kopf, und da sind die nicht böse drum, und das werden sie aber auch nicht akzeptieren. Zum anderen haben sie das Problem, das sie kein richtiges türkisch reden. Auch wenn sie sagen, sie sprechen ganz toll Türkisch. Dann gucke ich mir hinterher die Korrespondenz an und denke: Das darf nicht wahr sein! So schreibe auch ich. So schreibt dann kein Türke. Die haben dann schon teilweise die deutsche Mentalität so verinnerlicht, dass die auch mit Behörden oder mit irgend welchen Problemen nicht auf die türkische Art umgehen, und das kreiden die Mitarbeiter denen negativ an. Den Türken würden sie es nicht ankreiden. Uns als Ausländern auch nicht, weil sie sowieso davon ausgehen, das wir so denken, aber diese Leute haben einen speziellen Status, und dann wird es schwierig. Also, die Adaption dieser Leute ist sehr schwierig. Sie haben es selbst sehr schwer, haben viele Probleme. Wenn sie es geschafft habe, ist okay, dann haben sie einen steinigen Weg zurückgelegt. Äh, die Meisten schaffen es eigentlich nicht.

Sagen wir es mal so: Wenn sich Dinge ändern oder voranschreiten, wir haben sehr viele Türken in Deutschland äh, wir haben sehr viele deutsch-türkische Beziehungen, ähm, wobei ich feststellen muss, dass die früher nur bei den großen Firmen vorhanden waren und sich jetzt verlagern auf die Mittelgröße. Äh, das kommt dadurch, dass der Wirtschaftsmarkt sich eigentlich geöffnet hat. Äh, dass die Türken, die sowieso immer eine sehr gute Produktion hatten, es verstanden

German and Turkish Managers in Joint Ventures 183

> haben, in den letzten Jahren, ihre Produkte mit dem besseren Finish auch an den Mann zu bringen. Also die Produktivität ist gestiegen. Die Qualität der Produkte ist verbessert worden, und ist auch dem Geschmack der europäischen Länder angepasst. Das hat auch damit zu tun, dass die Generation der Türken jetzt am Ruder ist quasi in den Familienbetrieben, die also jetzt ausländische Schulen besucht, besucht hat oder in der Türkei die Schulen besucht hat, wie eben Bosporus, äh französisch amerikanische Schulen, die also weltoffener sind. Das ist jetzt aber nicht nur Europa oder Deutschland. Das ist jetzt generell. Ich habe also sehr viele Betriebe, da sind sehr viele Leute. Wir, wir, wir holen im Moment, Teile aus, aus Südamerika. Wir haben Export nach Japan. Äh, wir machen Messen nach Europa, Belgien, Frankreich, Dänemark, was-weiß-ich für Länder. Äh, das gab es vor zehn Jahren noch nicht in dem Sinne. Die Türkei öffnet sich insgesamt. Natürlich ist es – das durch den vorhandenen Bevölkerungsstopp, der eigentlich da ist, in Deutschland, ist es so, also, dass die Beziehungen eigentlich sehr eng sein sollten, was sie aber nicht sind. Ich kenne viele Leute, die sagen: Es sind ja die Türken nach Europa gegangen, die irgendwo aus dem Osten kommen. Und die westlichen Türken, die an der Westküste sind, für die ist das immer noch so eine andere Klasse. Und der Handel spielt sich bei denen immer noch mit den Europäern, mit den Deutschen und so ab. Die würden nie versuchen über die, über die türkische Schiene in Deutschland Geschäfte zu machen. Die machen direkt mit den Deutschen Geschäfte, weil die das auf ihrer eigenen Ebene betrachten. Sie kennen bestimmt sehr viele Leute in İstanbul, die auch kulturell sehr intensiv die Beziehungen pflegen, die werden ihnen genau das Gegenteil erzählen. Aber ich kann ihnen nur erzählen, was ich jetzt vom Geschäftlichen gesehen habe, von den praktischen Abwicklungen, die ich jetzt in den Firmen habe, die ich betreue. Und da habe ich selten, also, die – Sache, das die Türken jetzt explizit einen Türken suchen, der da angesiedelt ist, über den sie dann ihre Sache abwickeln. Entweder die kennen den irgendwo aus dem Studium oder von der Schule oder Verwandtschaft, aber die würden jetzt nie irgendwo hingehen und sagen: Geben Sie mir mal die Adressen der türkischen Firmen, die hier ansässig sind. Ich möchte jetzt hier Geschäfte machen. So gehen die nicht vor. Die holen sich bei der Kammer, hier wie drüben die Adresse. Im Zweifelsfall laufen die über Messen und recherchieren, wo sie ihre Produkte verkaufen können. [...]

German-Turkish interaction has also increased as a consequence of growing mutual ambitions in economic, institutional, personal and organisational transactions. The comments, statements and opinions of the informants underline the streams of ongoing processes with respect to economic, institutional, social and personal interests in interactions between partners and enterprises in trans-state linkages and relations. Governmental positions, on the other hand, are not as far developed as the continuous flow of mutual interaction and co-operation between German and Turkish business partners.

184   *Transnational Social Spaces*

The viewpoints of eighteen managers and consultants who are involved in transnational business relations show social linkages in terms of mutual knowledge, social ties and human resources within their settings and business life.

On the other hand, the increasing interaction in Turkish-German contexts – be they economically, organisationally or individually motivated – works beyond the immanent expectations and points of view of individuals. One could describe it in terms of a nationally-orientated state of mind. There is no need for a verification of existing social spaces and transnational linkages in the Turkish-German dimension. Streams and flows automatically continue. The question is how the Turkish and German governments and the populace is able to acknowledge continuing linkages in terms of professional, human and social capital which automatically develop in the business world.

Transnational Linkages among Turkish and German Colleagues in Elite Positions

It is impossible to discuss business relations among Turkish and German colleagues in elite positions on Turkish territory without referring to their various roles, functions and responsibilities in the continuation of shared goals as managing the transfer of resources and goods, the exchange of services, know-how, and technical knowledge. The informants articulated their motivation to optimise business settings and to minimise inconvenient moments in communicative, culturally, socially or politically orientated situations, e.g. getting to know the relevance of horizontal or vertical hierarchy, the question of decision-making processes or the management of prejudices and assumptions. Besides their experience with respect to everyday occurrences and inclinations in business settings, the selected excerpts convey the need to articulate questions and patterns which are primarily based on social and mental representations of the Turkish and German partners. This refers to attitudes, habits and opinions of business partners involved. It also means the adaptation of various roles, behaviour and attitudes to their respective partners. Especially the behaviour and attitudes of German managers towards their Turkish partners seems to play an important role. The question whether dissimilar or different cultural elements in Turkish-German interaction have a decisive impact on successes and failures in business is secondary. Viewed retrospectively, the behaviour of the partners, predominantly of the German managers, influences their business relations. Furthermore, the partners are interacting within and beyond Turkish and German contexts in the interest of their businesses. Macro-economic positions such as power, hierarchy, prestige and educational background are obviously not irrelevant in the interaction process. They are decisive factors which influence – consciously or subconsciously – the interaction within inherent expectations, connotations or attitudes, e.g. arrogance, anger or discomfort with regard to trust and loyalty. The interpretation – consciously or subconsciously – of the behavioural patterns of the partners seems to be the crucial question while the partners are negotiating. However, it might be too simple to summarise as typical or problematic a common discourse on German-Turkish business relations as a matter of dissimilarities. Nonetheless, habits, state of mind and streams of awareness, mindfulness and consciousness have a decisive impact on the process of co-operation and communication, especially in terms of biased opinions, attitudes, expectations and presuppositions of German and Turkish managers as business partners or colleagues.

It goes without saying that the successful management of a supportive and efficient climate in Turkish-German business relations has to take several aspects into consideration. These include the socio-economic and institutional structures, the socio-cultural patterns and individual attitudes of the partners involved. Here, the role of language or foreign languages in communication seems to have no tremendous impact on styles of communication patterns. Person *L* was the only one who mentioned the unqualified or insufficient knowledge of English of his German partner. Other informants did not mention language problems in German or English at all. What does seem to have a tremendous impact on Turkish-German business relations, however, is the behaviour in relation to the hierarchical position and socio-economic standing of the interacting partners. Different or dissimilar cultural elements were not a predominant topic in the interviews. Neither was religion. Nonetheless, it is an open empirical question whether Turkish-German settings with their socio-economic preconditions are likely to change mutual attitudes, especially those of German actors on Turkish territory.

The most important step regarding business relations can be seen in providing further possibilities for direct communication, personal contact and physical participation as mentioned by managers, especially by the Turkish informants. By this is meant not only getting a broader point of view of the business partner; it means broadening one's existing opinions, presuppositions and prejudices in order to overcome implicit judgements, for instance that the German manager may per se be better informed than the Turkish colleague.

Successful interaction, successful communication and co-operation is an ideal-type situation. However, one result of this study points to the importance of an awareness and acknowledgement of the influence of local environmental conditions. The German and Turkish actors have to accommodate themselves to local conditions at work. This refers partly to the German colleagues, but also to the Turkish partners. A decisive aspect seems to be the question whether the German partner is in a position to interact and cope with the different characters of partners which were described as rational or emotional types. For German and Turkish colleagues in management positions, the key to optimising their interaction can be seen in their capability and tactical ability to cope with the attributions and local conditions of the working place.

References

van Dijk, Teun A. (1977), 'Context and Cognition: Knowledge Frames and Speech Act Comprehension', in *Journal of Pragmatics*, Vol. 1, pp. 211-32.

van Dijk, Teun A. (1993), 'Principles of Critical Discourse Analysis', in *Discourse and Society*, Vol. 4(2), pp. 249-83.

van Dijk, Teun A. (1998), *Critical Discourse Analysis*, www.hum.uva.nl/~teun/cda.html, status: 2001.

Erickson, Frederik and Schultz, Jeffrey (1982), *The Counsellor as Gatekeeper. Social and Cultural Organization of Communication in Counselling Interviews*, Academic Press, New York.

Fairclough, Norman L. (1989), *Language and Power*, Longman, London.

Geertz, Clifford (1994), *Dichte Beschreibung*, Suhrkamp, Frankfurt am Main.

Goodenough, Ward H. (1964), 'Cultural Anthropology and Linguistics', in Dell Hymes (ed.), *Language in Culture and Society. A Reader in Linguistics and Anthropology*, Academic Press, New York, pp. 36-40.

Gudykunst, Bill W. and Ting-Toomey, S. (1988), *Culture and Interpersonal Communication*, Sage, Newsbury Park.

Gudykunst, William B. and Kim, Young Y. (1997), *Communications With Strangers. An Approach to Intercultural Communication*, McGraw-Hill, New York.

Gumperz, John J. and Levinson, Stephen (1996), 'The Linguistic and Cultural Relativity of Conversational Inference', in *Rethinking Linguistic Relativity*, Cambridge University Press, Cambridge, pp. 375-406.

Thieme, Werner M. (2000), *Interkulturelle Kommunikation und Internationales Marketing*, Peter Lang, Frankfurt am Main.

PART III

CULTURE, MEDIA AND EVERYDAY SOCIAL LIFE

Chapter 8

Good Guys and Bad Guys:
Turkish Migrant Broadcasting in Berlin

Kira Kosnick

The rapid development of new communication technologies is often cited as a key dimension of contemporary globalisation phenomena. It is especially their potential to circulate information and intensify communication across state borders that has been stressed within this context, and this seems to be particularly relevant for migrant populations. However, technological change has also transformed the conditions for electronic broadcasting on local and national levels in nation-states such as Turkey and Germany. Beyond satellite television imports that have become available to Turkish migrants all over Western Europe, there exists in Germany and particularly in Berlin a vibrant landscape of Turkish-language radio and television programmes produced locally. A part of this programming, such as for example the Turkish-language programme on Berlin's *Radio MultiKulti*, owes its existence to the older, so-called 'guestworker programmes' that were produced by public-service broadcasting corporations in Germany from the 1970s onwards (Kosnick, 2000). Another part, however, has come into being through the initiative of migrants themselves, in the domains of private, commercial and open-access broadcasting. Today, Berlin also has its own 24-hour Turkish radio station, a 24-hour Turkish television channel, several small commercial Turkish television projects broadcasting a few hours per week, and a host of Turkish-language programmes on Berlin's open-access television channel, the *Offener Kanal Berlin* (OKB). Much of this programming could not exist without the political support of Berlin's federal state parliament or crucial institutions such as the state media council for Berlin and the adjoining state of Brandenburg (*Landesmedienanstalt*). The reasons given for this support tend to centre on one major theme, that is, the *local* dimension of these Turkish-language broadcasting projects, as distinct from the satellite imports that are available to migrants from Turkey. Locally produced Turkish programming is expected to discuss the local dimensions of migrant life, thereby tying people closer to their place or country of residence. Satellite imports, on the other hand, are seen as an obstacle to integration, since programmes from Turkey have little to say on life in Germany, or tend to convey a rather negative image (Becker, 1998 and 2001; Greiff, 1995; Heinemann and Kamçılı, 2000).

190 *Transnational Social Spaces*

However, locally produced Turkish-language broadcasts also differ from each other in important respects. When asked to compare the Turkish programmes being produced on the *Open Channel* with those on *Radio MultiKulti*, the director of the *OKB* said to me, somewhat jokingly, 'They have the good guys, we have the bad guys'. In this essay, I want to make sense of this statement in the light of two axes that shape the space within which Turkish migrant life is situated in Berlin: the politics of multiculturalism as a dominant paradigm of integration for ethnic minorities, and the transnational, or trans-state dimensions of migrant life.

Good Guys: 'Berlinliyim, Çok Kültürlüyüm, her Gün Radio MultiKulti'yi Dinliyorum.'

I am a Berliner, I am multicultural, I listen to Radio MultiKulti every day.

This jingle appears regularly during the daily hour of Turkish broadcasting on *Radio MultiKulti*, and it neatly describes both the self-conception and the desired audience of the station. *Radio MultiKulti* is part of the public-service corporation *Sender Freies Berlin* (SFB), which provides Berlin with four different radio stations and a television channel. The radio station was created as a new kind of media experiment designed both to serve immigrants in their native languages and to increase public tolerance of ethno-cultural difference among the non-immigrant majority population (Busch, 1994; Mohr, 1996; Vertovec, 2000). It has received much public attention and international praise for its innovative programming format (Voß, 1995). Eighteen different languages are represented on *Radio MultiKulti*, with broadcasting time allotted according to the relative size of the respective immigrant population in the city. Given the number of Turkish-speaking residents in Berlin, Turkish naturally plays an important role on the station, with an hour of programming every afternoon at five p.m. However, Turkish-language broadcasting is not a new development at the SFB either. The Turkish programme, produced by the same group of editors as 25 years ago, goes back to the early days of labour migration. Its mission has changed over the years, however; the focus of the programme nowadays is on life in Berlin, no longer as an aid to orientation for newcomers, but rather as a service for an ethnic group firmly established in the city.

A typical daily programme might include a report from the Berlin Film Festival, a review of the main stories in Berlin newspapers, news items such as the opening of an exhibition against racism at a Berlin youth centre, a report on the latest matches of local Turkish soccer clubs, and the local weather forecast. Once a week, there is also a newspaper review from Turkey, and first-division soccer results are not omitted, but generally the emphasis is clearly on events in Berlin. In an interview, one of the younger Turkish editors of the programme, Cem Dalaman, described the targeted audience to me in the following terms:

We want listeners who identify with Berlin, with the life here. Who think of themselves as Berlin Turks. [...] We want to reach people who understand themselves as part of this society, not as part of the society in Turkey. Either you live here, we think, or in Turkey.

For Dalaman, seeing oneself as part of this society means to identify oneself as a Berlin Turk, not as a Turk from Turkey but also, significantly, not as a German Turk. 'Living here' refers to the city rather than to Germany as a whole, and this is in keeping with the local orientation of *MultiKulti*'s programmes. Multiculturalist campaigns in Germany often emphasize the local in the sense of a community of residence, the place where people of different ethnic and cultural backgrounds can belong.[1] The second important aspect of Dalaman's statement pertains to his categorization of Turkish immigrants as 'those who live here' and 'those who live in Turkey', thereby referring not to an actual place of residence but rather to people's interests and identifications. In contrast to other Turkish-language broadcasts available to immigrants, *MultiKulti* is for those who identify with life in Berlin. For Dalaman, this is a question of 'either-or', and to him, programmes which report on Turkey are 'backward-oriented'. Maintaining ties with Turkey, and identifying as a Turk from Turkey appears residual, something that characterised the early period of immigration but should no longer dominate people's identities. Life in Turkey should no longer be a major focus of interest to Turks in Berlin, Dalaman argues, and he criticises the orientation of Berlin's oldest Turkish television station *TD-1*:

That was not the point when TD-1 got a licence back then. The idea was not to show some strange films from the 1960s and then one and a half hours of news from Turkey. From the remotest corners, where a water-pipe has burst in some village and suchlike.

The local cable television station *TD-1* rebroadcasts the news programmes shown by Turkey's news channel *NTV* several times a day. While *MultiKulti's* programme also features news from Turkey, it does so in limited and narrowly circumscribed ways, Dalaman stresses:

---

[1] Berlin has been particularly active in this area, with public campaigns that have targeted public conceptions of who can belong in the city. To give just one example, in the early 1990s a poster campaign showed portraits of smiling people, of different skin colour, style of clothing, age groups. The heading stated, 'We are Berlin'. Such campaigns still continued. It is only recently that campaigns have also claimed national citizenship for people who tend to be categorized as foreigners, and this is a direct result of the transformation of citizenship and naturalization laws, in part intended to encourage those now qualifying for German citizenship to apply for it.

192 *Transnational Social Spaces*

> We have a weekly report from Turkey on Thursdays, four or five minutes, on what happens there, but we try to keep it relatively moderate. And we try to create a balance by reporting the day after, on Fridays, also from Amsterdam, Stockholm and Paris. As if one could take it for granted. Meaning about Turkish life in these three metropoles. But of course also from İstanbul and Ankara. In this context.

'Creating a balance' by reporting from other Western European cities in which there is a substantial immigrant population from Turkey: the particular angle from which issues pertaining to Turkey are addressed is one that primarily focuses on cities – İstanbul and Ankara. Secondly, these cities are presented as two locations among others located in Western Europe that creates a map of Turkish life within, but importantly, also outside of Turkey. While the Turkish *MultiKulti* programme focuses primarily on Berlin, reporting from other immigrant cities is an attempt to encourage a consciousness of a sort of Turkish 'diaspora' (this term is not much used by Turks themselves) in Europe which has come to be termed '*Türk Avrupalı*', Turkish European. This concept has become important particularly in Turkish academic circles in Western Europe, and suggests a secular and westernized community that is not so much seeking to maintain ties with Turkey as to form influential networks of co-operation across Western European nation-states. The Turkish *MultiKulti* programme thus nowadays deliberately tries to avoid what once was one of the main staples of public-service broadcasting for labour migrant populations since the 1960s: creating 'a bridge back home', at once assuming and encouraging identification with their respective country of origin (Kosnick, 2000). For *MultiKulti*, Turks in Berlin should think of themselves primarily as Turkish Berliners, and secondly as Turkish Europeans.

During the 1970s and for much of the 1980s, the Turkish public-service radio programmes like that of the SFB had a virtual monopoly on Turkish-language broadcasting in Germany. This situation changed dramatically with the advent of television and radio imports from Turkey in the early 1990s, mostly via satellite. Quantitative studies have revealed that Turkish households in Germany have a pronounced preference for these programme imports, and that German-language channels, but also Turkish-language broadcasts offered in the public-service domain have declined in the ratings.[2] Critics have interpreted this new preference for programme imports from Turkey as a dangerous development which ties migrants closer to their country of origin instead of their country of residence, an assessment shared by the producers of *MultiKulti*'s Turkish programme. Their understanding of the migration process converges with dominant migration paradigms: migration is seen as a process of slowly changing identifications that accompanies an initial uprooting, movement, and eventual 'spreading of roots' in

---

[2] Studies also show that people will often combine different kinds of media both from Turkey and Germany, rather than focus exclusively on media from one country only (ZfT, 1997). However, particularly in the area of television channels from Turkey capture a large Turkish audience in Germany (Eckhard, 1996).

Good Guys and Bad Guys 193

the destination locality. Accordingly, watching satellite television from Turkey constitutes one way of 'being there', of not engaging in life in Berlin but identifying as 'part of the society in Turkey', as Cem Dalaman has put it. 'Either you live here, we think, or in Turkey', he states, and just as a person cannot actually be in two locations at once without being physically torn in two, so the entry into the mass-mediated imaginary territory of Turkey seems to entail leaving Berlin. *Radio MultiKulti's* Turkish programme is intended to counter such 'backward-oriented' tendencies by encouraging local identifications.

However, the Turkish-language programme on *Radio MultiKulti* is less firmly tied to the local than it seems. This becomes evident less from the programme 'content' – in terms of what kinds of topics are presented – than from the language in which these topics are addressed. It is *Öztürkçe* – 'pure Turkish' as defined by the Turkish Language Association – that is enforced as a standard for the Turkish programme. Whereas the German-language programmes on *Radio MultiKulti* use 'foreign accents' to express and authenticate their multicultural dimension,[3] the standard for the Turkish programme is different. Passing on the Turkish language in its pure form: this educative aim was and is in certain aspects still central to the Turkish programme of *MultiKulti*, as it is for other Turkish broadcasting projects in the city. It can in fact be regarded as part of the general mission of foreign-language productions at *MultiKulti*, namely to aid in the 'cultivation' of cultural identity, which is a main principle of the station's overall mission (Voß, 1996). In light of the changes the Turkish population in Germany is undergoing at present, with a relative decline in the use of Turkish and certainly in its proficiency among younger generations, maintaining 'high' standards of Turkish is deemed a growing necessity by the editorial staff. In fact, the more 'pure Turkish' grew into decline among the programme's audience, the more urgent it seemed to provide this audience with 'pure Turkish' as a corrective in the context of broadcasting. As a result, however, the programme increasingly had to edit the voices of Turkish Berliners to render them fit for representation in the broadcasts. Up until three years ago, producers for the Turkish programme would edit out all instances of 'incorrect Turkish' before interviews with Turkish Berliners were broadcast. Cem Dalaman stated:

> Back then [...] we were very adamant that the Turkish language should be broadcast in its pure, I don't know, perfect form. [...] For example, I remember that from my own productions, whenever young people mixed German words into their statements or interviews, that would be cut out immediately (Cem Dalaman, 1998-02-06).

---

[3] See the extensive discussion of the deployment of 'foreign voices' on *Radio MultiKulti* in my doctoral thesis, submitted to the Department of Anthropology, New School University, New York, September 2002.

194 *Transnational Social Spaces*

The younger generation of editors became more and more uncomfortable with this practice, feeling that it did not correspond to the reality of language use among Turkish Berliners. Today, now that some of the older generation have retired, German words remain in the interview materials.

However, for the journalists themselves, different standards apply. Whereas the German-language programmes of *Radio MultiKulti* regard the somewhat imperfect German of their moderators and commentators as an asset,[4] this is not at all the case in the context of the Turkish-language programme. The programme might no longer enforce the rule of 'perfect Turkish' for material gathered among informants, but it is very much enforced for the journalists and presenters. This affects the very composition of the staff. Among young people of Turkish origin born and raised in Germany, it is extremely difficult to find anyone whose Turkish will meet the required standard, as editors repeatedly told me. This is put down not only to a factual 'creolization' process, in which German and Turkish is interwoven into everyday conversations,[5] or to the additional lack of opportunities to speak Turkish, but also to the variants of Turkish spoken among the parent generation.[6] The Turkish defined as 'pure Turkish' by the editorial staff of *Radio MultiKulti's* Turkish programme is the Turkish regarded as 'correct Turkish' by state representatives and elites in Turkey.[7] As a result, almost all of the staff members of the Turkish *MultiKulti* team, including those working on a freelance basis, have been raised and at least partially educated in Turkey, with the exception of one young woman who spent just a part of her childhood there. Several members of the staff worked for newspapers or television channels in Turkey prior to their employment at *MultiKulti*.

At first sight, the Turkish programme of *Radio MultiKulti* presents a paradoxical case in which a particular 'local' agenda – maintaining a linguistic identity – sets in motion a recruitment process which necessarily has a transnational dimension. As an organisation, it is not transnationally oriented, but it nevertheless relies on transnational cultural capital in order to fulfil its local agenda.[8] With regard to the maintenance of linguistic identity, it defends 'pure Turkish' against the widespread syncretic forms that mix Turkish and German, but it can do so only with people who have acquired skills and knowledge in both Turkey and Germany. Staff members are required to have a double transnational

---

[4] 'We speak with an accent' is a slogan to be found in promotional material published by the station. See also Vertovec, 2000.

[5] For a discussion of the concept of cultural creolization, see Hannerz, 1987.

[6] The majority of migrants has had only limited schooling in Turkey, and many of them came from regions in which different dialects or in fact other languages such as forms of Kurdish or Arabic are spoken.

[7] *Öztürkçe* reflects the transformation and modernization enforced by the Turkish Language Association after the birth of the Turkish Republic, which has led to a continuous process of expelling Arabic and Persian influences from the language and replacing them with words that have – imagined or factual – Turkic roots.

[8] For a discussion of cultural capital in transnational contexts, see Faist, 2000, p. 30.

Good Guys and Bad Guys

competence in the sense that they have to have a command of 'pure Turkish', which can only be acquired in Turkey, and a familiarity with Berlin affairs, which can only be acquired after a few years of residence in that city.[9] This double competence is, however, not to be confused with other forms of cultural syncretism and hybridity often claimed to characterise immigrant life in Germany. The '*Kanaksprak*', a term created and celebrated by the influential writer Feridun Zaimoğlu, thereby referring to the emergence of a kind of Creole language that mixes German with Turkish influences, constitutes a very different combination of cultural repertoires that have different nation-state origins. It has a definite class ascription, and if its users do not simultaneously have command of those linguistic repertoires defined as correct and high-standard in Turkey or particularly Germany, it actually hinders their upward social mobility. It is only those who have full command of these 'high cultural' repertoires who can benefit from switching and combining them advantageously.

The Open Channel

The open-access television channel *OKB* is another non-commercial site of Turkish-language television production in the city where mainly amateurs make use of broadcasting opportunities, which are free of charge. Open Channels exist all over Germany, and have been instituted as local forums of communication where 'normal citizens' can address the public with their concerns. Their first rule is that the Open Channels may not interfere with programme contents, or prevent anyone from using facilities and broadcasting programmes. Turkish-language programmes are produced at the *OKB* in large numbers: in the first half of 1998, their share of the overall broadcasting time was as high as 26 percent. Many immigrants are active on the Open Channel, which only requires its so-called users to have a residence permit in Germany in order to be given broadcasting time. As already stated, the Open Channel Berlin is very popular with Turkish producers, but this is not at all the case the other way around. In the view of broadcasting officials, politicians and other immigration experts in the city, and certainly the Turkish staff of *Radio MultiKulti*, Turkish programmes on the Open Channel are seen as 'backward oriented', politically extremist, aimed at indoctrination and hindering integration. In fact, on the Open Channel many groups are active whose political and religious positions are not represented by other broadcasting projects in the city. The majority of Turkish-language programmes focus on Islam, ranging from Nurculuks, followers of Kaplan and various Sufi groups, to several different Alevi programmes, some of which are seen by their producers as more cultural or political than religious. Ranking second are a range of nationalist programmes produced at the *OKB*, with a focus on either right-wing Turkish nationalism or

---

[9] A second aspect pertains to their ability to produce programmes that conform to the standards of quality and objectivity as defined by public-service broadcasting in Germany.

196 *Transnational Social Spaces*

Kurdish nationalism.[10] There also exists a minority of programmes produced by groups and individuals ranging from youth initiatives and soccer clubs to a retired journalist. It is the first two groups of programmes that constitute a major problem for the Open Channel.[11] Intended as it was as a medium for the local 'grass-roots' concerns of citizens who otherwise do not gain easy access to the public sphere, the appearance of allegedly extremist groups whose political roots originate in Turkey or elsewhere seems to contradict the democratising intentions of the Open Channel.

The principle of Open Channel communication being local, an expression of 'grass-roots concerns' of citizens who live in a particular city or region, is an important and largely unquestioned tenet of Open Channel ideals. Local citizen involvement is taken to exemplify accessibility and equal opportunity in mass media production. Many Open Channels require their 'users' to be local residents of their particular area of distribution. The Open Channel Berlin has a different requirement to ensure local ties: all programmes have to be produced by the 'users' themselves, and live programmes get better scheduling slots. In other words, migrants are not allowed to submit videotapes that have been recorded elsewhere or show programmes produced by other television stations from abroad. And this is a constant source of conflict between channel management and migrant producers. Rather than introducing 'foreign' material and issues, migrants are encouraged to address local concerns and present themselves as part of a multicultural and multi-ethnic Berlin. It is hoped that migrant activities on the Open Channel will promote their integration in local resident communities. This is expressed very clearly in a soundtrack that accompanies the broadcast of the daily programme schedule, in which the Berlin Deputy for Foreigner Affairs (*Ausländerbeauftragte*) Barbara John is featured making the following statement:

> When you look at the development of minorities in their new society they have to go through a long phase during which they move only within their own group. At first they are totally focused on their own family, then they start to form organisations, but most would never think of going public. I think that an important part of successful integration can be traced back to many non-German groups seizing the opportunity to use the Open Channel and using their energies there. By dealing with the opponents of their programmes, they grow and learn to have political exchanges in a democratic society.

This perspective firstly suggests that the particular opinion articulated by migrant producers is not in itself valued as a contribution to public debate. Rather, it is the learning process the producers themselves go through that is seen as

---

[10] I can only speak about those Kurdish programmes here that are presented in Turkish. There are some others that use *Kurmanci*, which was not accessible to me.

[11] Open Channels in areas with large immigrant populations report similar problems, such as the Open Channel Hamburg and Frankfurt/Offenbach.

Good Guys and Bad Guys   197

valuable.[12] This is in keeping with the general goal of Open Channels to strengthen the 'communicative competence' of those who usually tend to be mere consumers of mass media productions. But what is more, and more importantly in this context, it also reflects a particular vision of integration and the multicultural society that underlies this perspective. Migrants are expected to grow local roots, develop a local life and contribute to public debates of 'society', meaning their city or their new country of residence. Here, no thought is given to transnational connections, because these are expected to lessen over time.

However, as mentioned before, the foreign-language programmes, and particularly the Turkish-language ones, also pose serious problems for the Open Channel. Early in the year 2000, the Berlin parliament even debated whether to abolish the Channel, with critics claiming that the programmes were highly problematic (*Tagesspiegel*, 2000-03-25). While the Open Channel claims to make important contributions to a democratic culture of public debate, the actual broadcasts have little to offer, it was argued. Instead of grass-roots commitment, critics complained of egocentric banalities, or even worse, fundamentalist and extremist positions being broadcast.

Far from the democratic ideals the Open Channel is supposed to stand for, the Islamic and nationalist programmes are suspected of trying to mobilize viewers against those very ideals, and of promoting authoritarian politics. Among the audience, it is particularly the Turkish viewers who complain about specific programmes to the *OKB* management or to the state media council. Many of them argue that in Turkey such broadcasts would not be permitted, and they are quite right in the case of many Islamic and Kurdish-nationalist programmes. The criticism levelled against the political establishment in Turkey would certainly be deemed to promote *bölücülük*, separatist or divisive tendencies which threaten the unity of the Turkish state and nation, explicitly prohibited in Article 14 of the Turkish constitution,[13] or else be seen as a threat to the secularist foundations of the Republic. The strength of the Turkish protest against such broadcasts can in fact only be understood in the context of political conflicts originating in Turkey. No other issues polarize public debate in Turkey as much as the (re-)appearance of political Islam in the country, and of course Kurdish separatism (Erzeren, 1997; Schiffauer, 2000). Both issues attack the very heart of the Kemalist Turkish state, which was founded on the sometimes violent separation of Islam from the state and on secularism as the guiding principle of public life.[14] The treatment of Kurdish-nationalist or culturalist aspirations by the Turkish state has been abundantly

---

[12] For a more detailed account of this 'learning process', see Kosnick, forthcoming 2004.

[13] '*Anayasada yer alan hak ve hürriyetlerden hiçbiri, Devletin ülkesi ve milletiyle bölünmez bütünlüğünü bozmak, ...amacıyla kullanılamazlar.*' ('None of the rights and freedoms stated in the constitution may be used ...for the purpose of destroying the indivisible integrity of the state and nation', Article 14, *Türkiye Cumhuriyeti Anayasası*, 1995).

[14] Though see the work of Günter Seufert and others with regard to how Islam has in fact been reincorporated into the political establishment.

198   *Transnational Social Spaces*

documented (Amnesty International, 1996; Berger et al., 1998; İçduygu et al., 1999). Germany as well as other Western European countries have emerged as a location for politics-in-exile, and a number of studies underline the importance of organising operations abroad for Kurdish-nationalist activities or the campaigns of the Refah/Fazilet Partisi in Turkey to flourish (Karakasoğlu, 1996; Mertens, 2000; Van Bruinessen, 2000). With regard to mass media, the case of MED-TV/Medya TV providing Kurdish-nationalist programming via satellite to Turkey but also to migrants in Western Europe is well known.[15] However, migrants in Berlin have also made use of their local opportunities to engage in political and religious media activism. On the *OKB*, some of the programmes state their orientation quite clearly in their title: '*Ülkücü Gençlik diyor ki Türk Milleti mutlaka uyanacaktır*' ('The Idealist Youth says that the Turkish nation will definitely arise/come to consciousness'), '*Ben Kürdüm, Sen Kimsin?*' ('I am a Kurd, who are you?'), '*Türk'ten Türk'e TV*' ('TV from Turk to Turk'), 'Kurden und Kurdistan' ('Kurds and Kurdistan'), '*Her şey Türk için Türk'e göre Türk tarafından*' ('All for the Turks, from the point of view of Turks, out of the position of Turks').[16]

Obviously, specific organisations that programme-makers might be affiliated with, such as the PKK or KOMKAR, the MHP or others, will focus their attention mainly on Turkey. Islamic programme-makers also often address and criticise political events in Turkey such as, for example, the issue of Islamic clothing at universities, Turkey's role in the Gulf War, or the status of *Imam Hatip* schools. Several of the programme-makers I interviewed were convinced that in Turkey they would have been imprisoned for their broadcasts, and some thought that they were under surveillance by MİT, the Turkish National Intelligence Organisation. Many of them have received threats of violence, and a few have even been physically attacked by oppositional groups. Given the strong links many programme-makers have with groups and organisations that are either directly active in Turkey or network with organisations there, it is not surprising that the Open Channel rule of allowing only self-produced broadcasts does not go uncontested. Programme formats differ widely: while some producers such as Şerafet Duman, responsible for the '*Ben Kürdüm*' programme, simply sit down in front of the camera in the *OKB* studios and speak for an entire hour, in Duman's case accusing the Turkish state of persecuting Kurds, others drop off pre-recorded tapes. It is not always easy for the *OKB* to monitor whether or not programme-makers have in fact produced the material themselves, for instance when the makers of 'Evrensel Din Islam' ('universal religion Islam') show amateur recordings of the modern mystic Ahmed Hulûsi addressing an audience in Turkey. Others, such as the producers of 'Saadet TV', make use of internet webcams to transport the sheik of their Sufi order, who is presently based in the United States, live into the local context of *OKB* television broadcasting (see below).

---

[15] For an 'insider' account, see Tabak, 2001.
[16] This last programme name takes up a slogan promoted by the journal *Bozkurt* in the 1970s, which was connected with the Nationalist Action Party (Landau, 1995, p. 169).

Sometimes, however, *OKB* rules are overtly breached, and material taken from other television stations is shown. In late March 1998, the makers of 'Türk'ten Türk'e' were commemorating Alparslan Türkeş, leader of the right-wing MHP party in Turkey, who had died a year before. In their programme, they showed material taken from the local Berlin television station TD-1, who in turn had copied and broadcast a news programme from Turkey's station TGRT. Thus, trickling down to the *OKB* were the images of the masses who had gathered in front of the hospital in Ankara where Türkeş had died, shouting '*Başbuğlar ölmez*' ('Leaders never die'). This material was combined by the producers with pictures of Türkeş, taken at different stages of his life, which they had put up on the studio walls of the *OKB*, and a soundtrack with *ülkücü* political music celebrating the struggle of Turkish right-wing nationalists.

Apart from disagreeing with Turkish or Kurdish nationalist and Islamist politics, the Turkish producers at *Radio MultiKulti* and other critics often describe such programming as 'backward oriented', particularly with regard to Islamic programmes. Backward has a double meaning here. Firstly, it refers to the orientation of Open Channel producers toward Turkey instead of Germany, thus taking 'a step back' in the process of integration within the paradigm of migration outlined above. Second, within the context of politics in Turkey Islamist positions are often described as backward, since the trajectory of Kemalism has sought to reduce the allegedly 'anti-modern' influence of religion in public life and politics in Turkey (Göle, 1996; Heper, 1997; Margulies and Yıldızoğlu, 1997). A part of the Turkish-nationalist spectrum is also described as backward by left-wing or liberal secularists, in the sense that it stresses Turkish continuity with Ottoman times or pan-Turkish roots dating back thousands of years.

It would be wrong, however, to regard these activities simply as politics conducted abroad, oriented entirely toward Turkey and showing no interest in the social, cultural and political issues of the country (or city) of residence. Kurdish-nationalist, Turkish-nationalist and Islamist programme-makers do not equally portray Germany as a place of exile. If this were the case, life in the country and city of residence would be addressed only – or at least predominantly – in the context of 'home' affairs. Kurdish-nationalist programmes exhibit the strongest tendency to address their audience only as part of a Kurdish diaspora, geographically dispersed but united in its longing and struggle for Kurdistan, imagined as the homeland from which it has been exiled. Programmes such as '*Ben Kürdüm*', '*Welat TV*', '*Azadi TV*' and '*Kurden und Kurdistan*' on the Open Channel rarely take up issues that are not related to this political struggle, and Kurdish life in Berlin or Germany is usually shown in a context that feeds into this struggle, such as a youth group learning Kurdish folk dancing at a local community centre and other activities that represent forms of cultural nation-building. Interest in 'local' affairs exists – as far as the programmes are concerned – only in so far as they can be represented as evidence of the vitality, magnitude and determination of the Kurdish diaspora.

Türk'ten Türk'e

The same does not hold true for other kinds of programmes that have, to varying degrees, explicit political links and aspirations with regard to Turkey. In the following, I want to return to a Turkish-nationalist programme, '*Türk'ten Türk'e*' and its producers, in order to show how a right-wing nationalist agenda that has its political origins in Turkey is combined with and inform a 'local' agenda that pertains to the life of Turkish migrants in Germany. The example of the coverage by '*Türk'ten Türk'e*' of the death of Alparslan Türkeş described above gives little indication that these 'local' dimensions hold an importance in their own right. But the themes chosen for the monthly programme vary. The main organiser and person signing himself responsible (*V.i.S.d.P.*, responsible in accordance with press laws) for the programme is Abdullah Güneş, who came to Germany in 1980 at the age of 16. Güneş, who readily identifies himself as a Turkish nationalist, claiming his nationalism to be primarily oriented toward defending Turkish culture in Germany, describes the main goal of his programme as follows:

> We want to put a person, a Turkish child living in Berlin, in the position to be able to say 'I am a Turk' when asked, without fear, without shame.[17]

In order to do so, Güneş feels the need to fight in two directions with his programme. He has to make people aware of German political efforts to assimilate the Turks and erase their cultural identity, and he has to fight tendencies within the Turkish population to stress the differences that exist among them instead of standing united. With regard to the first point, he regularly translates articles printed in German newspapers in his television programme that pertain to Turks and integration issues.

> In Berlin right now there is a politics of assimilation going on against foreigners, all in the name of integration. And nobody is aware of it. [...] [They want] foreigners to assimilate! Because we already have integration! I already respect German laws. Integration is something else!

For Germany, Güneş defends a model of ethnic pluralism, in which people of different national cultures enjoy special minority rights that enable them to maintain their separate identities. The objective of the German state, he suspects, is however assimilation and the absorption of 'foreigners' into a German majority culture. Turks in Berlin thus have a vital interest in following local and national politics in Germany, and Güneş regards the effects of satellite television in much the same way as the editors of the Turkish programme at *Radio MultiKulti*. Asked whether he has a satellite dish at home, he stated:

---

[17] Personal interview with Abdullah Güneş, 1998-06-03.

Good Guys and Bad Guys 201

> I insist on not getting one, and why? Because it distances people from what is happening here in Berlin. Some of the troubles in Turkey actually don't interest me that much! More the troubles that exist in the society I live in. Ok, I put up a satellite dish, I watch Star. Sports from Turkey. So ok, maybe it is a bit important to me, but what is going on in Berlin, in Germany, is more important.

Even though a Turkish nationalist identity seems almost automatically to imply a focus on the Turkish nation-state, Abdullah Güneş' understanding of himself as a 'cultural nationalist' (*kültür milliyetçisi*) widens his area of concern to all locations where Turks live or where he suspects the influence of Turkish culture. His identification with the Turkish state remains strong: when it comes to international relations and Turkey's position with regard to Arab or European countries, he always speaks in terms of 'we' and 'us'. But he does not long to return, or see himself as exiled from the homeland, nor does he maintain that Turkish culture can only flourish in the context of a particular territory or state structure. Protecting Turkish identity might take the form of defending the integrity of the Turkish nation-state, but might just as well consist of demanding minority rights in the migration context. Whether it is 'dividers' from within the society in Turkey, among the Turkish community in Germany, or German politicians wanting to assimilate immigrants, the task is essentially the same in Turkey and abroad: to guard the unity of Turks and strengthen their identification with Turkishness. Fighting the alleged enemies of such unity is a task that unites the '*Türk'ten Türk'e*' producers with their MHP allies in Turkey.

> I say the Turkish nation is done for by this process of dividing it into smaller and smaller groups. They cut it up. But if the society is united, then you cannot ruin it. They call you rightist. They call you leftist, and the other one Alevi, Kurd, Sunni. [...] And then when they are separated into tiny groups it is easier to assimilate them or kill them! But if not, if they are united, they cannot do that. And that applies not only here, but also in Turkey.

Güneş links the conflicts dividing the population in Turkey to their situation in Germany: those who introduce divisions – by insisting on their identity as Kurds, Alevis, left-wing or right-wing – not only weaken the Turkish state but also the Turkish nation outside of Turkey. German efforts to assimilate the Turks and turn them into Germans are aided by those who emphasize the divisions among immigrants from Turkey. If the Turks were united, those efforts would fail. It is thus not just Turkey that is under attack by those who in the eyes of Turkish nationalists want to split up the country, but also the Turkish nation abroad. Güneş sees an unholy alliance between German assimilationists and Turkish 'divisionists', resulting in a joint onslaught against the Turkish nation as a national and cultural minority in Germany. The German state actively promotes conflict among the Turkish migrant population through its asylum policies, Güneş claims, and he provides an example:

202   *Transnational Social Spaces*

> There is a home for asylum-seekers over there. They visit me here, those kids who
> have come from the Southeast of Turkey. "My son, why did you come here?" "Well,
> ağabey, you know about the conditions in Turkey. We've come for the money." "So
> what did you tell them, why did they accept you as refugees?" "We said we are
> Kurdish, that we are persecuted in Turkey. The Germans expect such an explanation
> anyway. They gave us asylum." "But weren't you ashamed when you said that? How
> can you claim something that doesn't exist?" "What can I do? [...] If I had said, my
> friend, there is no work for me in Turkey, that's why I came, they would have kicked
> me out."

The story confirms two central convictions for Güneş: firstly, that the alleged persecution of Kurds and other minorities in Turkey does not actually exist, as the refugees themselves seem to admit. Secondly, the German state promotes separatist tendencies among the migrant population in order to further its own assimilationist agenda. Obviously, the respect that he demands for Turkish culture in Germany as a minority within a multicultural society is not warranted, in his mind, for the often quite similar demands that Kurds or Alevis make in Turkey. Whereas in the German context, Güneş sees integration politics as a form of assimilation and eradication, in Turkey the national identity has to override all differences, be they religious, ethnic or even political.

However, the point I want to pursue here is not to reveal the contradictions in this Turkish nationalist line of arguing, but rather to look at the way in which Turkish nationalist positions are articulated for a minority rights agenda in the German context. Commemorating the death of Alparslan Türkeş in Turkey is perfectly compatible with such an agenda. The televised images of demonstrators grieving on the streets of Ankara and shouting '*Başbuğlar ölmez*' – 'leaders live forever' are not shown to transport migrant viewers to Turkey, but rather to remind them of a collective endeavour, namely an ongoing project of establishing Turkish unity and strength, even under seemingly adversarial circumstances such as those presented by the migration context. Güneş has no illusions regarding a possible return of the migrant population to Turkey, and even expects future generations to identify more strongly with Germany.

> Germany is our second mother country, really! Maybe in three, four years, ten years,
> fifty years our children will say, Germany is our first mother country. But they will
> say so as Turks!

While Güneş plans to retain his Turkish citizenship, he does not object to his brother and his entire family acquiring German passports. The passport, in his view, does not change their culture, nor does it diminish the loyalty they feel toward the Turkish nation. Güneş does not further elaborate with regard to the possible consequences of naturalisation, but his culturally essentialist understanding of Turkishness renders cultural assimilation a much greater threat than the change of citizenship. On a more general level it has been argued that state actors in Turkey, who in the eighties still feared that naturalisation would lead to a loss of loyalty among Turkish migrants, now in fact advocate it, in order to create a more powerful lobby that could act in Turkey's interests abroad (Seufert for the example of *Diyanet*, 1999, p. 288). Güneş, however, is not just interested in migrants' loyalty toward the Turkish nation-state, but in their loyalty toward the Turkish nation, whose interests need to be defended on German ground as well. This conception is also supported by the pan-Turkism that has been a strong element in right-wing extremist politics in Turkey, whose most notorious leader Alparslan Türkeş already stated in the 1960s that the nationalist principle of idealism, *ülkücülük*, meant struggling for Turks everywhere so that they could determine their own fate in any state context whatever (Türkeş, 1965; see also Landau, 1995). Accordingly, the broadcasting rationale of 'Türk'ten Türk'e' does not oppose the Turkish nationalist struggle to migrant interests in Berlin, but regards the two as closely interrelated. The local efforts represent part of the wider Turkish-nationalist aspirations which extend to all countries in which Turks are thought to reside, but as local efforts they are very specific and respond to the particular socio-political environment that Berlin Turks live in.

Saadet TV

A third example, again taken from the Open Channel and its 'bad guys', presents yet another take on Turkish migrant programming which further undermines the opposition between 'life here' and 'life in Turkey' as mutually exclusive orientations. *Saadet TV* is an Islamic programme produced on the Open Channel since 1997. Even though the religious group which produces the programme has its roots in Turkish Sufism, neither Turkey nor migrant life in Berlin nor Germany form significant points of reference in *Saadet*'s broadcasts.

Saadet can be translated roughly as happiness, and is also used to refer to the era of the Prophet. Himmet Kabak, the producer, is a follower of the *Sheyk Efendi Hazretleri İskender Ali Mihr*, the founder and leader of the *tasawwuf* Mihr Foundation that has its centre in Ankara, the capital of Turkey. *Tasawwuf* can be described as the 'phenomenon of mysticism' in Islam (Encyclopaedia of Islam, Vol. X, p. 313) which goes back to the times of the Prophet. Very simply put, knowledge of the inner self and experiencing the love of God can be achieved, it is claimed, by special means which could include poetry, music, and dance among other activities. Starting in the 12th century, mystical Islam became increasingly organised in orders which continue until the present day. Following a strict hierarchy, they put great emphasis on the relationship between teacher and student, which is marked by complete obedience as the only way to arrive at higher levels of religious knowledge. Different forms of mystical Islam existed in the Ottoman Empire and they continued into the Turkish Republic, even though the orders were officially abolished in 1925. The *Sheyk Iskender Ali Mihr*, who claims to be a

204 *Transnational Social Spaces*

descendant of the Prophet, established his *Mihr Foundation* 1989 in Ankara, but now also has official branches in Izmir, in the USA, and in Germany.

Himmet Kabak and his family became attracted to his teachings in 1995, when they tried to return to Turkey for good. They went back to Germany because of the educational opportunities for the children, Himmet Kabak says. The Mihr order has no more than a handful of members in Berlin, centred around his family, but they have close contacts with other members in Germany and of course with their Sheyk and his followers in Turkey and the United States. Himmet Kabak began Open Channel programming shortly after his return from Turkey, having seen other Muslim groups producing programmes on the Open Channel. Initially, he taped speeches of an Imam based in another German city who is a student of the Sheyk, and then submitted the tapes for broadcasting on the Open Channel.

Saadet Television follows a simple format: Sometimes there is a musical introduction with images of blossoming flowers, flowing rivers and other things documenting the beauty of nature. Then the Imam appears on screen, always seen from the same camera angle, and addresses his audience, speaking freely on particular subjects of Islamic instruction. Mostly, *Hadis Dersi* is given, that is, instruction on the life of the Prophet. The programme is produced exclusively in Turkish. Unlike other Islamic programmes, *Saadet TV* features no-one but the Imam as the only person ever to appear on screen, with the production team leaving no trace beyond signing themselves responsible for the broadcast.

The visual absence of other members of the *Mihr* order from the actual broadcast is linked to their particular perception of religious authority and learning: it is only the authorized representative of the Sheyk or the Sheyk himself who can interpret and transmit religious truth. Himmet Kabak and his team do not even appear as students, as one can sometimes see on other Islamic programmes. Instead, they let the Imam directly address a general audience. The fact that the programme is broadcast in Turkish alone is due to the restricted linguistic competence of the Imam rather than a particular vision of their audience: the message is for all religiously interested people who seek to know the truth about Islam, says Himmet Kabak.

In 1998, the group was already making use of sophisticated communication technology for their internal communication. At home, the Kabak family used the internet to hold video conferences with members in other German cities and Turkey. During a visit to the their home, my main interview partner, the Imam based in another German city, was introduced to me on the television screen, with the same arrangement of camera, computer and TV set up at his end.

Given the dispersal of members across Turkey, Germany and the United States, they have been at the forefront of communication technologies in order to be able to communicate across vast distances. By the year 2000 they had introduced these new technologies into their programme on the Open Channel as well. *Saadet TV* now provides a live internet broadcast that is fed into the Berlin cable system – the first Islamic programme to make use of internet technology as an integral part of their broadcasts. Other programmes announce email addresses

Good Guys and Bad Guys

and websites as a means for making further contact and obtaining information, but *Saadet TV* has introduced the internet directly into Open Channel programming. The programme shows somewhat staggered pictures, a sound that is sometimes difficult to understand and always lags behind the person talking. But this typical webcam format is still quite acceptable for the programme, given the general lack of different camera angles and complicated editing techniques. The technical production effort is still substantial: Himmet Kabak and his assistants have to arrive early at the Open Channel studios to set up the connection. During the entire broadcast and beforehand, they talk on their mobile phones with their partners overseas, in order to give feedback on sound and picture and solve any problems that might occur.

Saadet introduces the internet as a means of producing live programmes, and this gives an interesting twist to the aims of Open Channel officials: live programmes are promoted not just because they tend to be more interesting to audiences, but also to ensure that it is the 'users' of the Open Channel themselves who appear in their programmes and talk about issues of local interest, rather than dropping off tapes with broadcasts produced elsewhere. So it was the local dimension of broadcasting that was to be ensured through live programming. The internet, however, allows remote people and their messages to be brought live on air and into the local context of Open Channel production, without breaching the Open Channel rules. So immediacy is no longer tied to a physical presence in the studio. Despite the physical remoteness of the key presenter, the programme nevertheless qualifies as a live broadcast, with all the benefits tied to live programmes at the *OKB*. Instead of having to bring religious authorities to the studio space, any location in the world can be the point of origin, as long as Himmet Kabak and his team manage to establish the connection, even across national boundaries.

The way in which the programme addresses its imagined audience also gives an indication of the 'universal' conceptualisation that underlies *Saadet's* transmission of religious truth: no reference at all is made in the programmes to the particular circumstances of life, political, social, or otherwise, in specific regions, states or localities. Unlike many Islamic programmes on the Open Channel which criticise political life in Turkey and debate the particular challenges of being Muslim in Germany and so on, the teachings of *Saadet TV* claim universal applicability, appropriate to any local context the programme reaches. The dispersal of *Mihr* members is not addressed. The truth of Islam, the programme suggests, is the same for everyone, and local or national particularities are just challenges to be overcome.[18]

---

[18] The internet pages of the Mihr Foundation (http://www.mihr.com) support the conception of a deterritorialized religious truth that can be transmitted to any location around the globe without modification or adaptation. A 'virtual university' has been set up on the internet (http://www.universityofallah.org), with a four-year programme to which one can apply on

206   *Transnational Social Spaces*

The programme forms part of a wider network of communication that is organised in strict hierarchy, with lessons being transmitted via different media to an ideally unrestricted audience. *Saadet TV* differs from other Islamic programmes on the Open Channel not just through its use of internet technology, but also, as already mentioned, through its neglect of the particular dimensions of local life. The community of Muslim believers is defined only by its relationship to the prime religious authority, the Sheyk, from whom it receives the truth of Islam. New communication technologies are put in the service of this relationship, helping to establish and support the bond between Sheyk and student by transmitting his teachings directly, without further intermediaries.

Conclusion

> We want to reach people who understand themselves as part of this society, not as part of the society in Turkey. Either you live here, we think, or in Turkey.

This statement of an editor of the Turkish programme on *Radio MultiKulti*, with whom my discussion of different types of migrant broadcasting began, articulates a basic assumption which underlies much thinking about the integration of migrant populations in different parts of the world. Whether integration is thought of in terms of assimilation, ethnic pluralism or segmented insertion, the dominant expectation has been that migration processes end with the cutting of ties to the former country of origin, and the growing of local 'roots' (Malkki, 1992 and 1995). This perspective has been challenged since the 1990s by a variety of academic disciplines, noting the continued importance of affiliations that link migrants in different ways to their countries of origin or other diasporic locations (for an inexhaustible list of writings that have influenced the discipline of anthropology in particular, see Appadurai, 1996; Basch et al., 1994; Bhabha, 1994; Clifford, 1994; Glick-Schiller et al., 1992; Hannerz, 1996; Kearney, 1995). However, notwithstanding the influence of the concepts of transnationalism, Diasporas and transmigrants upon academic thinking, the policies and integration initiatives aimed at migrants as yet show few traces of such influence. This is certainly the case for the German politics of migrant broadcasting in Berlin. 'Turning migrants into locals' continues to be the dominant strategy that informs integration efforts in the arena of broadcasting.

Radio MultiKulti is exemplary for this strategy, addressing people 'who identify with the life here in Berlin' and deliberately encouraging such identification. Cultural diversity is represented as a quality of Berlin, an ethnic mosaic of immigrant groups. Its representations of migrant life in the city for the most part inscribe ethnicity as a salient marker, turning it into a lens through which

---

the web in English, German, or Turkish. The courses consist of the very same lectures that are broadcast on *Saadet* television.

migrant life can be understood. The emphasis is on local affairs, both in the German language programme that represents ethnic minorities to the majority population and in the Turkish language programme that sees itself as broadcasting for Turkish Berliners, not just Turks in Berlin. The space allotted to reporting on events from the 'home country' is carefully circumscribed. It is only when these events gain an importance that makes them newsworthy across a range of German mainstream media that more reporting space is given to them, for example the last major earthquake in Turkey or the capture of PKK leader Abdullah Öcalan. The emphasis on local life is in keeping with an understanding of multiculturalism that is defined in terms of ethnic pluralism within the country of immigration, or, more narrowly, within a particular city of residence. Migrant organisations, events and initiatives that appear to further integration where they now live are given more broadcasting time than those that appear hostile to it, for example Islamic and nationalist groups. This orientation separates the 'Good Guys' from the 'Bad Guys' in Turkish migrant broadcasting. However, its parallel mission of cultural cultivation forces the station to breach its strictly local orientation and 'import' the cultural capital required for the task of cultivation from Turkey, as it were.

On the Open Channel, there are no restrictions or guidelines concerning permissible orientations. Turkish language producers can address whatever issues seem relevant to them, and present them as they see fit. The channel is thus the ideal 'outlet' for positions that are not represented in other realms of broadcasting, be it that their orientation is not acceptable in those other realms, or that they are articulated by a minority within the minority, or both. Like *Radio MultiKulti*, the *OKB* was intended as a medium of local communication, ideally fostering migrant participation in a local public setting and getting them involved in local affairs. Yet these expectations have not been fulfilled, giving rise to the 'Bad Guys' image. Rather, it can be argued that the Open Channel represents a case in which 'multicultural policies of the countries of settlement are conducive to upholding immigrants' transnational ties' (Faist, 2000, p. 200) instead of rendering them void. As a liberal broadcasting institution designed to encourage pluralism in the public sphere, the Open Channel sees its role for migrants as an integrative one, linking migrants closer to local community life and allowing them to participate in public debates at their place of residence. However, the very policies designed to facilitate that local integration are used by migrants to build and participate in transnational social spaces, by addressing their *vatandaşlar*, fellow countrymen, criticising the government in Turkey, or creating Muslim transnational audiences that draw viewers in Berlin into a wider network of religious learning and transmission of knowledge.

208 *Transnational Social Spaces*

References

Amnesty International (1996), *Türkei - Unsichere Zukunft ohne Menschenrechte*, Amnesty International, Bonn.

Appadurai, Arjun (1996), *Modernity at Large: Cultural Dimensions of Globalization*, University of Minnesota Press; Minneapolis.

Basch, Linda G., Glick-Schiller, Nina and Blanc-Szanton, Cristina (1994), *Nations Unbound: Transnational Projects, Postcolonial Predicaments, and Deterritorialized nation-states*, Gordon and Breach, Langhorne, PA.

Becker, Jörg (1998), 'Die Ethnisierung der deutschen Medienlandschaft - Türkische Medienkultur zwischen Assoziation und Dissoziation', in Siegfried Quandt and Wolfgang Gast (eds.), *Deutschland im Dialog der Kulturen: Medien, Images, Verständigung*, UKV Medien, Konstanz, pp. 295-302.

Becker, Jörg (2001), 'Zwischen Integration und Abgrenzung: Anmerkungen zur Ethnisierung der türkischen Medienkultur', in Jörg Becker and Reinhard Benisch (eds.), *Zwischen Abgrenzung und Integration: Türkische Medienkultur in Deutschland*, Evangelische Akademie Loccum, Loccum, pp. 9-24.

Berger, Andreas, Friedrich, Rudi and Schneider, Kathrin (1998), *Der Krieg in Türkei-Kurdistan*, Lamuv, Göttingen.

Bhabha, Homi K.(1994), *The Location of Culture*, Routledge, London and New York.

van Bruinessen, Martin (2000), 'Transnational Aspects of the Kurdish Question', *EUI Working Papers*, European University Institute, Vol. 22, pp. 3-33.

Busch, Jürgen C. (1994), *Radio Multikulti: Möglichkeiten für lokalen Ethnofunk Berlin - Deutschland - Großbritannien*, Vistas, Berlin.

Clifford, James (1994), 'Diasporas', *Cultural Anthropology*, Vol. 9(3), pp. 302-38.

Eckhardt, Josef (1996), 'Nutzung und Bewertung von Radio- und Fernsehsendungen für Ausländer', *Media Perspektiven*, Vol. 8, pp. 451-61.

Erzeren, Ömer (1997), *Der lange Abschied von Atatürk*, ID-Verlag, Berlin.

Faist, Thomas (2000), *Transstaatliche Räume: Politik, Wirtschaft und Kultur in und zwischen Deutschland und der Türkei*, transcript Verlag, Bielefeld.

FU:N (1995), 'Radio MultiKulti: Babylon auf dem Äther', in *FU-Nachrichten. Zeitung der freien Universität Berlin*, Vol. 8-9, p. 23.

Glick-Schiller, Nina, Basch, Linda and Blanc-Szanton, Cristina (1992), *Towards a Transnational Perspective on Migration: Race, Class, Ethnicity, and Nationalism Reconsidered*, Annals of the New York Academy of Science, New York, NY.

Göle, Nilüfer (1996), *The Forbidden Modern: Civilization and Veiling*, University of Michigan Press, Ann Arbor.

Greiff, Nannette (1995), *Türkische Medien in Deutschland*, Media Watch, Berlin.

Hannerz, Ulf (1996), *Transnational Connections: Culture, People, Places*, Routledge, London and New York.

Hannerz, Ulf (1987), 'The World in Creolization', *Africa*, Vol. 57(4), pp. 546-59.

Heinemann, Lars and Kamçılı, Fuat (2000), 'Unterhaltung, Absatzmärkte und die Vermittlung von Heimat. Die Rolle der Massenmedien in deutsch-türkischen Räumen', in Thomas Faist (ed.), *Transstaatliche Räume: Politik, Wirtschaft und Kultur in und zwischen Deutschland und der Türke*, transcript Verlag, Bielefeld, pp. 113-57.

Heper, Metin (1997), 'Islam and Democracy in Turkey: Toward a Reconciliation?', *Middle East Journal*, Vol. 51(1), pp. 32-45.

Good Guys and Bad Guys 209

İçduygu, Ahmet, Romano, David and Sirkeci, Ibrahim (1999), 'The ethnic question in an environment of insecurity: the Kurds in Turkey', *Ethnic and Racial Studies,* Vol. 22(6), pp. 991-1010.

Karakasoğlu, Yasemin (1996), 'Turkish cultural orientations in Germany and the role of Islam.', in David Horrocks and Eva Kolinsky (eds.), *Turkish Culture in German Society Today*, Berghan Books, Providence and Oxford, pp. 157-79.

Kearney, Michael (1995), 'The local and the global: the anthropology of globalization and transnationalism', *Annual Review of Anthropology*, Vol. 24, pp. 547-65.

Kosnick, Kira (forthcoming 2004), '"Extreme by definition": Turkish Migrant Broadcasting on Berlin's Open Channel', in *New German Critique*, page numbers still unspecified.

Kosnick, Kira (2000), 'Building bridges - media for migrants and the public-service mission in Germany', *European Journal of Cultural Studies,* Vol. 3(3), pp. 321-44.

Landau, Jacob (1995), *Pan-Turkism: From Irredentism to Cooperation*, Indiana University Press, Bloomington and Indianapolis.

Malkki, Liisa (1992), 'National geographic: the rooting of peoples and the territorialization of national identity among scholars and refugees', *Cultural Anthropology*, Vol. 7(2), pp. 24-44.

Malkki, Liisa (1995), 'Refugees and exile: from 'refugee studies' to the national order of things', *Annual Review of Anthropology*, Vol. 24, pp. 495-523.

Margulies, Ronnie and Yıldızoğlu, Ergin (1997), 'The resurgence of Islam and the Welfare Party in Turkey', in Joel Beinin and Joe Stork (eds.), *Political Islam: Essays from Middle East Report*, University of California Press, Berkeley and Los Angeles, pp. 144-53.

Mertens, Ilja (2000), 'Von einer „Inneren Angelegenheit", die auszog, Europa das Fürchten zu lehren. Transstaatliche politische Mobilisierung und das „Kurdenproblem"', in Thomas Faist (ed.), *Transstaatliche Räume: Politik, Wirtschaft und Kultur in und zwischen Deutschland und der Türkei*, transcript Verlag, Bielefeld, pp. 159-99.

Mohr, Inge (1996), 'SFB 4 MultiKulti: Öffentlich-rechtliches Hörfunkangebot nicht nur für Ausländer.', *Media Perspektiven,* Vol. 8, pp. 466-72.

Schiffauer, Werner (2000), *Die Gottesmänner. Türkische Islamisten in Deutschland*, Suhrkamp, Frankfurt am Main.

Seufert, Günter (1999), 'Die Türkisch-Islamische Union der türkischen Religionsbehörde - Zwischen Integration und Isolation', in Günter Seufert and Jacques Waardenburg (eds.), *Turkish Islam and Europe: Europe and Christianity as reflected in Turkish Muslim discourse & Turkish Muslim life in the diaspora*, Franz-Steiner Verlag, İstanbul and Stuttgart; pp. 261-93.

Tabak, Hikmet (2001), 'The Kurdish Television Station MED-TV', in Jörg Becker and Reinhard Behnisch (eds.), *Zwischen Abgrenzung und Integration: Türkische Medienkultur in Deutschland*, Evangelische Akademie Loccum, Loccum, pp. 149-72.

Türkeş, Alparslan (1965), *Dokuz Işık*, Dokuz Işık Yayınları, İstanbul.

Vertovec, Steven (2000), 'Fostering Cosmopolitanisms: A Conceptual Survey and A Media Experiment in Berlin', *Transnational Communities Working Paper Series*, http://www.transcomm.ox.ac.uk, Vol. 6, pp. 1-31.

Voß, Friedrich (1996), 'Low Budget and High Level', *Wort, Bild & Ton*, Vol. 1, p. 6.

Zentrum für Türkeistudien (ZfT) (1997), *Kurzfassung der Studie zum Medienkonsum der türkischen Bevölkerung in Deutschland und Deutschlandbild im türkischen Fernsehen*, Zentrum für Türkeistudien, Essen and Bonn, Vol. June.

Chapter 9

Transnational Ties
of the Second Generation:
Marriages of Turks in Germany

Gaby Straßburger

Introduction

Transnational ties to one's country of origin are generally assumed to be of less importance to the offspring of immigrants, since most second-generation youngsters have spent their entire lives in the destination country and only visited the country of origin for relatively restricted periods of time. Compared to the immigrant generation, the social ties of the second generation are probably located to a much greater degree within the destination country, while transnational ties with family, kin, and friends in the country of origin might easily narrow down to only a few contacts. Social networks of the second generation are likely to be located for the main part in the destination country with only minor extensitys back to the country of origin. This assumption also seems to hold for many second-generation Turks in Germany. Various factors, like for example the long distance to Turkey, having grown up largely in Germany, and a dense social network of family, friends, colleagues and others who live in Germany, contribute to a declining importance of transnational ties. Nevertheless, there are also indications of the existence of relatively strong transnational ties in the second generation. One such indication is the incidence of transnational marriages with partners who lived in Turkey prior to marriage.

An analysis of the marriage behaviour of the second-generation Turks is therefore likely to help answer the question whether transnational ties and networks exist and function beyond the first generation of immigrants (Faist, chapter 1, this volume). Continued transborder interaction in the second or third generation would primarily be guaranteed by the existence of strong transnational ties, for instance through relationships between close relatives in the sending and receiving countries. By binding migrants and non-migrants together in a complex web of social roles, kinship networks are channels of mutual information and of social and financial assistance (Boyd, 1989). The intensity of transnational kinship ties may be sustained by ongoing migration and return migration, of which the most prominent pattern nowadays is family-forming migration induced by transnational marriages.[1] Statistical data indicate that over half of the second-generation Turks continue to choose their spouses from Turkey. Most transnational marriages result in migration to Germany, thus sustaining, reinforcing and constituting transnational familial ties between Turkey and Germany.

As we shall see, the interrelation of marriages and networks is manifold because transnational marriages not only strengthen existing social ties or establish new ties by bridging the network of the partner in the country of origin with that of the partner in the destination country. Transnational marriages in general should also be seen as a result of transnational social ties that were already existent prior to marriage, since such networks provide the social space in which potential spouses may meet. Consequently, transnational marriages constitute both the cause and the result of transnational social ties. Moreover, they reaffirm these relationships, and since it is probably individuals embedded in transnational ties who are most willing to enter into transnational marriages, this kind of marriage can contribute to the self-perpetuation of migration and the maintenance of a transnational social space. It therefore seems worthwhile to find out more about the causes of transnational marriages as compared to marriages within the Turkish migrant population and to interethnic marriages, both of which are the predominant alternative marriage options of the second generation – apart from not marrying.

The central questions are therefore: What are the underlying causes of the relatively high percentage of transnational marriages in the second generation? And what might be said about the quality of their transnational ties? Are transnational marriages indeed induced by potential migrants in Turkey with a view to procuring a residence permit for Germany via marriage, as is often assumed in public debates? If so, this would indicate that transnational obligations and solidarity are so strong that second-generation Turks value the desire of potential migrants more than their own freedom to choose an appropriate partner themselves. It could then also be assumed that transnational ties hinder integration into Western society. Such assumptions are often based on culture-bound theories. Broadly speaking, such theories claim that patriarchal traditions are responsible for arranged marriages across borders.

By contrast, we might find other, more appropriate factors that explain why most second-generation Turks apparently opt for transnational marriages. These could, for instance, be individual preferences, demographic factors, and social ties that provide opportunities to meet potential marriage partners in Turkey who appear to be in some way more attractive than potential spouses in Germany.

This leads us the question whether the transnational ties of the second generation are generally of a strong or a weak quality. In other words, are second-

---

[1] Family-forming migration is of particular importance in countries like Germany where up until 2000 the new immigration of adults was only accepted in the context of a marriage. Since then the so-called Green Card option for highly qualified computer experts has completed the agenda.

Transnational Ties of the Second Generation   213

generation Turks personally embedded in a transnational system of reciprocity that encourages them to accept transnational marriages even if they mainly function as a means of support for potential migrants? Or, in contrast, are second-generation Turks simply using transboundary ties as an additional opportunity to meet potential partners? In the first case this would require quite strong ties, while in the second case transnational ties may be assumed to be quite weak.

For a discussion of these questions, I shall first present a statistical analysis of Turkish marriages in Germany. The main part of the article, however, is focussed on the reasons why most second-generation Turks opt for transnational marriages. Beginning with a description of the common discourse on transnational marriages, which differs according to gender, I shall go on to argue that the majority of transnational marriages is influenced by factors which are quite different from what is often assumed. Similarities and differences between the cases studied here are engendered by individual factors such as gender, socio-economic background, biographical background, as well as personal experiences and expectations. Furthermore, personal ties to friends, neighbours, and kin in Turkey are very important for transboundary marriage behaviour, since they provide opportunities to meet potential spouses.

Turning to the first question whether transnational family ties operate beyond the first generation of immigrants, the paper argues that transnational kinship ties change in quality over time. Prolonged periods of residence in Germany obviously weaken personal transnational ties to kin and to the group of origin, and it can therefore be assumed that transnational marriages with members of such a network will probably continue to decline. However, we are at the same time faced with an apparently increasing proportion of transnational marriages which are not based on kinship ties or other pre-migratory relationships to the respective group of origin. These kinds of transnational marriages seem to be an outcome of a diversified transnational network, that is, they are no longer restricted to kinship and other pre-migratory ties as they were in the earlier stages of immigration from Turkey to Germany, but are meanwhile complemented by friendships and other post-migratory ties that are established after migration to Germany. Marriage to someone belonging to a post-migratory transnational network further contributes towards strengthening post-migratory transnational ties by transforming them from friendships into family and kinship ties. Therefore, it is argued in this paper, we are confronted with a shift in the importance and the inner structure of transnational kinship ties.

The study presented in this paper examines the marriage behaviour of Turks who are permanent residents of Germany, most of them born and raised there. The findings are derived from a statistical analysis of demographic data and from detailed qualitative case studies. The aim of the qualitative analysis is to explore the entire logic of decision-making processes concerning choice of partner and to show the variety of marriages. Second-generation Turks in Germany may choose from three main categories of marriage options:

214 *Transnational Social Spaces*

1. They could either enter into marriage with a partner who is a resident of Turkey (i.e. transnational marriage), or
2. they could choose a spouse from among the Turkish population in Germany, especially from the second generation (i.e. marriages within the Turkish migrant population), or
3. they could marry someone outside their group of origin (i.e. interethnic marriages).

As compared to their parents they have many more options and are more likely to marry a partner of different origin and biographical, social, cultural or religious background. Besides, they might choose to marry either someone from within the second generation or someone living in their country of origin. In the latter case, they will have to decide whether to join their spouse in Turkey or to move to Germany. In comparison to the first generation, which generally got married in Turkey, the marriage market of the second generation, which grew up in Germany, is socio-culturally diversified – i.e. it includes the option of interethnic marriages – and spatially extended – i.e. it has become transnational.

Distribution of Marriage Patterns

This section attempts to show to what extent second-generation Turks make use of these different marriage options. Turning to the official marriage statistics, it is difficult to determine the quantitative significance of the marriage options considered here since we lack sufficient statistical data. One of the most important reasons why the statistical information available is full of gaps is that the transnational dimension of migrants' marriage behaviour is not covered by national statistics. Since most of the civil marriage contracts of Turkish migrants are concluded either outside of Germany or at a Turkish consulate, only a small percentage is registered in German marriage statistics. Most marriages are registered in Turkish statistics, but in these cases it is of course not possible to distinguish marriages involving permanent residents of Germany from other marriages.

Other ways must therefore be sought in order to at least estimate how many civil marriages are contracted, how many of them are interethnic or transnational, and how many are established within the Turkish population in Germany. I tried to solve this problem by summing up

1. civil weddings of Turkish nationals at German registry offices,
2. civil weddings of Turkish nationals at Turkish consulates in Germany, and
3. visas issued by German consulates in Turkey to residents of Turkey for the purpose of joining their non-German spouses in Germany.

Transnational Ties of the Second Generation 215

Although I am well aware that this estimate includes many problematic points – which I have already discussed in other papers (see Straßburger 2000 and 2001) – I assume it to be the best one available to date.

For the year 1996, Table 9.1 lists around 29,000 marriages of Turkish nationals residing in Germany. The data refer to 1996, because this was the first year in which the number of visas was specified that were issued for the purpose of family unification and especially for the purpose of joining one's spouse. Besides, 1996 is a year in which the number of naturalizations of former Turkish nationals was still quite low, while it increased in the following years and made the estimate even more problematic.

In 1996, approximately 16 percent of all marriages taking place at German registry offices which involved Turkish citizens were German-Turkish marriages, 2.6 percent were mixed marriages with third-country nationals and around 3 percent were Turkish-Turkish marriages. In addition, approximately 17 percent were Turkish-Turkish marriages registered at Turkish consulates in Germany. The last item listed are family-unification visas granted for the purpose of joining one's spouse. These visas represent slightly more than 61 percent.

Table 9.1 Civil weddings of Turkish nationals residing in Germany 1996

	Absolute Numbers	Percentage
German-Turkish marriages at German registry offices	4,657	16.1
Marriages between Turkish nationals and third-country nationals at German registry offices	747	2.6
Turkish-Turkish marriages at German registry offices	917	3.2
Turkish-Turkish marriages at Turkish consulates in Germany	4,920	17.0
Visas issued by German consulates in Turkey to residents of Turkey for joining their non-German spouse in Germany	17,662	61.1
Total	28,903	100.0

Sources: Federal Statistical Office, Turkish Consulate General, Foreign Office

If one assumes that most of these weddings concern marriages of the children of immigrants, the statistical data indicate that obviously over half of the second generation continue to choose their partners from among the residents of Turkey. So transnational marriages, bridging the country of origin with that of residence clearly represent the most popular marriage option, followed by marriages within the Turkish population of Germany. German-Turkish marriages come third.

This distribution implies that family-related migration has not yet come to an end but is still substantial enough to guarantee continued interaction between Turkey and Germany through the constant integration of new family members who grew up in their country of origin. Yet, the inner structure of this continued interaction and the quality of the transnational ties have still to be discussed.

We now have to establish the underlying causes of transnational marriage behaviour. This includes the question whether individuals who opt for a transnational marriage have certain characteristics that differ from individuals who prefer marriage within the migrant population. The starting point for our discussion will be gender.

By separating the data already presented above along gender lines (Figures 9.1 and 9.2), two differences are striking: German-Turkish weddings account for 18.3 percent of the male Turkish population resident in Germany, but only for 6.5 percent of female Turks.[2] However, Turkish-Turkish weddings within the migrant population – registered at German registry offices or Turkish consulates in Germany – represent only 28.7 percent of the male, but 40.5 percent of the female population.

---

[2] Here, it should be noted that - contrary to the figures presented which refer to all Turkish nationals - I have also found some evidence that second-generation men and women enter German-Turkish marriages at a similar percentage. See Straßburger, 1999 and 2000.

Transnational Ties of the Second Generation 217

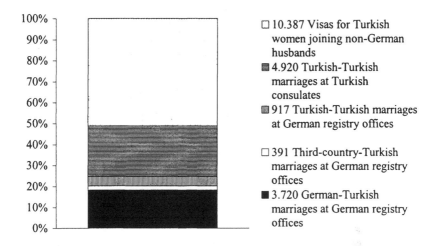

Figure 9.1 Civil weddings of male Turkish nationals residing in Germany 1996

Sources: Federal Statistical Office, Turkish Consulates in Germany General, Foreign Office

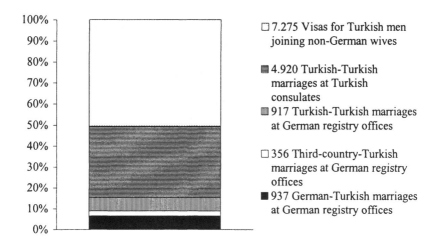

Figure 9.2 Civil weddings of female Turkish nationals residing in Germany 1996

Sources: Federal Statistical Office, Turkish Consulates General, Foreign Office

218 *Transnational Social Spaces*

These differences are probably primarily an outcome of the unbalanced sex ratio in the Turkish population of Germany. According to official statistics, the group of unmarried (single, divorced, or widowed) women aged 15 years or more is just half as large as the group of men with the same characteristics. For every hundred unmarried Turkish men there are only 48 unmarried women, and while women may find marriage partners within the migrant population relatively easily, men are faced with a skewed ethnic marriage market in Germany.

Corresponding to this shortage of potential spouses (marriage squeeze), one might expect more men than women to marry German partners. However, the sex ratio imbalance does not seem to overwhelmingly encourage male intermarriage with Germans. If this were the case, the number of intermarriages would be much higher, but the vast majority of men appear to prefer transnational marriages with women from Turkey, rather than consider intermarriage.[3]

The demographic factor 'sex ratio' may largely explain the higher percentage of German-Turkish marriages on the male side, just as the higher proportion of transnational marriages may partly be caused by the skewed ethnic marriage market. But since we still need an explanation for transnational marriages of Turkish women, it seems we have to consider other factors as well. Lacking statistical data for Germany, it seems worthwhile to examine the situation in Belgium explored by Lievens (1999). His analysis of the 1991 census (see Table 9.2) shows the distribution of married couples for which at least one partner had Turkish nationality, was 18 or older, and had either migrated at least two years prior to marriage or was born in Belgium. Taking into account the fact that such individuals were in a position to marry a partner from their country of origin, Lievens calls them 'potential importers'.

Table 9.2 Distribution of potential importers by origin of partner and sex in Belgium

Origin of Partner	Men		Women	
	Absolute Numbers	Percentage	Absolute Numbers	Percentage
Western European	413	5.6	90	1.8
Turkish group in Belgium	1,455	19.7	1,452	29.5
Imported partner	5,510	74.7	3,392	68.7
Total	7,378	100.0	4,934	100.0

Source: Lievens 1998, p. 123

---

[3] For a similar situation in the Pakistani population of Great Britain see Basit (1996, p. 15) and Stopes-Roe and Cochrane (1990).

Transnational Ties of the Second Generation 219

Similar to the Turkish group in Germany, their counterparts in Belgium also show a large preference for transnational marriages with so-called 'imported partners',[4] followed by marriages within the Turkish group, while marriages to Western Europeans cover a very small percentage. However, there are differences between the German and the Belgian sample: the percentage of transnational marriages is much higher and that of interethnic marriages much lower in Belgium. I assume this to be at least partly a reflection of the time factor, since the marriages examined in Belgium were contracted much earlier. So the proportion of 'potential importers' who grew up largely in Turkey is expected to be much higher in the Belgian than in the German sample.

In order to gain insight into the underlying causes of transnational marriages, Lievens analysed the effects of socio-cultural characteristics like 'age at marriage' and 'educational attainment' on the probability of being married to a partner from Turkey. He observed clear differences between men and women. For Turkish men he found the *lowest* probability of a transnational marriage for those men who married at a higher age and held a higher education diploma. In sharp contrast, Turkish women with the same characteristics showed a *higher* probability of a transnational marriage than women who married at a lower age or had a lower level of education.

Explaining Transnational Marriages

To explain the gender differences observed, Lievens refers to the patrilocal tradition and the supposed strong influence of the husband's family in Turkish culture. He states that when a woman marries she is expected to become a member of her husband's family, and the new couple often lives for a while with the parents of the husband. During this period the woman is, as Lievens puts it, strongly influenced by her in-laws, especially by her mother-in-law to whom she shows obedience. Lievens notes that

> when a woman from the migrant group marries a man from the migrant group, the chances are high that she will end up in such a situation. By marrying a man from the country of origin, however, she can free herself from the direct influence of her in-laws, since they are far away. She can also temper the influence of her own parents because it is not accepted for a man to live with his wife's parents (1999, p. 728).

---

[4] The expression 'imported partners' is also common within the Turkish population, where the term '*ithal damadı*' (import groom) is used.

220   *Transnational Social Spaces*

This culturalistic approach has a certain appeal when Lievens states that

> the means of achieving this goal [to secure more independence through marriage G.S.] may at first glance look traditional, but the intended goal itself is not always so traditional (1999, p. 741).

However, this culture-bound theory has a flaw, at least when examining the situation in Germany in the late nineteen-nineties: it is simply not the case that women who marry within the second generation necessarily move in with their in-laws. Of course there still are certain social environments in which they are expected to follow this patrilocal tradition but it is highly probable that highly educated girls in particular are able to refuse to do so and thus have no need to seek emancipation via transnational marriages. Nor is it true that grooms who come over from Turkey never move in with their in-laws. On the contrary, since they generally do not know the German language and, furthermore, are legally restricted from directly entering the labour market, the phenomenon of the so-called '*içgüvey*' (son-in-law living in the household of his in-laws) is rather widespread among 'imported partners' from Turkey.

Although I do not agree with his culturalistic notion, I want to underline Lievens' observation that second-generation women may have their own reasons for marrying someone from their country of origin. This important finding contradicts many commonly held assumptions found in public discourses on the causes of transnational marriages. Such theories differ according to gender: while second-generation women are generally deemed to be pressured into transnational marriages to help someone to settle in Germany via family unification, second-generation men are assumed to prefer transnational marriages in order to avoid marrying emancipated women who grew up in Germany.

These gender-specific mainstream discourses are each part of a separate social discussion. The discourse on transnational marriages of second-generation women is part of an immigration debate, as transnational marriages are often suspected of being arranged especially to assist somebody in moving to Germany who would otherwise not legally be allowed to live there. This theory primarily sets out from the assumption that transnational marriages result from continuing emigration pressure in Turkey which might best be offset by family-forming migration. It implicitly accuses the settled immigrant population of acting against the interests of the German state by fostering new immigration that is considered to be an economic and social burden. Obviously, transnational marriages contradict the political goal of reducing family-forming migration to Germany. They thus challenge one of the main functions of states, i.e. to control the border and decide how many people are allowed to cross it for the purpose of permanent settlement. This challenge seems to be an important reason why transnational marriages of second-generation women are frequently discussed along with the issue of sham marriages or marriages of convenience.

The discourse on transnational marriages of second-generation men, however, is commonly part of an integration or assimilation debate. When men marry someone from their country of origin they are assumed to simply follow a traditional pattern and to be poorly adapted to modern life. Their marriage decision is interpreted as a refusal to marry women from the migrant group who are allegedly considered to be too modern and behave too liberally in the eyes of traditionally oriented men (e.g. see Lievens, 1999, p. 728). In this case, transnational marriage behaviour is clearly seen to be working against integration.

Some other connotations of these widespread generalizations on the underlying causes of transnational marriage behaviour shall only be listed here:

1. Transnational marriages are commonly expected to be arranged, not self-determined.
2. Furthermore, transnational marriages of second-generation women are usually assumed to be embedded in strong ties of solidarity within the specific group of origin, and primarily kin.
3. Moreover, is it generally expected that due to a supposed overwhelming emigration pressure in Turkey, every man who gets the opportunity to migrate to Germany for the purpose of family unification will take advantage of this chance and settle down in Germany.
4. The discourse is further based on the generalizing assumption that it is primarily the demand from the Turkish marriage market which so frequently gives rise to transnational marriages of second-generation women.

Besides, it is supposed that the demand is met because parents of marriageable immigrant daughters prefer transnational marriages and are therefore willing to meet the demand from Turkey. So it is generally the parents who are expected to decide, not the young women themselves.

Determinants of Transnational Marriages: an Exploratory Approach

In order to reach a more detailed insight into the reasons and motives for transnational marriages, I have carried out a qualitative analysis that focuses on reasons why so many of the second generation opt for transnational marriages. These reasons include structural and demographic factors, social and cultural resources, and individual preferences.

The aim of the exploratory biographical analysis was to outline the diversity of influences that lead to transnational marriages, and to contrast them with commonly held theories on the underlying causes. In order to be able to examine a certain variety of marriages despite a rather limited number of interviews, I decided not to use the snowball-sampling-method to find potential interviewees, since this method would probably have led to a rather restricted range of cases. Instead, I based the sampling on the examination of data on each Turkish citizen in

222   *Transnational Social Spaces*

a middle-sized town in Franconia (Bavaria, Germany) with 70,000 inhabitants, including 1,400 Turkish nationals. These personal data were provided by the municipal foreigners' registration office. They contained enough information to single out all persons who might be relevant informants for this research, because they belonged to the second generation and got married not more than seven years prior to the study, which was carried out in 1997. I then tried to get into contact with each of these 35 potential interviewees. However, some no longer lived at the given address or were never at home when I tried to contact them, while others said that they had no time for an interview or did not want to be interviewed anyhow.

Finally, I was able to carry out 14 in-depth interviews with nine women and five men of different ages and educational levels and with different religious (*Sunni* and *Alevi*) and ethnic (*Turkish* and *Kurdish*) backgrounds, who had been living in Germany for various periods of time. All of them belonged to the second generation, which – for the purpose of this study – had been defined as individuals who were either born in Germany or immigrated to Germany at or under 13 years of age. Some of their marriages had been arranged, others had been completely self-determined, but most of them were based on a mixture of both modes of partner choice. Three men and five women had transnational marriages, two women were married to partners of non-Turkish origin while the others had chosen partners among the Turkish population in Germany.

This range of cases with different modes of partner choice and marriage options provides a good database for a comparative analysis, but its results are obviously not representative at all. The aim of this exploratory analysis, however, is not to make general statements. Its goal is much more modest. The study aims to show a variety of examples and to give a thick description of their complexity. To this end I used a biography-oriented hermeneutic approach and tried to single out the relevant influences and reconstruct the interconnectedness of the underlying causes. I then analysed similarities and differences of the cases and set up some profound hypotheses about various marriage options.

In the following the outcome of this analysis will be contrasted to some of the widespread generalizations on the underlying causes of transnational marriage behaviour. It will be shown that the transnational marriages that have been analysed in this study can be attributed to factors which are quite different from what is often assumed, and that there are similarities and differences between the cases, which are influenced by factors like gender, socio-economic background, life-cycle or biographical background, as well as individual experiences and expectations.

Individual Preferences

Unlike the mainstream discourses outlined above that attribute transnational marriages mainly either to emigration pressure in Turkey or to traditional marriage patterns, I have preferred to examine the subject from the perspective of the second generation and to investigate their motivations. My investigation revealed quite

Transnational Ties of the Second Generation

plainly that – apart from exceptional cases of suppression that certainly exist but are by no means typical – women decide mainly on their own free will to marry someone from their country of origin. One major factor among others in opting for a transnational marriage can be experiences with second-generation men that have not been very satisfactory. This was apparently the case for Berrin (21 years old, born in Germany). She states:

> Men from here are not OK. That is the reason why I have decided not to look for a partner from here!

As her statement indicates, she clearly preferred a transnational marriage rather than a marriage with one of the young men in her immediate surroundings in Germany. It is doubtful whether this decision was always as clear as she described it in retrospect during the interview, but she had apparently been well aware of the advantages and disadvantages of her transnational marriage. Her marriage decision had been the result of a teenage romantic love affair with Bülent, who is one year older than herself and lived in Germany during his childhood. He had later returned to the small town in the European part of Turkey where Berrin's parents come from. The couple got to know each other when Berrin was twelve. At first it had merely been a holiday flirt between adolescents. But within a few years, things had changed into a serious relationship which was kept secret to Berrin's parents until Bülent's family asked them for Berrin's hand when she had reached the age of 17.

Bülent would have preferred Berrin to take up residence in Turkey but she did not agree. So he came over to Germany and moved in with her parents for one year. When she became pregnant the young couple moved into an apartment next door and Berrin gave up her working permit in favour of Bülent who could then start a regular job at a factory.

This case obviously contradicts some of the assumptions cited above: the marriage was not arranged and Berrin's husband did not actually intend to leave Turkey, but gave in to Berrin's plans and agreed to live with his in-laws. In this respect Berrin's case is not exceptional, since most of the transnational marriages which I have analysed were more or less self-determined. Moreover, I also found two other husbands who first tried to persuade their fiancées to join them in Turkey. One of them succeeded – his wife agreed and returned to Turkey, but after two years they both finally came back to Germany. These examples show that obviously many men are well aware of the economic problems they might face in Germany. In addition, social problems might occur, because contrary to women – who when joining their husband after marriage comply with virilocal or patrilocal tradition – men joining their wives (and in-laws) contradict gender roles. Instead of being bread-winners, they risk – at least initially – being dependent on their wife's or in-laws' income. This is another reason why at least some men try to avoid joining their wives in Germany.

Contrary to the common expectation that women do not actively decide to enter a transnational marriage, men who are married to a partner from Turkey are

224 *Transnational Social Spaces*

usually assumed to have explicitly preferred this option. This assumption is contradicted by statements of interviewees like Faruk (28 years old, in Germany since the age of eight), who emphasized that he preferred a marriage partner from among the second generation:

> If I had met the right one, I would probably have married in Germany because she would have already known the German language and would have been used to the surroundings here. Such a marriage would have been much easier.

Statements like this clearly indicate that transnational marriages cannot be simply equated with a rejection of marriage to someone from among the second generation. Rather, at least a certain percentage of these marriages is caused by the fact that the search for an appropriate partner within the immigrant population remained unsuccessful. In this respect, transnational marriages are not always the first but sometimes only the second choice.

Demographic Factors

As already mentioned above, the unbalanced sex ratio among the Turkish population in Germany somehow forces men to extend their search for a partner from the marriage market in Germany to Turkey. To find a marriage partner among the Turkish population in Germany is much more difficult for men than for women. Faced with this demographic imbalance, second-generation men's individual preferences for either marrying within the second generation or marrying someone living in their country of origin seem to be much less important than often expected.

Of course, none of the interviewees pointed to this demographic context or explained their transnational marriage in such terms. They merely stated that they could not find an attractive partner among the second generation, although they and their families had looked for a spouse within the Turkish population in Germany. Faruk, for example, explained that compared to other Turkish youngsters he had even been in an advantaged position because he is a musician. He had therefore attended lots of Turkish weddings in Germany, events which provide ideal opportunities to meet potential marriage partners. Finally, he got married to the daughter of his sister's neighbours in Adana. As the marriage had been arranged by his sister, who had known that girl for a long time, Faruk was sure that his future wife was 'from a good family and has been raised in the Islamic tradition'.

His statement could simply be interpreted as an expression of conservative ideas. This would even fit Faruk's self-perception. So his traditional and religious orientation could be seen as the reason for his transnational marriage. However, such an interpretation would neglect the fact that he had first tried to find an appropriate spouse in Germany. Therefore, in order to gain more insight into the background of individual statements like Faruk's, we also have to be aware of the

Transnational Ties of the Second Generation 225

demographic structure of the marriage market. Otherwise we might fail to acknowledge important factors underlying these decisions and might instead just perpetuate the widespread assumption that second-generation men are not satisfied with the migrant marriage market and prefer women from Turkey.

Social Networks

Until now, we have concentrated on individual preference and demographic factors to examine the underlying causes of transborder marriages. In the following, however, we will focus on the role of social ties and see that preferences and structure are not the only crucial determinants of the second generation's marriage behaviour. Networks are very important as well. Social ties affect the chances of making acquaintance with potential marriage partners in Germany and Turkey. They are the connecting links between socio-structural conditions and individual preferences.

Transnational networks of family, kin or friends provide many opportunities for second-generation Turks to meet potential spouses in Turkey. It should therefore come as no surprise that among the transnational marriages which I have analysed all except one are based on personal ties to friends, neighbours, and kin in Turkey. Only one relationship started with a flirt at the beach during summer vacation. All the other couples met each other at weddings, in a group of friends or cousins, or they were introduced to each other on family visits, which were sometimes especially arranged for this purpose.

Whether second-generation Turks make use of such opportunities to look for marriage partners in Turkey depends, among other factors, on the ideas they have about transnational marriages and how they qualify them as compared to marriages within the second generation. (Here, the connection between network-based opportunities on the one hand, and individual attitudes on the other, becomes apparent.) In general, one might see advantages and disadvantages in both types of marriage which are similar to those Stopes-Roe and Cochrane summarize in their study on what Asian-British people usually think about imported partners and partners from among the second generation:

> To a family deeply concerned with cultural traditions there were advantages in a young in-law from the country of origin. Such a young person would be fluent in the family's native language, would be well accustomed to the appropriate routines of family life and relationships, respect, obedience, duty to parents and joint living, and would be uncontaminated by much contact with other life styles. On the other hand, a young person brought up in Britain would have more competence to deal with circumstances here; he or she would be fluent in English, would understand about jobs and the requirements of daily living, could be more help to the family in maintaining itself here, and would understand better the situations that faced his or her partner (Stopes-Roe and Cochrane, 1990, pp. 137f).

226   *Transnational Social Spaces*

Second-generation Turks in Germany usually reflect upon similar issues. Therefore, an analysis has to take into account questions like: do they expect to fulfil their future plans more easily with someone who has grown up in Germany or in Turkey? How do they judge the effect of socialization in these socio-cultural contexts on the future prospects of the marriage? Do they regard the lifestyle of potential marriage partners to be compatible with their own? Since ideas about such issues are not shaped in a vacuum but affected by experiences made within a social context, it is necessary to examine the personal networks of second-generation Turks.

With respect to social ties that might be relevant for a transnational marriage decision, it is important to study the socio-economic background of the Turkey-based networks. Here, the crucial point must be the socialization of individuals who might eventually become partners in a transnational marriage. If they were raised in Istanbul, Ankara or Izmir, their lifestyle might, in the eyes of the second generation, easily be qualified as adaptable to Germany. The contrary might be the case if they grew up in an Anatolian village. The attitude of second-generation youngsters towards transnational marriages is probably influenced positively if their personal transnational networks provide contact to individuals who have qualities that they regard as necessary and favourable for a good marriage.

These qualities include in general the individual cultural capital that a potential imported partner could transfer to Germany. Reflecting often on problematic experiences with transnational marriages among elder siblings and friends, a growing number of second-generation Turks is well aware that it is essential for imported partners to have cultural resources such as education, language proficiency and occupational skills. That such cultural capital is indeed a decisive factor in the selection of imported partners becomes apparent when we consider the Belgian case, where it seems that second-generation women show a clear preference for educated spouses.

> Migrant bridegrooms are generally better educated than their reference population in Turkey, and thus show a positive instead of a negative or neutral selection (Reniers, 1997, p. 19).

Another aspect which second-generation Turks often regard as important is the transferability of the cultural capital available. Most cultural resources, however, cannot easily be transferred to another country (see Faist, 1997). Such potentially transferable cultural capital is highly valued primarily in male imported partners, since they are usually expected to be the bread-winners of the future household. This became apparent during the interviews when women showing a positive attitude towards marriage with a partner from Turkey noticeably implied that he should have an urban background and a high level of education, including professional experience. Correspondingly, women who refused a transnational marriage generally justified their refusal by referring to problems that might occur when an imported partner has to be integrated into the labour market but either

Transnational Ties of the Second Generation

lacks the required qualifications or cannot make use of them because he lacks language skills.

Anticipated problems such as these might be a reason for avoiding transnational marriages, but anticipated problems with a marriage partner from among the second generation might likewise promote transnational marriages. As an example, the transnational marriage of Gülay (23 years old, born in Germany and permanently resident there for the last 16 years) is based on her reluctance to marry someone of the second generation:

> I never thought about a husband from here. Their eyes are open, they already know everything. This is not the case in Turkey. Their minds are – how should I say – somehow innocent.

When Gülay states that men who have been socialized in Germany have 'open eyes' (*gözü açık olmak*), she actually means that these men have a lot of experience and are hence of a 'calculating' kind. Those grown up in Turkey, on the other hand, she regards as 'innocent' which in this context means unspoilt (*bozulmamış*).

In Turkey, Gülay's 'open-eyes' argument is generally used by men to differentiate between the qualities of young women who have been raised in an urban area and those raised in a village. It conveys the image of an appropriate marriage partner who cannot be spoiled because she (or he – as in the case of Gülay) has always been living in controlled surroundings. By transferring this argument to the German-Turkish context, Gülay implies that she regards Turkey to be a controlled space while Germany lacks effective social control. Besides, her case provides an example which shows that a negative attitude towards marriage with a partner from among the second generation is not only found among males, as is often stressed by widespread theories, but might occur among females as well.

Another aspect that has to be taken into account when studying how social networks might influence marriage decisions is solidarity. As stated above, transnational marriages among second-generation women are usually assumed to be embedded in strong ties of solidarity to their parents' community of origin. According to this notion, it is mainly the demand of prospective migrants in Turkey which causes transnational marriages of second-generation women to occur so frequently.

This aspect was mentioned quite a few times during the interviews. Several women said that they have been asked again and again to marry a specific person in order to give him access to Germany. Nevertheless, none of them agreed because they did not see any reason why they should accept a marriage under these conditions.

On the other hand, one has to take into account the results of an ethnographic field study undertaken in the late nineteen-eighties in the Netherlands by Böcker (1995). The study indicates that in certain parts of the Turkish population it was quite common to arrange transnational marriages mainly with the

228   *Transnational Social Spaces*

intention of bringing someone over to the Netherlands.[5] The imported partners were mostly male members of the specific community of origin, especially kin. In these cases the marriage functioned as a means of support and was embedded in a system of mutual solidarity. Yet the marriages described by Böcker involved not the second generation, but a generation between the first and the second. These women had spent their childhood and also in most cases considerable parts of their youth in Turkey and had migrated relatively late to the Netherlands. Therefore, most of them were still personally embedded in the system of solidarity and reciprocity.[6]

However, this is not the case for second-generation women who were born in Germany or settled in Germany when they were quite young. Having grown up largely in Germany they are hardly part of a system of exchange relationships characterized by solidarity and reciprocity. Thus they could not be expected to feel personally responsible for the faith of their kin or the community of origin when they come to Germany. Under such circumstances the crucial point is obviously not the mere existence of transnational ties but their quality. All in all, a decline in the significance of transnational solidarity and reciprocity can be observed.

We can, moreover, perceive a certain diversification of the transnational social ties of the Turkish population in Germany. Transborder relationships of the second generation are no longer restricted to kin or to the respective community of origin. Instead, 'old' transnational kinship and community ties – which had already existed prior to immigration – are increasingly complemented by 'new' transnational ties of friendships that start during summer vacations or on similar occasions. While on the one hand 'old' transnational ties are gradually loosing importance, 'new' transnational ties are established on the other. We are thus not faced with a transnational social space that is vanishing, but with one whose inner structure and quality are changing.

---

[5] For similar observations in Sweden see Engelbrektsson (1995).

[6] Another important characteristic of the community studied by Böcker in Nijmegen is the utmost importance of chain migration. This particular mode of immigration has strongly contributed to the perpetuation of transnational exchange relationships on the one hand, and to the effectiveness of social control within the rather homogenous local Turkish community on the other. Böcker clearly shows the close connection between chain migrations at the beginning of the immigration process and subsequent chain migrations in later times, which are then often facilitated by transnational marriages. The same mechanisms have been observed in Sweden by Engelbrektsson (1995).

Both ethnographic analyses could also be read the other way round. In this case, they indicate that the underlying causes of transnational marriages will probably differ in communities which are not primarily based on chain migration but on individual immigration which has often been induced by formal recruitment. Transnational marriages might under these circumstances be influenced much less by solidarity and much more by individual decisions and other factors. This hypothesis is further supported by the comparison between the primarily chain-migration based Turkish community of Colmar in France and the primarily recruitment-based Turkish community in Bamberg in Germany (see Straßburger, 1998; Straßburger, Unbehaun and Yalçın-Heckmann, 2000).

The ongoing diversification of transborder networks is also reflected by a rise in the number of transnational marriages not with members of 'old', but of 'new' transnational ties. My observations of Turkish migrant families that if we compared the marriage behaviour of siblings, we might expect that the probability of marrying someone from one's respective community of origin (especially kin) depends on

1. the age at which someone migrated,
2. his or her position in the siblings' order, and
3. how long she or he has been living abroad.

Since all these life-cycle factors pertain to time, there seems to be a shift from transnational marriages within the specific community of origin to transnational marriages with members of other groups in Turkey. The former seem to be more widespread in the transnational marriage behaviour of elder siblings, while the latter are probably more strongly represented in the marriage behaviour of younger siblings.

Nevertheless, transnational marriages still often take place between kin, although a decline in their importance can be observed. Nowadays, such marriages are only seldom regarded as a favoured option. Rather, those of the second-generation men and women interviewed who are married to kin distanced themselves from idealising such marriages. Instead, they pointed to their practical advantages and described relatives as primarily an important network, providing opportunities to meet potential spouses.[7]

Transnational Ties of the Second Generation

To summarise the above line of argumentation, a prolonged period of residence in Germany obviously weakens 'old' personal transnational ties to kin and to the specific community of origin. This results in a shift to transnational marriages with other residents of Turkey. In addition, in the eyes of the second generation ongoing integration into German society seems to decrease the value of social and cultural capital which cannot be transferred from Turkey to Germany, while it increases the value of capital which is already linked to Germany. Therefore transnational marriages are expected to decline, while marriages within the second generation will probably increase.

Nevertheless, transnational marriages will continue to constitute a significant number of the marriages of the second generation and will therefore further contribute to the maintenance and expansion of transboundary social spaces between Turkey and Germany. However, the quality of transnational familial ties

---

[7] Similar shifts have been observed by Stirling and Incirlioğlu (1996) in a population of internal migrants in Ankara.

230 *Transnational Social Spaces*

might be quite different in the second generation from what it was when the first generation began to settle down in Germany.

Intimate transnational social networks of immigrants and their descendants that were once rather restricted to kin and to members of one's respective community of origin have meanwhile been complemented by 'new' transnational ties to friends in Turkey outside the community of origin. These 'new' ties are increasingly strengthened by marriages, so their value will steadily increase. Thus it might be assumed that they will gain importance as an alternative to 'old' transnational ties.

This diversification of intimate transnational ties is paralleled by a decreasing significance of the community of origin. The quality of these 'old' pre-migration ties has gradually altered from a relationship of solidarity and reciprocity, that was widely based on mutual dependence, to a relationship characterized by another kind of emotional solidarity which is practised much more voluntarily than before. This new kind of solidarity is obviously not strong enough to directly influence such serious decisions as partner choice of the second generation.

Acknowledgements

Research for this paper was conducted within the framework of the Interdisciplinary Post-Graduate Research Programme 'Migration in Modern Europe' at the Institute of Migration Research and Intercultural Studies, University of Osnabrueck. It was funded by a doctoral dissertation grant of the Deutsche Forschungsgemeinschaft (*German Research Council*). Moreover, this paper has benefitted from the very useful comments and suggestions made by the organisers and participants of the German-Turkish Summer Institute 2000-2001 in Bremen and İstanbul and by participants of the workshop on 'Muslim Networks and Transnational communities in and across Europe' at the Second Mediterranean Social and Political Research Meeting at the European University Institute in Florence. Last but not least, I want to thank Can Malatacık who helped me to tighten up my analysis.

References

Basit, Tehmina N. (1996), '"Obviously I'll have an Arranged Marriage": Muslim Marriage in the British Context', in *Muslim Education Quarterly*, Vol. 13, pp. 4-19.

Böcker, Anita (1995), 'Migration Networks: Turkish Migration to Western Europe', in Rob van der Erf and Liesbeth Heering (eds.), *Causes of International Migration. Proceedings of a workshop, Luxembourg, 14th-16th of December 1994*, Luxembourg, pp. 151-71.

Transnational Ties of the Second Generation

Boyd, Monica (1989), 'Family and Personal Networks in International Migration: Recent Developments and New Agendas', in *International Migration Review*, Vol. XXIII(3), pp. 639-70.

Engelbrektsson, Ulla Britt (1995), *Tales of Identity: Turkish Youth in Gothenburg*, Centrum för forskning om internationell migration och etniska relationer (CEIFO), Stockholm.

Faist, Thomas (1997), 'Migration und der Transfer sozialen Kapitals oder: Warum gibt es relativ wenige internationale Migranten?', in Ludger Pries (ed.), *Transnationale Migration*, Baden-Baden, pp. 63-83.

Lievens, John (1998), 'Interethnic Marriage: Bringing in the Context through Multilevel Modelling', in *European Journal of Population*, Vol. 14, pp. 117-55.

Lievens, John (1999), 'Family-Forming Migration from Turkey and Morocco to Belgium: The Demand for Marriage Partners from the Countries of Origin', in *International Migration Review*, Vol. 33(3), pp. 717-44.

Reniers, Georges (1997), *On the Selectivity and Internal Dynamics of Labour Migration Processes: A Cross-Cultural Analysis of Turkish and Moroccan Migration to Belgium*. Department of Population Studies, Universiteit Gent, IPD-Working Paper No. 97(7).

Stirling, Paul and Incirlioğlu, Emine Onaran (1996), 'Choosing Spouses: Villagers, Migrants, Kinship and Time', in Gabriele Rasuly-Paleczek (ed.), *Turkish Families in Transition*. Peter Lang, Frankfurt am Main, pp. 61-82.

Stopes-Roe, Mary and Cochrane, Raymond (1990), *Citizens of This Country: The Asian-British*, Paperback 15th October 1990, Multilingual Matters, Clevedon.

Straßburger, Gaby (1999), 'Türkische Migrantenkolonien im Einfluß der Aufnahmegesellschaften: ein deutsch-französischer Vergleich', in Holger Preissler and Heidi Stein (eds.), *Annäherung an das Fremde: XXVI. Deutscher Orientalistentag* (25th-29th Semptember 1995 in Leipzig), Franz Steiner, Stuttgart, pp. 442-51.

Straßburger, Gaby (1999), '"Er kann deutsch und kennt sich hier aus": Zur Partnerwahl der zweiten Migrantengeneration türkischer Herkunft', in Gerdien Jonker (ed.), *Kern und Rand: Religiöse Minderheiten aus der Türkei in Deutschland*, Das Arabische Buch, Berlin, Studies 11, pp. 147-67.

Straßburger, Gaby (2000), 'Das Heiratsverhalten von Personen ausländischer Nationalität oder Herkunft in Deutschland', in Sachverständigenkommission 6. Familienbericht (ed.), *Familien ausländischer Herkunft in Deutschland: Empirische Beiträge zur Familienentwicklung und Akkulturation. Materialien zum 6. Familienbericht* (Sixth Official Family Report about Families of Foreign Origin in Germany), Leske + Budrich, Opladen, Vol. 1, pp. 9-48.

Straßburger, Gaby (2001), 'Transnationalität und Einbürgerung: Defizite in der statistischen Erfassung der Eheschließungen von Migranten', in Jürgen Dorbritz and Otto Johannes (ed.), *Einwanderungsregion Europa?*, Conference Proceeding of Deutsche Gesellschaft für Bevölkerungswissenschaft (DGBw) and Institute for Migration Research and Intercultural Studies (IMIS), University of Osnabrück, Series: Materialien zur Bevölkerungswissenschaft of Bundesinstitut für Bevölkerungsforschung beim Statistischen Bundesamt, Leske + Budrich, Leverkusen, Vol. 99, pp. 81-95.

Straßburger, Gaby, Unbehaun, Horst and Yalçın-Heckmann, Lale (2000), *Die türkischen Kolonien in Bamberg und Colmar: Ein deutsch-französischer Vergleich sozialer Netzwerke von Migranten im interkulturellen Kontext*, in Lehrstuhl für Türkische Sprache, Geschichte und Kultur, University of Bamberg (ed.), Online-Series: Turkologie und Türkeikunde, http://elib.uni-bamberg.de/volltexte/2000/2.html, Vol. 1.

Index

activism 16, 44, 54, 198
actors 1, 3-6, 9, 12, 14-6, 18, 21-2,
  44-6, 49, 51-2, 54, 62, 65, 69,
  75-6, 122, 146, 165, 185, 202
Anatolia 20, 50, 81, 113, 133, 145-6,
  226
anti-imperialist 43-4
assimilation 21, 23-4, 28, 121,
  200-2, 206, 221
Australia 20, 38, 46-7, 49, 51-3, 55,
  59, 70
authority 3, 6, 116-7, 119, 135, 171,
  204, 206

Berlin 20, 24, 26-7, 31, 38, 50, 60,
  62, 73-4, 78, 84-7, 102, 106-8,
  133, 189-201, 203-27
Bosphorus Germans 92, 100, 103
broadcasting 26, 94, 189-190, 192-3,
  195, 198, 203-7

capital 2, 5-8, 11, 19, 21, 37, 107,
  145, 150-2, 156, 194, 207, 226,
  229
  Social capital 30, 144, 153, 165,
    184, 229
circles 30, 91, 171, 192
citizenship 4-6, 9, 54, 62, 92,
  96-101, 103-6, 108, 125, 203,
  191
  dual 24, 98, 103, 105-6
collaboration 30-1, 68, 70, 73, 82-3
communication 3-6, 11, 17, 21-2,
  26-7, 31-2, 43, 48, 51-3, 66-8,
  72, 74-7, 80-2, 108, 156, 163,
  165-6, 169, 171-2, 185, 189,
  195-6, 204, 206-7
communism 144, 120, 133

community 1-3, 5-7, 9-12, 15-6, 19,
  21, 30-1, 54, 60, 64, 69, 92, 108,
  111, 117, 152, 174, 191-2, 196,
  199, 201, 206-7, 227-230
conflict 9, 12-3, 15-6, 24, 37-9, 41,
  48, 53, 55, 68, 80-1, 112-3, 131,
  133-4, 196-7, 199, 201, 203
co-operation 1, 6, 15-7, 30-2, 67-82,
  133, 151, 163, 165, 171-2, 176,
  183, 185, 192
Çorum 20-1, 144-6, 151-7
culture 5, 12-3, 22-4, 28-32, 60,
  78-80, 104, 121, 135, 164, 171,
  174, 197, 200-2, 212, 219, 220
cyanide 38-40, 42-5, 47-55

democracy 18, 32, 43, 55, 72, 76,
  124, 148
demographic factors 212, 218, 221,
  24-5
denizen(ship) 93, 97
development, economic 11, 106,
  144-6, 148-151, 154
diaspora 6, 10, 192, 199-200
Die Brücke 18, 101-8, 110
diffusion 5-9, 12, 15, 22, 27
  cultural 3, 9, 22-3, 27
discourse 9, 15, 24, 30, 32, 37, 42-4,
  67, 114, 116-7, 123-4, 127-8,
  132-3, 135-6, 164-5, 174, 177,
  179, 185, 213, 220-2
discrimination 9, 12, 21, 60, 98, 106,
  120
domestic violence 61-2, 70, 73, 77,
  79

economic realm 12, 14, 20, 24
economy 20, 60, 128, 144-152

234 *Transnational Social Spaces*

emotion 9, 179, 185, 230
employment 18, 21, 40, 59-62, 69,
  71, 79, 94-5, 97, 101, 113, 145-7,
  151, 154, 156
entrepreneurs(hip) 13, 15-7, 20-1,
  143-4, 146, 148-157
environment 1, 9, 15, 39, 42-54, 69,
  79, 143, 152, 173, 185, 203, 220
equality 11, 67, 69, 71, 76, 80, 171,
  174
ethics, work 171, 177
Eurogold 15, 37-40, 48, 52, 56
Europa-Kolleg 18, 104, 108
Europe 3, 6, 9, 11-5, 18-9, 22-5, 27,
  29, 32, 50, 59, 63, 73, 76, 79, 98,
  106, 108-9, 112, 122-4, 128,
  131-6, 143, 151-2, 169, 177, 189,
  192, 198, 201, 218, 219, 223,
  230
European Union 4, 9, 13, 49, 53, 63,
  75-6, 91, 95-6, 106-7
exchange 3-8, 12, 19, 23, 32, 51, 77,
  79, 122, 144, 166, 184, 196, 228
  cultural 23, 100
  Information 16, 47, 51-2, 63, 66-
    7, 70, 74-5, 78-81, 102, 156
  transboundary 2-3, 5, 51, 63
exile 134, 198-9, 201
expansion 6, 10, 17, 26, 37, 52, 55,
  76, 92, 163, 229
  border-crossing 1
  transboundary 3-4, 6, 12, 23-4,
    28, 31, 45, 56, 144
export 12, 21, 143-4, 147, 149, 151-
6
extensity/intensity 3, 5, 22, 38, 46,
  49, 51, 54, 97, 99, 111, 122, 144,
  155, 211

fascism 111, 113-6, 118-9
FIAN 40, 46-7, 49-52
formalisation 7, 45, 49

generation 17, 20, 28-9, 31, 06, 62-4,
  100, 111, 115, 130, 193-4, 202,
  211, 213-4, 228, 230
  second 20, 24-5, 28-30, 61, 64,
    81, 100, 211-5, 220-30
  third 24, 28, 62-3, 100, 121, 211
German-Turkish Summer Institute 2-
  3, 27, 30-32, 66, 230
globalisation 3-4, 11, 24, 37, 55, 76,
  97, 108, 112, 144, 151, 156, 169,
  189
Greece/ greek 10, 25, 53, 55, 151
Grey Wolves 115-8, 123, 129-132

hemşerilik 28, 63
hierarchy 6-7, 9, 45-6, 49, 66, 118-9,
  134, 164-5, 171, 174, 184-5, 203,
  206
hybridization 23, 27

idealism 111, 119, 123, 203
identification 191-3, 201, 206
ideology 4, 19, 25, 60-1, 67-8, 71,
  97, 111-5, 118, 122, 128-30,
  135-6, 164
immigration 2, 6, 8-10, 12-3, 17, 19-
  21, 23-31, 59-66, 68, 74, 77-8,
  80-1, 84, 86, 92, 94, 97, 111-2,
  120-1, 128-9, 133, 136, 147, 153,
  155, 158, 190-2, 195, 201, 206-7,
  211, 213, 215, 220-2, 225, 228,
  231
imported partners 218-20, 225-6,
  228
independence 10, 43-4, 54, 60, 220
infrastructure 3, 5, 16, 20, 26, 28, 51,
  54, 67, 76, 81, 157, 164
institutionalisation 1-4, 6-8, 12-3, 16,
  27, 29-30, 43, 52, 63, 72, 75, 81,
  108, 111, 119
institutions 1-2, 4, 7, 12, 14, 18, 24,
  26-7, 62, 67, 69, 78, 95, 99, 101,

Index

106, 151, 155, 157, 189
integration 11-4, 21, 24, 26, 28, 32,
     76, 104, 108, 120-1, 189-90,
     195-200, 202, 206-7, 212, 216,
     221, 229
interaction 3-6, 8-9, 21-2, 43, 47,
     60, 65, 157, 163-5, 183-5, 211,
     216
     business 163-5, 172, 176
     cultural 21-2
intercultural encounters 163
interests 4, 14, 19, 38-9, 45, 55,
     118-9, 132-3, 136, 183, 191, 203,
     220
international relations 3, 13, 15, 201
internet 16-7, 26, 43, 52, 66, 72, 108,
     112, 198, 204-6
investment 1, 11, 55, 70, 91, 143,
     146, 158
Islam 10, 19, 21-4, 27, 32, 104, 112,
     121, 123, 125, 129-32, 136, 177,
     195, 197-9, 203-7, 224
İstanbul 2, 18, 21, 30-1, 44, 50, 68-9,
     77, 87-8, 100-2, 104-5, 123, 163-
     8, 174, 183, 192, 226, 230
İzmir 38, 46, 48, 102, 104, 204, 226

joint ventures 20-1, 77, 83, 99, 163,
     166

kinship 6-8, 19, 21, 28-30, 155, 211,
     213, 228
Kurdistan/ Kurdish/ Kurds 8, 10,
     12-3, 18, 25, 27, 32, 62, 113,
     132, 196-9, 201-2, 222

labour market 18, 20, 60, 93-5, 97,
     99-100, 106-7, 143, 220, 226
language 4-6, 8, 12, 19, 22, 24-8, 31,
     52, 62, 64, 73, 98-9, 103-4, 122,
     126-7, 153, 164, 166-9, 185,
     189-97, 207, 220, 225-7
leadership 118-9, 125-6, 131, 133-4,
     136
link(ages) 1, 4-5, 9, 16-7, 21, 23,

38-40, 45-9, 51, 54-5, 63, 65-6,
     74-5, 92, 108, 165, 183-4, 198,
     200, 206-7, 225, 229
livelihood 42, 44, 48, 54, 59
lobbying 16, 18-9, 70, 72, 85, 102,
     104-8, 131-2, 136, 203
local 4, 15, 21-2, 26-8, 32, 37-42,
     52, 55, 67-8, 71-2, 79, 82, 104,
     127-8, 143, 145, 150-6, 164, 169,
     171-2, 185, 189-203, 205-7, 228
loyality 29, 165, 184, 202-3

Man in the Street 116-7, 123, 132-3
manager 21-2, 154, 163-8, 171, 177,
     179-80, 184-5
marriage 28-30, 61-2, 70, 91, 93, 98-
     9, 211-6, 218-30
media 13, 18, 22-8, 32, 39, 47, 49,
     104, 122, 172, 189-90, 196-8,
     206-7
migration/ migrant 1-2, 6, 8-9, 11,
     17, 19-21, 25-6, 28-9, 59-67, 73-
     7, 79, 81, 83, 91-5, 97, 99-107,
     113, 143-151, 153, 156-7, 189-
     90, 192, 196-203, 206-7, 211-9,
     221, 225-30
     German 24-5, 92-3, 95-6, 101-4,
          106, 108
     family-forming 212, 220
     international 1, 10-1, 19, 22-3,
          28, 59, 97, 99, 143-4, 146-7
     labour 59, 81, 143, 190, 192
military 6, 13, 39, 68, 100, 115, 117-
     9, 121, 123, 126-7, 132, 135
minority 10, 12, 17, 22, 24, 26, 28,
     62, 64, 103, 196, 200-2, 207
mobilisation 10, 13, 16, 38-9, 55,
     112-3, 116
motivation/ motive 40, 42-5, 54-5,
     61, 106, 130, 184, 221-2
multiculturalism 12, 26-8, 163, 190-
     1, 193, 196-7, 203, 207

nation (-state) 4, 10, 12, 15, 22, 25,
     43, 76, 97, 111-8, 201-3, 128,

131, 133, 136, 177, 189, 191, 195, 197-9, 201-3
nationalism 12, 24, 97, 113-4, 123, 129, 132, 195-6, 200
naturalisation 18, 97-8, 202-3
Network of Foreign Spouses 18, 98, 202-3
networks 3-7, 9, 11, 15-8, 26, 28-31, 37, 40, 45-7, 49, 52-5, 60, 63-5, 69, 71-2, 76, 81, 92, 98, 101-2, 105-6, 108, 111, 144, 149-50, 154-5, 192, 198, 206-7, 211-3, 225-6, 227, 229-30
    advocacy 1, 9, 16, 54, 69
    issue 2, 7, 9-10, 16, 19, 37-8, 45-7, 49, 53, 55, 72
NGOs 1, 9-10, 16-7, 37, 40-1, 46, 49, 54, 59, 61, 65-7, 69-78, 80-1, 83

Open Channel/ OKB 27, 190, 195-9, 203-7
organisations, transnational 9-10, 16, 43, 45-7
Ottoman Empire 6, 22, 25, 92, 101, 199, 203

patterns, linkage 5, 9, 51, 55, 92, 108
peasants 15, 38-44, 47-9, 52, 55, 119
petty bourgeoisie 113-4
pluralism 23, 24, 26, 200, 206-7
prejudice 22, 113, 163-4, 173, 184-5
programme 18, 61, 66, 68-70, 74, 79-80, 107, 120, 123, 189-200, 203-7, 230
pure Turkish 26, 193-5

Radio MultiKulti 26, 189-95, 199-200, 206-7
reciprocity 4, 8, 19, 29, 163, 165, 213, 228, 230
Red Apple 115-6
regulation/ law/ policies 1, 3-6, 9, 11-5, 17-18, 22, 26-7, 29, 31-2,

37, 43, 46, 51-2, 68-71, 79, 92, 99, 119, 191, 201, 206-7
religion 6, 10, 13, 22-3, 25, 105, 108, 135, 185, 198-9
remittance 8, 19-20, 124, 143-4, 147-8, 159-60
resistance see demonstrations
Rights 12-3, 15-8, 38-9, 43, 63, 76, 95, 97, 100, 107, 121, 128, 131-2, 134, 136, 200-2
    human 1-2, 9, 13-6, 18, 43, 45-7, 54, 61, 63, 71, 74-5, 80
    women's 61, 63, 71, 74-5, 77

Saadet TV 198, 203-6
Schumpeter, Joseph 148-9, 152, 154
skills 80, 103, 150-1, 194, 226, 228
social movement 1, 8, 15, 37, 40-1, 45, 49, 76
solidarity 4, 8, 10, 16, 19, 28-9, 64, 67-8, 81, 121, 165, 212, 221, 227-8, 230
struggles see conflict
subsidiaries 27, 163, 166
syncretism 22-3, 26, 195

ties 1-6, 8, 11-3, 16, 18-20, 23, 26, 28-30, 38, 44-5, 49, 51-2, 54-6, 63-7, 74-5, 77-9, 82, 91-2, 106, 108, 111, 121-2, 152, 155, 163, 165, 191-2, 196, 206-7, 211-3, 216, 221, 225, 227-30
    social 4, 8-9, 23-4, 28, 165, 185, 211-2, 225-6, 228
    symbolic 4, 8-10, 23-4, 28, 165
time-space compression 3-5, 49
transaction 3-5, 8, 11, 19, 23, 29, 65, 108, 122, 150, 155, 165, 183
transnational (social) spaces 1-4, 6-7, 9, 11-3, 17, 22-4, 27-9, 32, 44-5, 47, 51, 53, 55, 64, 69, 76, 82, 92, 97, 144, 151, 155, 157, 163, 165, 168, 179, 184, 207, 229
transnational families 8, 10

transnational relations 1, 45-6, 122
Türkeş, Alparslan 112, 114-5, 118-9,
123, 134-5, 199-200, 202-3
Turkish Law on Foreigners 92-3, 98,
105
Türk'ten Türk'e 198-201, 203

ülkü Ocaklari 112, 122, 124, 126-8,
130, 133-4

ülkücülük/ ülkücü/ MHP 19, 111-
136, 198-9, 201, 203

welfare 61-4
women 17-8, 29, 43, 59-88, 98-9,
103, 105, 114, 129-31, 218-229